teach®
yourself

american english
as a foreign
language
sandra stevens

assistant author:
bismarck vallecillo
language consultants:
john shepheard,
richard a. spears

For over 60 years, more than
40 million people have learnt over
750 subjects the **teach yourself**
way, with impressive results.

be where you want to be
with **teach yourself**

3 1257 01633 9904

For UK order enquiries: please contact Bookpoint Ltd, 130 Milton Park, Abingdon, Oxon OX14 4SB. Telephone: +44 (0)1235 827720, Fax: +44 (0)1235 400454. Lines are open from 09.00–18.00, Monday to Saturday, with a 24 hour message answering service. Details about our titles and how to order are available at www.teachyourself.co.uk

For USA order enquiries: please contact McGraw-Hill Customer Services, PO Box 545, Blacklick, OH 43004-0545, USA. Telephone: 1-800-722-4726. Fax: 1-614-755-5645.

For Canada order enquiries: please contact McGraw-Hill Ryerson Ltd, 300 Water St, Whitby, Ontario L1N 9B6, Canada. Telephone: 905 430 5000. Fax: 9 430 5044.

Long renowned as the authoritative source for self-guided learning   with more than 40 million copies sold worldwide – the **teach yourself** series includes   r 300 titles in the fields of languages, crafts, hobbies, business, computing and educatic

British Library Cataloguing in Publication Data
A catalogue record for this title is available from The British Library

Library of Congress Catalog Card Number: On file

First published in UK 2001 by Hodder Headline Plc, 338 Euston Road, Lon   n, NW1 3BH.

First published in US 2001 by Contemporary Books, a Division of the   IcGraw-Hill Companies, 1 Prudential Plaza, 130 East Randolph Street, Chicago, IL 60601 ISA.

This edition published 2004.

The **teach yourself** name is a registered trade mark of Hodder Headline Ltd.

Copyright © 2001 Sandra Stevens

Cover photo from Mike Stones
Typeset by Transet Ltd, Coventry, England.
Printed in The United States of America.

1 2 3 4 5 6 7 8 9 0 FGR / FGR 3 2 1 0 9 8 7 6 5 4

This book is printed on acid-free paper.

CONTENTS

ABOUT THE AUTHOR

Sandra Stevens has worked in English as a foreign language for the last 30 years, as a teacher, teacher trainer, trainer of trainers and materials writer. She has worked in the UK, France, Spain and Nicaragua with the British Council, Ministries of Education and private language schools. She has also made working trips to other countries, including Argentina, Hong Kong, Italy, Kuwait, Mexico, Poland and Uruguay.

Before becoming a teacher of English as a foreign language, Sandra was an interpreter/translator (English/French) and a teacher of French. She also speaks German and has taught herself Spanish.

In addition to teaching and training, Sandra is a Joint Chief Assessor of the Cambridge Certificate in English Language Teaching to Adults (UCLES, CELTA) and a committee member for the development of Certificates and Diplomas in English Language Teaching to Young Learners. She has been Examiner and Assistant Chief Examiner of the written paper of the Cambridge Diploma.

Acknowledgements

The author and Publisher would like to thank the following for their kind permission to use their copyrighted material in this book:

Thistle Hotels plc (p. 324)
London Underground (p. 216–7)

INTRODUCTION

What is 'Teach Yourself English'?

A complete course for learning English without a teacher.

Who is 'Teach Yourself English' for?

This course is for adult learners who want to understand and speak English with confidence.

How much English do I need to use this book?

You can follow this course with very basic English.

If you know a lot of English, this book teaches you how to use the language in real, everyday situations.

What is different about this book?

It is a real self-teaching course. We use a new method, devised especially for learners without a teacher.

How does this new method work?

The 'learn alone method' is carefully organised, step by step to help you *understand* and *use* new language.

- First, you listen to a conversation. The course follows a story, so you know the characters and the situation. Questions help you understand the conversation.
- Then you listen for some of the words and expressions they use in the conversation.
- Next we look at this new language (grammar, functions, vocabulary and pronunciation). The explanations are in clear, simple English.
- Finally, you practice the new language in lots of different situations.

What is special about this course?

- You learn English in English.
- The course is flexible. You decide where, when and how long you study. Each exercise has a complete title, so you can stop and start at any time. We recommend that you study little and often. Some people find it fun and helpful to work with a friend.
- The focus of the course is communication. You learn some grammar and you also learn how to do things in English, for example, *ask for information*, *offer to do something*, *accept or reject an invitation*, *make a suggestion* etc. This book also teaches 'the little things', for example how to attract attention. These 'little things' help learners feel more confident with their English.
- It teaches you how English-speaking people communicate their feelings and attitudes through language, stress and intonation.
- It prepares you to talk about yourself, your life, your family, your work or studies and your country.
- After every practice exercise, we give you the answers. You can check your progress immediately.

What is the structure of this course?

The complete course consists of this course book and two 60-minute cassettes containing all the listening and pronunciation material.

It is useful to have the recordings, if possible:

- They give you practice in listening and understanding.
- They are also a model for pronunciation.
- They include the guided pronunciation exercises.

All the material on the recording is in gray   .

What is in this book?

This course book contains ten **topic areas** and a **reference section**.

Each **topic area** starts with a box which lists the important new language in that topic. There are four main sections in each topic:

1 Understanding new language

Understanding the important information Listening to a conversation and understanding the key points.

Understanding more Listening again and understanding more details.

What do they say? Listening for some of the words and phrases they use. These are the important grammar points.

Find the words and phrases Listening/reading for useful words and expressions.

How do you pronounce it? Listening (for pronunciation) and practice.

What's the right word? Vocabulary and dictionary exercises on the topic.

2 Using the new language

Using these words and phrases Practicing some words and expressions from 'Find the words and phrases' above.

Grammar and communication Explanations and lots of practice from 'What do they say?' above. These are the main language points in the topic.

i **Culture** Information about life, customs and habits.

QA **Question and answer** Questions learners of English often ask, with answers.

! **Common mistake** Advice on problem spots for learners.

About you, your family and your country You talk about the topic in relation to you, your life and your country.

What would you say? We give you some practice in unusual situations.

Sections with a * These give you extra information about the language.

3 Revision

Join the conversation Another look at the first conversation in the topic. This time you participate.

Translation You translate into your language some examples of the main language points.

4 Test

The **reference section** at the back of the book has three sections:

1 A **glossary** The first time we use a grammar term it is in *italics*, with a short definition in parentheses ( ).

   In the glossary we give full definitions, with more examples, of these grammar terms.

2 A **quick reference section of phrases for communication**. This is in alphabetical order, to help you find words and expressions quickly.

3 A complete **index** With the help of the index, you can find a specific exercise quickly. This is particularly useful for teachers.

I study English in a school. Is this book useful for me?

Yes, you can use this course at the same time as other books, for extra practice.

I'm a business person. Can this book help me?

Yes. This book emphasises social competence in English in a variety of situations.

I want to travel. Is this book useful?

Yes. This book gives lots of practice in the language you need, for example, to order food and drink, find a hotel and use public transportation.

I'm an English teacher. How can I use this book?

- For reference
- As a course book
- As supplementary material
- The recorded material as a listening course
- For homework
- The grammar
      functions   } syllabus and exercises can be used alone
      pronunciation   } or in the combination you choose
      vocabulary
- The **Common mistake** exercises can help with persistent problem areas
- The **You, Your family and Your country** sections can be used for personalization
- The **Culture** sections can be starting points for comparisons with customs and habits in students' own countries/fluency work
- The **tests** can be used independently

1 | SAYING 'HELLO'

Grammar and communication
- Starting a conversation – question tags
- Continuing a conversation – short answers
- Continuing a conversation – saying more
- Invitations and offers – *Would you like...?*
- *A/Some* – countables and uncountables
- Offering more – food and drink
- Saying *yes* and *no* to offers

Vocabulary
- Food and drink

Pronunciation
- Introduction to intonation

Our story begins on a plane ...

The first conversation

→ If you have the cassette or CD, cover the text of Recording 1, *The Story*.
→ Read the sentences below.
→ Listen to the conversation 1, 2 or 3 times.
→ If you don't have the cassette or CD, read the text of the recording.
→ Choose the correct answer **a**, **b** or **c**.

1 It's **a** cold
    b sunny } in the plane.
    c hot

2 The conversation is about **a** London.
    b a drink.
    c dinner.

3 The woman would like **a** some Coke.
    b to sleep.
    c to eat.

Recording 1 (and 8) – The Story

Man	It's hot, isn't it?
Woman	Yes, it is – very hot.
Man	Would you like a drink?
Woman	M'm, yes, please.
Man	What would you like?
Woman	Some Coke, please.

☑ **Check your answers**

1c   2b   3a

What do they say?

→ Cover the text of Recording 1 again.
→ Read the sentences below.
→ First listen and complete the words.
→ Then read the text of the recording to help you.

1 a The man starts the conversation.
He says, 'I _' s/h _ _ /, i _ n' _ /i _ ?'

b The woman answers,
'Y _ _, i _ / i _ / – / v _ _ _ / h _ _ .'

2 a The man offers a drink.
He says, 'W _ _ _ d / y _ _ / l _ k _ / a / d _ _ _ k ?'

b The woman accepts.
She says, 'Y _ _ / p _ _ _ s _.'

3 a The man asks what drinks she wants.
He says, 'W _ _ _ / w _ _ _ _ / you / l _ _ _ ?'

b The woman answers,
'So _ e / C _ k _ /, p _ _ _ _ e.'

☑ **Check your answers**

1a It's hot, isn't it?   b Yes, it is – very hot.
2a Would you like a drink?   b Yes, please.
3a What would you like?   b Some Coke, please.

English pronunciation

Intonation

★ Intonation is very important in English. What is intonation? The *music* or movement of our voice. Sometimes our voice goes up ➤ (a rise) – sometimes our voice goes down ➤ (a fall). This is **intonation**.

★ Different languages express things in different ways. English uses intonation a lot for communication. A different intonation can give a different message. Is intonation important in your language? This book explains and gives practice in understanding and using intonation in English.

Intonation and Grammar – questions

Listen to Recording 2, part 1 and repeat the words. (**a** rises and **b** falls)

Recording 2, part 1

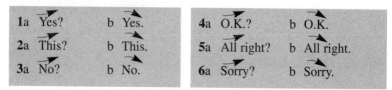

1a Yes?	b Yes.	4a O.K.?	b O.K.	
2a This?	b This.	5a All right?	b All right.	
3a No?	b No.	6a Sorry?	b Sorry.	

Q Is there a pattern here?

A Yes. In general, a rise is a question. (Some questions go down. See Topic 3.)

Q Where exactly is this rise or fall?

A On the **syllable** with **stress** or emphasis. (A **syllable** is a word or part of a word with a vowel sound.)

Intonation and feelings – voice movement

★ In English we use intonation to express **attitude** (our feelings).

★ In general, big voice movements express strong feelings.

★ Flat intonation expresses that you are not interested or that your attitude is **negative**.

Listen to Recording 2, part 2, and repeat the words. (**a** big movements = positive and interested, **b** small movements = not very positive, not interested, negative).

Recording 2, part 2

1a Yes	b Yes	4a O.K?	b O.K?
2a This?	b This?	5a All right	b All right
3a No	b No	6a Sorry	b Sorry

Find the right word

Drinks

→ Find seven drinks in this word search. The words go across → and down ↓.

→ Use the pictures and your dictionary if necessary.

o	w	r	m	c	s	z
s	i	j	b	o	g	w
v	n	e	n	f	o	a
y	e	m	w	f	a	t
j	u	i	c	e	t	e
l	a	l	b	e	e	r
c	o	k	e	r	a	p

☑ **Check your answers**

o	w	r	m	c	s	z
s	i	j	b	o	g	w
v	n	e	n	f	o	a
y	e	m	w	f	a	t
j	u	i	c	e	t	e
l	a	l	b	e	e	r
c	o	k	e	r	a	p

Grammar and communication 1

Starting a conversation – question tags

Example from *The Story*:

The man starts the conversation. He says, 'It's hot, **isn't it**?'

Q *What is 'isn't it?'*

A It's a **question tag**.

★ Question tags are very common in English.

Q *What are question tags?*

A Question tags are short questions at the end of a sentence.

Meaning

Q *Is this a real question?*

A No. The man knows it's hot. The falling intonation also tells us it's not a real question. Here, the question tag starts a conversation.

Form

★ We use the same tense in the main verb and the question tag.
★ With a **positive main verb**, we use a **negative question tag**.
   With a **negative main verb**, we use a **positive question tag**.

Grammar summary – Question tags with verb *be*			
Positive verb + negative tag		**Negative verb + positive tag**	
I am right,	aren't I?	I'm not wrong,	am I?
He She is English, It	isn't { he? she? it?	He She isn't English, It	is { he? she? it?
We You are happy, They	aren't { we? you? they?	We You aren't happy, They	are { we? you? they?

Q *And if there isn't a verb?*

A That depends. Here are some examples.

Positive	Negative
'It's good, isn't it?	It's not very good, is it?
OR	OR
'Good, isn't it? (Informal)	Not very good, is it? (Informal)

With an **adjective** we use a **negative question tag**.
With '*not*' + **adjective**, we use a **positive question tag**.

★ In informal spoken English, it is possible to start with the adjective. For example, 'It's interesting, isn't it?' is correct and always appropriate. 'Interesting, isn't it?' is correct and informal.

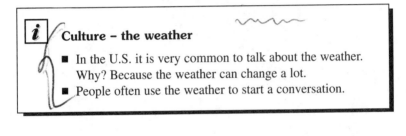

i **Culture – the weather**

■ In the U.S. it is very common to talk about the weather. Why? Because the weather can change a lot.
■ People often use the weather to start a conversation.

Question tags with falling intonation

→ Complete with the correct question tag.

1 It's really cold today, _____/___?
2 Nice and warm this morning, _____/___?
3 The weather's not bad today, ____/___?
4 Lovely day, ____/___?

☑ Check your answers *(Recording 3)*

1 It's really cold today, <u>isn't it?</u>
2 Nice and warm this morning, <u>isn't it?</u>
3 The weather's not bad today, <u>is it?</u>
4 Lovely day, <u>isn't it?</u>

How do you pronounce it?

Starting a conversation

→ Listen to Recording 3 above and start these conversations. Pay special attention to the falling intonation on the question tag.

Question tags with falling intonation

→ Match the pictures (1–9) below with the correct sentence a–i and complete the question tags.

a It's a very good film, _____ ?

b You're David, _____ ?
My name's Sam.

c The food's very nice, _____ ?

d This program's not very interesting, _____ ?

e She's beautiful, _____ ?

f This isn't right, _____ ?

g It's not very warm in here, _____ ?

h They're lovely, _____ ?

i He's a good singer, _____ ?

☑ **Check your answers** *(Recording 4)*

1	d	This program's not very interesting, is it?
2	g	It's not very warm in here, is it?
3	a	It's a very good film, isn't it?
4	b	You're David, aren't you? My name's Sam.
5	h	They're lovely, aren't they?
6	i	He's a good singer, isn't he?
7	e	She's beautiful, isn't she?
8	c	The food's very nice, isn't it?
9	f	This isn't right, is it?

More pronunciation practice

→Listen to Recording 4 above and start these conversations. Pay special attention to the falling intonation on the question tags.

Grammar and communication 2

Continuing a conversation – short answers

Example from *The Story*:

Man: '**It's** hot, **isn't it**?'   Woman: '**Yes, it is** – very hot.'

Yes, it is is a short answer.

Meaning

The woman wants to continue the conversation.

Form

Man: '**It's** hot, **isn't it**?'   Woman: 'Yes, **it is** – very hot.'

Here's a different example:

Man: '**It's not** very nice, **is it**?'   Woman: 'No, **it isn't**.'

Short answers

Q *Can I just say 'Yes'?*

A *Yes* and *No* alone can sound impolite. ☹

It can mean you are not interested in the conversation.

Q *The negative has two forms 'No, it isn't' and 'No, it's not'. Are they different?*

A No, they are the same.

⚠ Common mistake – short answers

'It's hot, isn't it?'

'Yes, it is.' (Not: '~~Yes, it's~~')

'It's' is the **contraction** (short form) of 'it is'. It is not possible to end a sentence with a positive contraction.

And in the negative?

'It isn't very hot, is it?'

'No, it isn't.'

This is correct. It is possible to end a sentence with a negative contraction.

Short answers

→ Complete the short answers with expressions from the box below.

Example: They aren't here, are they?   *No, they aren't.*

1 He's not there, is he?   No, _____

2 She's pretty, isn't she?   Yes, _____

3 This isn't difficult, is it?   No, _____

4 We're ready, aren't we?   Yes, _____

5 You're Paul, aren't you?   Yes, _____

6 They're in France, aren't they? No, _____

I am	*he isn't*	*it isn't*	*they aren't*	*she is*	*we are*

Grammar and communication 3

Continuing a conversation – saying more

★ It is very common to say more after short answers.

→ Look at these responses:

A Nice weather, isn't it?
B Yes it is,   OR   Yes, lovely.
           OR   Yes, it's lovely.
           OR   Yes, it is. It's lovely.
           OR   Yes, it is, isn't it.

→ Here are the sentences from Recording 4 (page 9) again.
→ This time match sentences **1–9** with responses **a–i** and complete the responses.

                                  Response

1 It's a very good film, isn't it? `f`   **a** Yes _____.
                                       They're beautiful.

2 You're David, aren't you? ☐   **b** Yes,_____.
                                       It's delicious.

3 The food's very nice, isn't it? ☐   **c** No,_____ Not at all.

4 This program's not very   ☐   **d** Yes,_____ I like him
   interesting, is it?   a lot.
5 She's beautiful, isn't she? ☐   **e** Yes, _____.
                                       She's wonderful.

6 This isn't right, is it? ☐   **f** Yes, *it is*. It's excellent.
7 It's not very warm in here, is it? ☐   **g** No,_____. You're not
                                       too good at math,
                                       are you?

8 They're lovely, aren't they? ☐   **h** Yes, that's right_____.
                                       And your name is …?

9 He's a good singer, isn't he? ☐   **i** No, _____. The
                                       window's open.

☑ **Check your answers**

1f Yes, it is. **2**h I am. **3**b Yes, it is. **4**c No, it isn't. **5**e Yes, she is.
6g No, it isn't. OR No, it's not. **7**i No, it isn't. OR No, it's not.
8a Yes, they are. **9**d Yes he is.

Grammar and communication 4

Invitations and offers – food and drink

Example from *The Story*:

The man suggests a drink.
He says, 'Would you like a drink?'

→ Listen to Recording 5 and practice your pronunciation and intonation.

🎧 *Recording 5*

Would you like a drink?
W...
Would...
Would you...
Would you like...
Would you like a...
Would you like a <u>drink</u>? ↘

What's the right word?

Food

→ Label these pictures. Use your dictionary if necessary.

☑ **Check your answers**

rice   chips   sandwich   bread

crackers   grapes   soup   hamburger

Grammar and communication 5

'A'/'Some'

The man offers a drink. He says, 'Would you like **a** drink?'

The woman wants Coke. She says, 'Yes, **some** Coke please.'

→ Look at these examples:

Would you like **a** sandwich?	**a** sandwich	*singular* (one sandwich)
Would you like **some** chips?	**some** chips	*plural* (more than one chip)
Would you like **some** bread?	**some** bread	*uncountable* (can't count bread)

★ '*A*' is for singular things, for example, a hamburger, a cracker.
★ '*Some*' is for plural things, for example, some grapes, some crackers, and things we can't count, for example, some soup, some rice.

A or *some*?

→ Write 1–10 next to the correct picture.

1 an ice cream cone
2 some ice cream
3 some ice creams
4 a cake
5 some cake

6 some cakes
7 a chocolate
8 some chocolate
9 some chocolates
10 a pizza
11 some pizza
12 a Coke
13 some Coke

☑ **Check your answers**

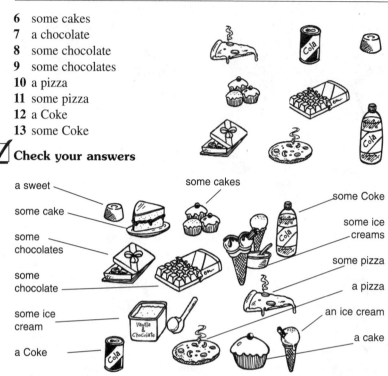

→ Now write invitations for these pictures.

1 Example: *Would you like a hamburger?*

✔ **Check your answers (Recording 6)**

> 1 Would you like a hamburger?
> 2 Would you like some bread?
> 3 Would you like some soup?
> 4 Would you like a sandwich?
> 5 Would you like some grapes?
> 6 Would you like a cracker?
> 7 Would you like some chips?
> 8 Would you like some rice?

→ Listen to the exercise above on Recording 6 and repeat the questions.

Invitations and offers – food and drink

Q *Can I say, 'Do you want a drink?'*

A *Do you want ...?*

★ The grammar is correct.
★ It is very informal.
★ You can sound rude. ☹

> **Tip:** Use *Would you like ...?*.
> Say *Do you want...?* only with people you know very well.

Q *Can I say 'Do you like...' for offers and invitations?*

A No.

Do you like...? is a general question about likes.

For example: '**Do you like** ice cream?' – **a general question**.
　　　　　　'**Would you like** some ice cream?' – **an invitation or offer**.

Grammar and communication 6

Offering more – food and drink

→ Look at the table below.

First offer	Second offer	
A sandwich?	**another** sandwich?	*singular*
Some chips?	**(Some) more** chips?	*plural*
Some water?	**(Some) more** water?	*uncountable*

→ Complete these offers with '*another*' or '*more*' or '*some more*'.

1 _____ drink?
2 Would you like _____/_____ chips?
3 _____ wine?
4 Would you like _____ cracker?
5 _____/_____ milk?

✔ **Check your answers**

1 Another drink? **2** Would you like some more chips? **3** More wine?
4 Would you like another cracker? **5** Some more milk?

> **𝑖**   **Culture – saying *yes* and *no* to offers**
>
> ■ People say *please* and *thank you* a lot in English.
> ■ It is the norm to say *Yes, please* or *No, thank you* (or *thanks*) to offers.
> ■ *Yes* or *no* alone can sound rude.
> ■ *Thanks* is a little more informal than *thank you*.

Grammar and communication 7

Saying *yes* and *no* to offers

→ Look at these examples.

Saying *yes*

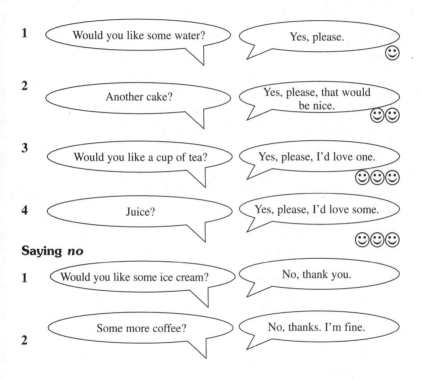

1   Would you like some water?   Yes, please. ☺

2   Another cake?   Yes, please, that would be nice. ☺☺

3   Would you like a cup of tea?   Yes, please, I'd love one. ☺☺☺

4   Juice?   Yes, please, I'd love some. ☺☺☺

Saying *no*

1   Would you like some ice cream?   No, thank you.

2   Some more coffee?   No, thanks. I'm fine.

Q *In an offer, for example, 'Would you like some tea?' can I answer, 'Yes, I would' or 'No, I wouldn't'?*

A The grammar is correct but they are not appropriate answers to offers. ☹ Say, 'Yes, please' and 'No, thank you' with offers.

How do you pronounce it?

Offers – rising intonation
Saying *yes* and *no*

→ Listen to Recording 7 and repeat the offers and answers.

 Recording 7

1 A Coffee?

   B Yes, please.

2 A Some more tea?

   B No, thanks.

3 A Would you like another drink?

   B Yes, please.

4 A More orange-juice?

   B No, no more thank you. I'm fine.

5 A Would you like some more bread?

   B Yes, please, I'd love some.

About you – food and drink. Answer these questions.

Are you hungry? Would you like something to eat?_____

What would you like?_____

Are you thirsty? Would you like something to drink?_____

What would you like?_____

What would you say?

Situation 1: You are in the street.
              A person says to you, 'Hello Chris.' You are not Chris.
              You say:_____

Situation 2: You are in a coffee shop.
              You want tea, your friend wants coffee.

The waiter says to you: 'Here's your coffee and tea for your friend.

You say: _____

Possible answers

1 Sorry, I'm not Chris. **2** Thanks, but the coffee's for my friend and the tea's for me.

Review

What is it in your language?

→ Here are some examples of the important points in this topic.
→ Translate the sentences below into your language in the spaces.
→ Remember – translate the idea, not the words.

1 It's hot, isn't it?

_____

2 Yes, it is – very hot.

_____

3 Would you like a drink?

_____

4 Yes, please.

_____

5 What would you like?

_____

6 Some Coke, please.

_____

Join the conversation

→ Look at Recording 1 on page 1 again.
→ Listen to Recording 8.
→ Say the **man's** words in the spaces.

That's the end of Topic 1.
Well done!
Now try the test.
There's one at the end of each topic.

TEST 1

Which one is right?

→ Choose the correct sentence, **a** or **b**.

1 **Starting a conversation**   **a** Nice day, is it?
                                b Nice day, isn't it?

2 **Offering**   **a** Would you like a drink?
                                b Do you like a drink?

   Saying *yes*   **a** Yes, I do.
                                b Yes, please.

3 **Starting a conversation**   **a** This topic's not very difficult, isn't it?
                                b This topic's not very difficult, is it?

4 **Starting a conversation**   **a** This soup are delicious.
                                b This soup's delicious.

   Responding   **a** Yes, it is, isn't it?
                                b Yes, it's.

5 **Offering more**   **a** Another bread?
                                b Some more bread?

   Saying *no*   **a** No thanks, I'm fine.
                                b No.

Write a dialogue

Situation: You are in the street with a friend. It's cold.

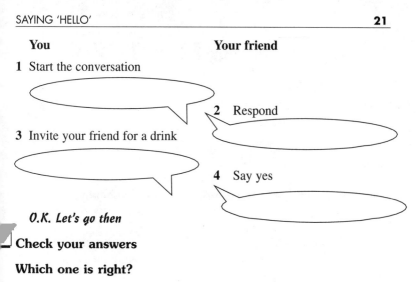

You	Your friend
1 Start the conversation	
	2 Respond
3 Invite your friend for a drink	
	4 Say yes

O.K. Let's go then

Check your answers

Which one is right?

1 Starting a conversation	**b**	Nice day, isn't it?
2 Offering	**a**	Would you like a drink?
Saying *yes*	**b**	Yes, please.
3 Starting a conversation	**b**	This topic's not very difficult, is it?
4 Starting a Conversation	**b**	This soup's delicious.
Responding	**a**	Yes, it is, isn't it?
5 Offering more	**b**	Some more bread?
Saying *no*	**a**	No, thanks. I'm fine.

Dialogue: model answers

1	**You**	Cold, isn't it?
2	**Your friend**	Yes, it is – very cold.
3	**You**	Would you like a hot drink?
4	**Your friend**	Yes, please.
		Yes please, that would be nice!
		Yes please, I'd love one.

2 | ASKING FOR THINGS

Grammar and communication
◆ Responding to offers
◆ Making decisions – *I'll*
◆ Asking for things, *Could I have...?*
◆ Ordering drinks
◆ Talking about availability
  – *have got, there is + some/any, any*
◆ Opinions and comparisons,
  What's... like?, smaller, etc.
◆ Asking for permission,
  Is it all right if I...?

Vocabulary
◆ Food and drink (2)

Pronunciation
◆ Introduction to
  stress
◆ Intonation and
  communication

The two passengers would like a drink ...

Understanding the important information

→ Cover the text of Recording 1.
→ Read the sentences below.
→ Listen and answer 'Yes' or 'No'.

1 The woman wants Coke   Yes/No
2 The man wants water   Yes/No
3 The woman wants ice   Yes/No
4 The man wants ice   Yes/No

Recording 1 (and 11) – The Story

Man	Excuse me.
Flight attendant	Yes, sir?
Man	Could I have a Coke and some orange juice, please?
Flight attendant	Of course. Would you like the Coke with ice?
Woman	Yes please.
Flight attendant	Ice for you, sir?
Man	No thanks.
Flight attendant	Here you are. One Coke with ice and one orange juice.
Man and woman	Thank you/Thanks.

Check your answers

1 Yes 2 No He wants orange juice 3 Yes 4 No

What do they say?

→ Cover the text of Recording 1 again.
→ Read the sentences on page 24.
→ First, listen to the recording and try to complete the words.
→ Then read the text to help you if necessary.

1   The man wants the attention of the flight attendant.
    He says, 'E _ _ _ _ _ / m _ .'

2   The man asks for the drinks.
    He says, 'C _ _ _ _ / I / h _ _ _ / _ / Coke and / s _ _ _ /
    o _ a _ _ _ j _ i c _ /, please?'

3   The flight attendant gives them the drinks.
    He says, 'H_ _ _ / y _ _ / a _ _ /.
    O _ _ /Coke with ice and / _ _ _ / orange juice.'

 Check your answers

1 Excuse me. **2** Could I have a Coke and some orange juice, please? **3** Here
you are. One Coke with ice and one orange juice.

---

i	**Culture – attracting attention**

- In English, we say, *Excuse me* to attract attention.
- Other ways, for example, a sound like 'ts,ts,ts', are impolite.

English pronunciation

Stress

 What is stress?

A Emphasis or accent. English has no written accents. It has stress on some
words and syllables. This book explains and gives practice in stress.

Word stress

Q *Where's the stress in words?*

A In words with two syllables or more, one syllable has stress.

   (**Q** What's a syllable?   **A** Part of a word with a vowel sound.)

   Examples from the conversation above are, 'ex<u>cuse</u>', '<u>o</u>range'.

→ Listen to the words below and <u>underline</u> the syllable with stress.

Recording 2, part 1

1 syllables
2 examples
3 conversation
4 above
5 important
6 information

Check your answers

1 <u>syl</u>lables 2 e<u>xam</u>ples 3 conver<u>sa</u>tion 4 a<u>bove</u> 5 im<u>por</u>tant 6 infor<u>ma</u>tion

Q *Where's the stress on a word? How do I know?*

A In some dictionaries, they show stress (') at the beginning of the syllable.
   For example, *above* / ə'b ʌ v /

Stress in phrases and sentences

Q *Where's the stress in phrases and sentences?*

A On the important or new information.
   For example, in *My name's Tom*, the stress is on <u>Tom</u>.

→ Listen to the phrases below and <u>underline</u> the syllable with stress.

Recording 2, part 2

1 Some Coke
2 To London
3 From David
4 For us
5 Does it change?
6 Ask them

Check your answers

1 Some <u>Coke</u>. 2 To <u>Lon</u>don. 3 From <u>Da</u>vid. 4 For <u>us</u>.
5 Does it <u>change</u>? 6 <u>Ask</u> them.

Q *What about the other syllables – the syllables without stress?*

A In these little words (for example, *some*, *to*, *from*, *us*, *does*, *them*), sometimes the vowel sound changes to the first sound in the word *above*. The name of that sound is *schwa*. We write it / ə /. We can say that some of the vowel sounds in English reduce to *schwa* when they are in unstressed syllables.

→ Listen to Recording 2, part 2 again.

How many / ə / sounds are there: 4, 5, 6, 7 or 8? Where are they?

 Check your answer

Seven. **1** S/ə/me Coke. **2** T/ə/o Lond/ə/on. **3** Fr/ə/om Dav/ə/id.

4 For /ə/us. **5** D/ə/oes it change? **6** Ask th/ə/em.

Reduced forms

Q *Is the pronunciation of, for example, the 'o' in 'to' always the same?*

A No. The full or stressed pronunciation is / ʊ /. We use this when 'to' is important. The reduced or unstressed pronunciation is / ə /. We use this when 'to' isn't important.

→ Listen to Recording 2, part 3 and repeat the phrases with these words. In **a** the vowel is weak, in **b** the vowel is strong.

🎧 *Recording 2, part 3*

1 Some	reduced			/ə/
			a	Some <u>Coke</u>
	full		**b**	Would you <u>like</u> some?
				/ə/
2 To	reduced		**a**	to <u>Lon</u>don
	full		**b**	Where <u>to</u>?
				/ə/
3 From	reduced		**a**	from <u>David</u>
	full		**b**	Who <u>from</u>?

4 Does	reduced	**a** Does /ə/ it <u>change</u>?
	full	**b** Yes, it <u>does</u>.
5 Them	reduced	**a** <u>Ask</u> them /ə/.
	full	**b** Ask <u>them</u>, not <u>me</u>.

? *Is the vowel sound in the word 'some' always the same?*

A Yes, It is a / ə / whether it is stressed or unstressed.
  → The vowels in some English words can be reduced to schwa when the words are unstressed.
  → Listen to Recording 2, part 3 and repeat the phrases with these words.

? *Why are reduced forms important for learners of English?*

A Learners often say 'I can't understand English people – they speak very fast and swallow their words'. One reason for this is reduced forms. This book explains and gives practice in understanding and using reduced forms.

What's the right word?
Food

  → Label the pictures with the food names.
  → Use your dictionary if necessary.

fish
chicken
beef
lamb
vegetarian
pork

☑ **Check your answers**

a beef b pork c chicken d fish e lamb f vegetarian

Our story continues... the flight attendant serves dinner

Understanding the important information

→ On Recording 3 the flight attendant serves eight passengers.
→ Listen and tick the right answer

Passenger 1	**a** chicken	**b** beef	
Passenger 2	**a** beef	**b** vegetarian	
Passenger 3	**a** fish	**b** pork	
Passenger 4	**a** lamb	**b** fish	
Passenger 5	**a** fish	**b** beef	
Passenger 6	**a** fish	**b** beef	
Passenger 7	**a** vegetarian	**b** chicken	
Passenger 8	**a** fish	**b** chicken	**c** a sandwich

🎧 *Recording 3 – The Story*

1	**Attendant**	Chicken or beef, sir?
	Passenger	Chicken, please.
2	**Attendant**	Beef or vegetarian, madam?
	Passenger	Beef for me, please.
3	**Attendant**	Would you like fish or pork, sir?
	Passenger	I'd like fish, please.
4	**Attendant**	What would you like to eat, madam, fish or lamb?
	Passenger	Could I have lamb, please?

5	**Attendant**	Is it fish or beef for you, madam?
	Passenger	I'll have beef, please.
6	**Attendant**	And for you, sir?
	Passenger	The same for me too, please.
7	**Attendant**	Would you like vegetarian or chicken, sir?
	Passenger	I don't mind. I like both.
8	**Attendant**	Would you like fish or chicken, madam?
	Passenger	Nothing for me thanks. I'm not very hungry. Could I have a sandwich instead?
	Attendant	Of course.

Check your answers

1 a chicken **2 a** beef **3 a** fish **4 b** lamb **5 b** beef **6 b** beef **7 a** or **b** we don't know **8 c** a sandwich

What do they say?

Responding to offers – food and drink

→ Cover the text of Recording 3, *The Story* again.
→ Read the questions and responses below.
→ Listen and try to complete the responses.
→ Then read the text of Recording 3 to help you if necessary.

1	**Attendant**	Chicken or beef, sir?
	Passenger	Chicken, / p _ _ _ _ _/.
2	**Attendant**	Beef or vegetarian, madam?
	Passenger	Beef / f _ _ / m _/ please.
3	**Attendant**	Would you like fish or pork, sir?
	Passenger	I' _ / l _ _ _ / fish, please.
4	**Attendant**	What would you like to eat, madam, fish or lamb?
	Passenger	C _ _ _ _ / I / h _ _ _ / lamb, please?
5	**Attendant**	Is it fish or beef for you, madam?
	Passenger	I' _ _ / h _ _ _ / beef, please.

Check your answers

1 Chicken, please. **b** Beef for me, please. **3** I'd like fish please. **4** Could I
have lamb, please? **5** I'll have beef, please.

→ Now listen to Recording 3, Passengers 1–5, and repeat the responses.

Grammar and communication 1

Responding to offers

→ Look at the text of Recording 3 on pages 28–9.
→ Complete the sentences below and answer the questions.

1 Asking for the same

In the mini-dialogues on pages 28–9, Passenger 5 wants fish.
                                        Passenger 6 wants fish, too.

  Passenger 5 says 'Could I have fish please?'
  Passenger 6 says, ' T_ _ / s _ _ _ / f _ _ / m _ / t _ _ , please.'

2 Verb *mind*

The flight attendant asks Passenger 7, 'Would you like vegetarian or
chicken, sir?'
He says, 'I don't mind…'

→ Choose the correct meaning below, **a**, **b** or **c**.

  a He wants vegetarian.
  b He wants chicken.
  c It isn't important. He likes vegetarian and chicken.

3 Saying *no*; talking about alternatives

The flight attendant asks Passenger 8, 'Would you like fish or chicken,
madam?' She isn't very hungry. She says, 'N _ _ _ _ _ _ / f _ _ / m _ , thanks.
I'm not very hungry. Could I have a sandwich i _ _ _ _ _ _ , please?'

Check your answers

1 Passenger 6 The same for me too, please. **2 c 3** Nothing for me, thanks.
I'm not very hungry. Could I have a sandwich instead, please?

Grammar and communication 2

Making decisions – *I'll*

Example from the listening exercise on pages 28–9:

The flight attendant asks Passenger 5, 'Is it fish or beef for you, madam? The passenger says, '**I'll** have beef, please.'

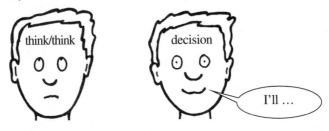

Tip: When you decide and speak, say *I'll... .*

→ Make decisions in these situations.

1 Would you like Coke or fruit juice?
__'__ / _____ fruit juice, please.

2 Which cake would you like, fruit or chocolate?
__'__ / ____ a slice of the chocolate one, please.

3 It's lunch time…I think__'__ / _____ some bread and cheese.

4 Are you tired?
Yes, I think __'__ go to bed.

5 The supermarket is closed now. __'__ / ___ tomorrow.

✓ Check your answers

1 I'll have fruit juice, please. 2 I'll have a slice of the chocolate one, please.
3 I think I'll have some bread and cheese. 4 I think I'll go to bed. 5 I'll go
tomorrow.

! Common mistake – negative decisions

It's time to go to work but you feel terrible. You decide to stay at home.

I **don't think**   **I'll** go to work. ✓
↑   ↑
Negative   Positive

Not: **I think**   **I won't** go to work. ✗
↑   ↑
Positive   Negative

Tip: Put the negative with *think*, not with *I'll*.

Grammar and communication 3

Asking for things (requests)

Example from *The Story*:

Oliver asks for the drinks. He says, 'Could I have a Coke and some orange juice, please?'

In Topic 1 we look at *a/an* and *some* with offers.
For example, 'Would you like some coffee?'

★ *Please* is very common when you ask for something.

→ Look at the examples below:

Singular

Offer	Would you like **a cup** of coffee?
Request	Could ⎰ I have **a cup** of coffee, please?
	Can ⎱

Plural

Offer	Would you like **some crackers**?
Request	Could ⎰ I have **some crackers**, please?
	Can ⎱

Uncountables

Offer	Would you like **some fruit juice**?
Request	Could ⎰ I have **some fruit juice**, please?
	Can ⎱

> **Tip:** The use of *a/an* and *some* is the same in offers and requests.

→ Complete the requests below. Put the words in the right order.

1 A Would you like a drink?
  B Yes,_____, please?
       have/I/coffee/some/could

2 A Would you like something to eat?
  B Yes, _____, please?
       sandwich/have/can/I/a

3 A What would you like to drink?
  B _____, please?
       have/something/we/can/cold

4 A Would you like some pizza?
  B Yes, _____, please?
       slice/have/I/could/small/a

5 Excuse me, _____, please?
       a/water/I/glass/could/have/of

6 A Would you like some grapes or some strawberries?
  B _____, please?
       grapes/could/have/I/some

Check your answers

1 Could I have some coffee, please? **2** Yes, can I have a sandwich, please?
3 Can we have something cold, please? **4** Could I have a small slice, please?
5 Excuse me, could I have a glass of water, please? **6** Could I have some grapes, please?

> **Tip:** Flight attendants and other people who work with food and drink don't always say *some*. They say 'Tea?', 'Chicken?, 'Fish or beef?', etc. for offers. This is practical and short.

How do you pronounce it?

Requests – intonation

★ Intonation is important with requests.
★ A big fall sounds polite.
★ Flat intonation can sound rude.

→ Listen to the requests on Recording 4. You will hear each one twice.
→ Listen to the fall on the syllable with stress. One is rude (flat intonation) and one is polite (big fall).
→ Circle 'R' for rude (flat intonation) → or 'P' for polite (big fall) ↘

Recording 4

A Could I have some coffee, please?
1 R/P **2** R/P
B Yes, can I have a sandwich, please?
1 R/P **2** R/P
C Can we have something cold, please?
1 R/P **2** R/P
D Could I have a small piece, please?
1 R/P **2** R/P
E Excuse me, could I have a glass of water, please?
1 R/P **2** R/P
F Could I have some grapes, please?
1 R/P **2** R/P

Check your answers

A	**1** Polite	**2** Rude
B	**1** Rude	**2** Polite
C	**1** Rude	**2** Polite
D	**1** Polite	**2** Rude
E	**1** Rude	**2** Polite
F	**1** Polite	**2** Rude

→ Now listen to Recording 5 and repeat the request.
→ Pay special attention to the big fall on **Coke**.

Recording 5

Could…
Could I…
Could I have…
Could I have some…
Could I have some Coke…
Could I have some Coke, please?

More requests

→ Ask for the things in the pictures.

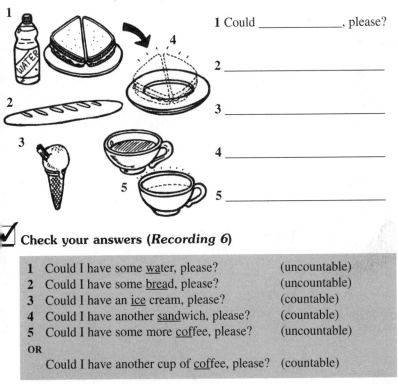

1 Could _____, please?

2 _____

3 _____

4 _____

5 _____

✓ **Check your answers (*Recording 6*)**

1	Could I have some <u>wa</u>ter, please?	(uncountable)
2	Could I have some <u>bread</u>, please?	(uncountable)
3	Could I have an <u>ice</u> cream, please?	(countable)
4	Could I have another <u>sand</u>wich, please?	(countable)
5	Could I have some more <u>coff</u>ee, please?	(uncountable)
OR		
	Could I have another cup of <u>coff</u>ee, please?	(countable)

→ Now listen to Recording 6 and repeat the requests.
→ Pay special attention to the big fall on the syllables with stress.

Grammar and communication 4

Ordering drinks

Situation You work in a coffee shop.

→ On Recording 7 on page 36, three customers are ordering drinks. What would they like?
→ Listen and write their orders.

Customer 1	Customer 2	Customer 3
_____	_____	_____
_____	_____	_____
	_____	

☑ **Check your answers** *(Recording 7)*

🎧
> 1 Three coffees and one tea, please.
> 2 Could I have four Cokes, two orange juices and one hot chocolate?
> 3 We'd like two teas, please.

Tip: It is common to omit *cup* and *glass* when you order drinks.

Asking for things

Q *What's the difference between 'Could I have...?' and 'Can I have...?'*

A ★ The grammar in both is correct.
   ★ *Could I...?* is always appropriate.
   ★ *Can I...?* is a little informal.

'*Give me...*' The imperative can be impolite. Use it only in informal situations and with people you know well. (See Topic 9.)

Our story continues... the flight attendant serves drinks

Understanding the important information

What drinks would these three passengers like?

→ Cover the text of Recording 8.
→ Listen and:
→ Write the drink they would like
→ Is it possible? Choose *Yes* or *No*.

   Passenger 1_____   Yes/No
   Passenger 2_____   Yes/No
   Passenger 3_____   Yes/No

Recording 8

Passenger 1
Would you like a drink with your meal? I've got some apple juice.
Yes, please.

Passenger 2
What would you like to drink with your meal, sir?
Have you got any cold beer?
Of course... Here you are.

Passenger 3
Could I have some white wine, please?
I'm sorry, madam. I haven't got any more white wine. Would you like red instead?

Check your answers

1 Apple juice – possible. **2** Beer – possible. **3** White wine – impossible.

Grammar and communication 5
Talking about availability – *have got*

→ Cover the text of Recording 8 again.
→ Listen and try to complete the words below.
→ Then read the text of the recording to help you if necessary.

Passenger 1
Flight attendant: I'_ _ / g _ _ / some apple juice.
Passenger 2
H _ _ _ / y _ _ / g _ _ / any cold beer?
Passenger 3
Flight attendant: I h _ _ _ _ ' _ / g _ _ / any more white wine.

Check your answers

1 I've got some apple juice. **2** Have you got any cold beer? **3** I haven't got any more white wine.

Meaning

★ *Have got* is about availability.

Form

Grammar summary – *have got*						
Affirmative						
I/you/we/they	have 've	got		a drink.		
He/she/it	has 's					
Negative						
I/you/we/they	haven't	got				
He/she/it	hasn't					
Questions						
Have Has	I/you/we/they he/she/it	got		a drink?		
Question tags					**Short answers**	
I you we they	've got…	haven't	I? we? you? they?	Yes,	I you we they	have
he she it	's got …	hasn't	he? she? it?	Yes,	he she it	has
I you we they	haven't got…	have	I? you? we? they?	No,	I you we they	haven't
he she it	hasn't got…	has	he? she? it?	No,	he she it	hasn't

→ Complete the sentences below with the correct parts of *have got*.
→ Use the table above to help you.

1 **A** What sort of drinks *have you got?*
  B I' _ _ / g _ _ / water, juice, beer or wine.

2 **A** Could I have chicken, please?
  B I'm sorry, we _ _ _ _ _ ' _ / _ _ _ / any more chicken.

3 A If you're hungry, I' _ _ / g _ _ / a pizza.
    B H _ _ _ / y _ _ ? Could I have some now, please?

4 A _ _ _ he _ _ _ any milk for the coffee?
    B Yes, he _ _ _. Here it is.

5 A We _ _ _ _ _ ' _ / _ _ _ any bread.
    B H _ _ _ _ ' _ / _ _ ? O.K. I'll go and buy some.

6 A I _ _ _ _ _ 't / _ _ _ chicken but I' _ _ / _ _ _ lamb.
    B No, thanks. Can I have a sandwich, instead, please?

7 A They' _ _ / g _ _ / Coke, h _ _ _ _ 't / they?
    B Yes, I'll ask for some.

8 A Why _ _ _ _ ' _ he / _ _ _ / any rice?
    B I don't know.

✓ Check your answers

1 I've got water, juice, beer or wine.
2 We haven't got any more chicken.
3 **A** If you're hungry, I've got a pizza.
   B Have you? Could I have some now, please?
4 **A** Has he got some milk for the coffee?
   B Yes, he has. Here it is.
5 **A** We haven't got any bread.
   B Haven't we? O.K. I'll go and buy some.
6 **A** I haven't got chicken but I've got lamb.
7 **A** They've got Coke, haven't they?
8 Why hasn't he got any rice?

Talking about availability – *there is/ there are*

What food or drink is it – tea, lemonade, etc.?
Have they got it?

→ Cover the text of Recording 9 on page 40.
→ Listen to these six mini-dialogues.
→ **a** Write the food or drink, and **b** choose Yes/No/We don't know.

Name of food/drink	Have they got it?
1 _____	Yes/No/We don't know
2 _____	Yes/No/We don't know
3 _____	Yes/No/We don't know
4 _____	Yes/No/We don't know
5 _____	Yes/No/We don't know
6 _____	Yes/No/We don't know

🎧 *Recording 9*

1 A What is there to drink?
   B There's some beer, if you like.
2 A Is there any bread?
   B Yes, it's in the cupboard.
3 A There isn't any cheese!
   B Yes, I know. I'll get some later.
4 A There are some cookies in the jar, aren't there?
   B I'm not sure.
5 A Are there any chips?
   B Sorry.
6 A There aren't any grapes.
   B Yes, there are. They're in the fridge.

✓ Check your answers

1 Beer – yes. 2 Bread – yes. 3 Cheese – no. 4 Cookies – we don't know.
5 Chips – no. 6 Grapes – yes.

Grammar summary – Availability – *there is, there are*	
Affirmative There is + *singular/uncountables* 's	There are + *plurals*
Negative There isn't + *singular/uncountables*	There aren't + *plurals*

Questions	
Is there? + *singular/uncountables*	Are there? + *plurals*

Question Tags
There's..., isn't there?
There isn't..., is there?
	Short answers
	Is there...? Yes, there is
	                      No, there isn't
	Are there...? Yes there are
	                      No, there aren't

'Some'/'any' with plurals and uncountables

→ Look at these examples with *there is* and *have got*.

→ Pay special attention to the words *some* and *any*.

Yes	There's **some** beer	I've got **some** apple juice
No	There isn't **any** cheese	I haven't got **any** wine
Question	Is there **any** bread?	Have you got **any** cold beer?

★ We use *some* to say yes.

★ We use *any* to say no.

★ We use *any* to ask questions.

→ Complete these sentences with *some* or *any*.

1 I've got _____ wine but there isn't _____ beer.

2 A Is there _____ more pizza?
   B No, but there's _____ bread.

3 A Are there _____ hamburgers?
   B No, but there are _____ sandwiches.

4 A Have you got _____ cookies?
   B No, and there isn't _____ chocolate either.

5 A Is there _____ soup?
   B Sorry, I haven't got _____ more.

☑ **Check your answers**

1 I've got some wine but there isn't any beer. **2 A** Is there any more pizza? **B** No, but there's some bread. **3 A** Are there any hamburgers? **B** No, but there are some sandwiches. **4 A** Have you got any cookies? **B** No, and there isn't any chocolate either. **5 A** Is there any soup? **B** Sorry, I haven't got any more.

Summary – Offering, choosing and asking for an alternative

Situation You're at home with a friend. It's time to eat.

→ Put this dialogue in the correct order.

→ Use your dictionary if necessary

_____ **A** Actually, I don't drink alcohol, so could I have some Coke, fruit juice or something like that instead, please?

_____ **B** I really don't mind. I like all vegetables.

__1__ **C** What would you like to eat? There's chicken or I've got some beef, too.

_____ **D** We've got some apple juice in the fridge. Could you get it for me?

_____ **E** And would you like something to drink? I've got some wine if you'd like some.

_____ **F** I'd like some chicken, please.

_____ **G** Of course. Here you are.

_____ **H** With peas or carrots?

☑ **Check your answers**

1 C What would you like to eat? There's chicken or I've got some beef too.
2 F I'd like some chicken, please.
3 H With peas or carrots?
4 B I really don't mind. I like all vegetables.
5 E And would you like something to drink? I've got some wine if you'd like some.
6 A Actually, I don't drink alcohol, so could I have some Coke, fruit juice or something like that instead, please?
7 D We've got some apple juice in the fridge. Could you get it for me?
8 G Of course. Here you are.

... and the story continues... the passengers have dinner.
The flight attendant talks to a passenger

→ Cover the text of Recording 10.
→ Read the questions below.
→ Listen and choose True or False.

1	The chicken isn't good.	True/False
2	More passengers eat beef.	True/False
3	More passengers eat chicken.	True/False
4	The passenger wants to try the beef.	True/False
5	The passenger wants to try the chicken.	True/False

Recording 10 – The Story

Passenger	This fish isn't very good at all. What's the chicken like?
Attendant	I think it's very good.
Passenger	Better than the beef?
Attendant	I think so, but the beef is more popular. In fact, beef is always the most popular dish on the plane.
Passenger	Could I exchange this fish then, please? Is it all right if I have a different meal?
Attendant	Of course. What would you like instead?
Passenger	Can I try the chicken, please, if that's O.K.?

✓ **Check your answers**

1 False 2 True 3 False 4 False 5 True

What do they say?

→ Cover the text of Recording 10 again.
→ Read the sentences below.
→ Listen and try to complete the words.
→ Then read the text to help you, if necessary.

1 The passenger isn't happy with the fish.
   She says, 'This fish / i _ _ ' _ / very good/ a _ / a _ _ .'

2 She wants an opinion about the chicken.
   She says 'W _ _ _ ' s / the chicken / l _ _ _ ?'

3 The flight attendant thinks it's very good.
The passenger asks for a comparison with the beef.
She says, 'B _ _ _ _ _ / t _ _ _ / the beef?'

4 The flight attendant thinks yes
She says, 'I think / s _ .'

5 But the passengers eat more beef.
'Beef is m _ _ _ / p _ _ _ _ _ _ than chicken. In fact beef is t _ _ /
m _ _ _/ p _ _ _ _ _ _ dish on the plane.'

6 **a** The passenger wants to exchange the fish.
He says, 'C _ _ _ _ / I / exchange this fish then, please?'

   b He wants to have a different meal.
He says, 'I _ / i _ / a _ _ / _ _ _ _ t / i _ / I have a different meal?'

   c He would like to try the chicken.
He says, 'C _ _ / I / try the chicken, please, if that's O.K.?'

☑ **Check your answers**

1 This fish isn't very good at all.
2 What's the chicken like?
3 Better than the beef?
4 I think so.
5 Beef is more popular than chicken. In fact beef is the most popular dish on the plane.
6 **a** Could I exchange this fish then, please?
   b Is it all right if I have a different meal?
   c Can I try the chicken, please, if that's O.K.?

Grammar and communication 6

Opinions and comparisons

Example from *The Story* above:

The passenger asks for an opinion about the chicken.
She says, 'What's the chicken like?'
The attendant thinks the chicken is **better/nicer than** the beef, but beef is **more popular** than chicken. In fact, beef is **the most popular** dish on the plane.

Grammar summary – comparisons
Comparing two Short adjectives → *adjective* + er + than → nicer than Long adjectives → more + *adjective* + than → more popular than
Comparing three or more Short adjective → the + *adjective* + 'est' → the nicest Long adjectives → the + most + *adjective* → the most popular

→ Complete these sentences.
→ Use the table above to help you, if necessary.

1　**A**　How big is Mexico City?
　　B　Well, it's b _ gg _ _ / t _ _ _ New York.

2　**A**　Which is the t _ _ _ _ _ building in the world?
　　B　The Empire State Building, isn't it?

3　Which is m _ _ _ / difficult, understanding English or speaking it?

4　He's t _ _ / m _ _ _ / interesting person I know!

✓ **Check your answers**

1 It's bigger than New York.　**2** Which is the tallest building in the world?
3 Which is more difficult, understanding English or speaking it?　**4** He's the
most interesting person I know.

! **Common mistake**

'Coffee is the most popular drink in the U.S.'
Not, 'Coffee is the ~~more~~ popular drink in the U.S.'

Tip: To compare three or more, say *the most* OR *the ...est*.

| *i* | **Culture – Food** |

- The most popular drinks in the U.S. are coffee and tea.
- Traditional U.S. food is meat, potatoes and vegetables, but nowadays there's a lot of international food from all over the world in the supermarkets.
- People usually eat a light lunch and a big meal in the evening.
- The most traditional dish is roast beef with mashed potatoes and vegetables. One of the most traditional desserts is called pie.
- Beer is very popular. People often go to a bar for a drink and to talk.

About your country: Food and drink

→ Write answers to the questions below or prepare to tell a friend.
→ Use the text above and your dictionary to help you.

1   What is the most common drink in your country?

_____

2   What is the most common food? Is it with rice, potatoes, pasta, etc.?

_____

3   Talk/write about the traditional drinks and dishes in your country.

_____

4   When is the biggest meal of the day – in the middle of the day or in the evening?

_____

Grammar and communication 7

Asking for permission

Examples from *The Story*:

The passenger wants to exchange the fish, have a different dinner and try the chicken.

He says, '**Could I** exchange this fish then, please?'
      '**Is it all right if I** have a different meal?'
      '**Can I** try the chicken instead?'

The flight attendant responds: '**Of course.**'

Ask for permission in these situations. You are in a friend's house.

1 You want to use the phone _____
2 You want to use the toilet _____
3 You want to smoke_____
4 You want to have some more bread_____
5 You want to watch T.V._____

✓ Check your answers

1		use the phone?
2	Can I	use the toilet?
3	Could I	smoke?
4	Is it alright if I	have some more bread?
5		watch T.V.?

Saying *yes* and *no* to requests

The attendant says, 'Of course.'
Another response: 'Yes, go ahead.'

Negative responses: *I'm sorry but* + reason, for example,
    'I'm sorry but my mother's on the phone at the moment.'

→ Complete these mini-dialogues.

1 **A** Is it all right if we go later?
  B Yes, o _ / c _ _ _ _ _ .

2 **A** Can I invite my friend?
  B I'm s _ _ _ _ . We've only got three tickets.

3 **A** Could I read your magazine?
   B Yes, g _ / a _ _ _ _.

4 **A** Is it all right if I borrow your car?
   B I'_ / _ _ _ _ _ . I don't think that's possible.

☑ Check your answers

1 Yes, of course. **2** I'm sorry. We've only got three tickets. **3** Yes, go ahead.
4 I'm sorry, I don't think that's possible.

What would you say?

Situation 1 You are a customer in a coffee shop
Another customer says to you, 'Excuse me, could I have two cups of coffee, please?'

Situation 2 In a restaurant
You ask the waiter for chicken. Then your friend says, 'Oh the chicken here isn't very good at all but the beef's wonderful.' Now you want beef. Talk to the waiter.

Possible answers

1 'I'm sorry, I'm a customer here too.'
   Advanced alternative: 'I'm sorry but I don't work here.'
2 'Excuse me, could I have beef and not chicken, please?
   Advanced alternative: 'Excuse me, would it be possible for me to have beef instead of chicken, please?'

Review

What is it in your language?

→ Here are some examples of the important points in this topic.
→ Translate the sentences below into your language.
→ Remember – translate the idea, not the words.

1 **A** Excuse me, could I have some bread, please?
   B Of course, here you are.

2 **A** Beer or wine? **B** I don't mind. I like both.

3 A I've got some coffee but I haven't got any milk.

  B There's some milk in the fridge, isn't there?

---

4 A Is it all right if I use your toilet, please?
  B Yes, go ahead.

---

5 One tea and two coffees, please.

Join the conversation

→ Look at Recording 1 (page 23) again.
→ Listen to Recording 11.
→ Say the **man's** words in the spaces.

TEST 2

Which one is right?

→ Choose **a** or **b**.

1 In a restaurant a Please, please, a Coke.
        b Excuse me, could I have a Coke, please?

2 I'll make you a cup of tea
  a Is it all right if I have water instead, please?
  b Is it possible I have water in the place of coffee?

3 Would you like some white wine or red?
  a Red for me, please.
  b Red to me, please.

4 Fruit juice or lemonade?
  a I don't mind.
  b I'm not mind.

5 a I think I go to the supermarket later.
  b I think I'll go to the supermarket later.

6 a Could I have some cookies, please?
  b Could I have any cookies, please?

7 **a** I haven't got some beer.
   b I haven't got any beer.

8 **a** There isn't any more cake, is there?
   b There isn't any more cake, isn't it?

9 **a** Would you like something for drink?
   b Would you like something to drink?

10 **a** Which test is the more difficult in the book?
   b Which test is the most difficult in the book?

Write a dialogue

Situation You are in a restaurant with a friend. It is the end of the meal.

1 **You**
   Offer your friend tea or coffee

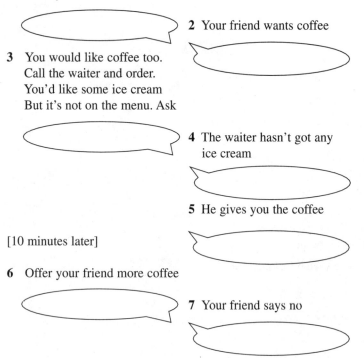

2 Your friend wants coffee

3 You would like coffee too.
   Call the waiter and order.
   You'd like some ice cream
   But it's not on the menu. Ask

4 The waiter hasn't got any
   ice cream

5 He gives you the coffee

[10 minutes later]

6 Offer your friend more coffee

7 Your friend says no

8 Call the waiter and ask for the bill

[The waiter brings the bill]

9 Ask if it's possible to pay by credit card

10 The waiter says yes

✓ **Check your answers**

Which one is right?

1 b 2 a 3 a 4 a 5 b 6 a 7 b 8 a 9 b 10 b

Dialogue: model answers

1	**You**	Would you like tea or coffee?
2	**Friend**	Coffee for me, please.
3	**You**	Excuse me, (Can/Could I have) two coffees, please?
		Have you got any ice cream?
4	**Waiter**	No, I'm sorry, we haven't.
5	**Waiter**	Two coffees.
6	**You**	Would you like some more coffee?
7	**Friend**	No thanks, I'm fine.
8	**You**	Excuse me, can/could I have the bill, please?
9	**You**	Is it all right if I pay by credit card?
10	**Waiter**	Yes, of course.

3 | MAKING CONVERSATION

<table>
<tr><td>

Grammar and communication
◆ Everyday activities – present simple
◆ Ability – *can*
◆ Expressing interest – echo questions

Vocabulary
◆ Countries, nationalities, languages

</td><td>

Pronunciation
◆ Intonation
  – 'wh' questions
  – expressing interest with echo questions
◆ Plurals with an extra syllable
◆ Stress and reduced forms
  – *can/can't*

</td></tr>
</table>

The conversation on the plane continues...

United States
Mexico
Brazil
England
France
Portugal
Spain
Germany
Poland
Italy
Egypt
China
Japan
Australia

Understanding the important information

→ Cover the text of Recording 1, *The Story*.
→ Read the sentence below.
→ Listen to the recording and circle ⬭ ALL the correct answers.

They talk about **a** countries
 b their families
 c nationalities
 d their names
 e languages

Recording 1 (and 10) – The Story

Woman	Where are you from?
Man	The United States. And you?
Woman	I'm from the States too.
Man	Oh, really? But your book isn't in English.
Woman	Well, actually, I live in South America, in Uruguay and so I speak Spanish.
Man	Do you? That's interesting!
Woman	Yes, I like it there. How about you? Do you speak any foreign languages?
Man	I can speak a bit of French.
Woman	Can you?
Man	Yes, I use it in my job sometimes – but I'm not really very good at it.
Woman	Oh, aren't you? I really like languages.

Check your answers

a countries **c** nationalities **e** languages

Understanding more

→ Cover the text of Recording 1 again.
→ Read the sentences on page 54.
→ Listen to the recording and choose the correct answer.

1	The woman's American.	Yes/No/We don't know
2	The man's American.	Yes/No/We don't know
3	She speaks Spanish.	Yes/No/We don't know
4	She uses her foreign language in her job.	Yes/No/We don't know
5	She lives in Rome.	Yes/No/We don't know
6	He lives in Rome.	Yes/No/We don't know
7	He can speak a little French.	Yes/No/We don't know
8	He uses his foreign language in his job.	Yes/No/We don't know
9	Languages are easy for him.	Yes/No/We don't know
10	She's interested in languages.	Yes/No/We don't know

☑ **Check your answers**

1 Yes **2** Yes **3** Yes **4** We don't know. **5** No – she lives in South America.
6 We don't know. **7** Yes **8** Yes **9** No **10** Yes

What do they say?

→ Read the sentences below.
→ Listen to Recording 1 again and try to complete the words.
→ Read the text of the recording to help you, if necessary.

1 Nationalities

   a The woman asks, 'W _ _ _ _ / a _ _ / y _ _ / f _ _ _?'
   b The man answers, 'The / U _ _ _ _ _ / S _ _ _ _ _.'
   c The woman says 'I'_ / f _ _ _ / t _ _ / _ . _ . / t _ _.'

2 Asking questions; expressing interest

   a The woman says, 'I'm from the U.S. too.'
      The man is interested. He says, ' Oh, r_ _ _ _ _ ?'
   b The woman says, 'Actually, I /l _ _ _ / in South America, in Uruguay.'
      The man is interested. He says, 'D_ / y _ _ ?'
   c The woman asks about languages.
      She says, ' D_ / y _ _ / s _ _ _ _ / any / f _ r _ i _ n / l _ n g _ a _ e s?'
      The man answers.
      'I / c _ _ / s _ _ _ _ / a / b _ _ / o _ / F _ _ _ _ h.'
      The woman is interested. She says, 'C _ _ / y _ _ ?'

Check your answers

1 a Where are you from?
   b The United States.
   c I'm from the U.S. too.
2 a Oh! Really?
   b Actually, I live in South America, in Uruguay.
      Do you?
   c Do you speak any foreign languages?
      I can speak a bit of French.
      Can you?

Find the words and phrases

→ Read the questions below.
→ Read the text of Recording 1 (page 53) and find the answers.

1 Asking the same question
   a The woman asks: 'Where are you from?'
      The man doesn't ask, 'Where are you from?' He asks, 'A _ _ / y _ _ ?'
   b The woman says, 'I speak Spanish.'
      She doesn't ask the man, 'Do you speak Spanish?' She asks,
      'H_ _ / a _ _ _ _ / y _ _ ?'

2 Making conversation
   The woman says, 'I speak Spanish.'
   Then she says, 'A _ _ _ _ _ _ y, I live in South America.'

3 The man doesn't speak French very well.
   He says, ' I speak a bit of French…but I'm not very good /_ _ / it.'

Check your answers

1 a And you?
   b How about you?
   ★ These two questions mean the same.
   ★ You can use both questions with all tenses.
   ★ The structure of the questions is always the same.
2 Actually, I live in South America.
3 I speak a bit of French… but I'm not very good at it.

Using these words and phrases

1 Asking about the same topic – *And you? How about you?*

→ Complete these dialogues.

1 A What's your name?
   B I'm Sam. _____?
   A My name's…

2 A I'm cold. _____?
   B I'm all right, actually.

3 A Here's the coffee bar. I'd like something hot to drink.
      _____?
   B I think I'll have the same.

✓ Check your answers

1, 2, 3 'And you?' or 'How about you?'.

2 Making conversation – *actually*

★ *Actually* makes the sentence less direct.

→ Make mini-dialogues. Match **1–5** below with **a–e**.

1 Terrible weather, isn't it?	**a**	Yes, actually the food here is always good.
2 Are you Japanese?	**b**	I don't mind, actually. I like both.
3 Tea or coffee?	**c**	Yes, I'm from Tokyo, actually.
4 Where is he?	**d**	Yes, it is actually, isn't it?
5 This is really delicious!	**e**	Actually, I'm not sure.

✓ Check your answers

1 d **2** c **3** b **4** e **5** a

❗ Common mistake – *actually*

Situation A tourist in Europe.
                 '~~Actually, I'm in Paris~~. Tomorrow it's Madrid.'

★ In some languages *actually* means *now*, *at the moment*.
★ In English *actually* does not refer to time.

Grammar and communication 1

Everyday activities – Present simple

Examples from *The Story*:

1 The woman says, 'I **live** in South America.'
2 The man says, 'I **use** my French in my job sometimes.'

Meanings

★ In sentence **1** above the present simple is for permanent situations.
★ In sentence **2** the present simple is for repeated actions.

Form – present simple

Affirmative (*yes*)			
I You We They	live	He/she/it	lives
Questions			
Do	I you we they	live?	Does he/she/it live?
Negatives (*no*)			
I You We They	don't live (do not)	He/she/it	doesn't live
Short answers			
	Positive I		**Negative** I
Yes,	you we they	do	No, you we they	don't
	he/she/it	does	he/she/it	doesn't

Question Tags					
I		I?	He	lives, doesn't	he?
You	live, don't	you?	She	doesn't live, does	she?
We	don't live, do	we?	It		it?
They		they?			

→ Complete the sentences about the two passengers.
→ Use the grammar summary to help you, if necessary.

She says   Talking about the woman:
1 'I speak Spanish.'   She _____ Spanish.
2 'I live in South America.'   She _____ in South America.
3 'I like it there.'   She _____ it there.

He says   Talking about the man
4 'I use French in my job   He _____ French in his job
   sometimes.'   sometimes.

Check your answers

1 She speaks Spanish. **2** She lives in South America. **3** She likes it there.
4 He uses French in his job sometimes.

Present simple – questions and answers

→ Look at the table above and complete the questions and answers about
  the two passengers. Use the information from *The Story* on page 53.

Example: Does she speak Spanish?   *Yes, she does.*

1 _____ she live in South America?   _____
2 _____ she like it there?   _____
3 _____ the man speak Spanish?   _____
4 _____ he speak French?   _____
5 _____ he live in South America?   _____
6 _____ they work together?   _____

About you
7 Do you speak Spanish?   _____
8 Do you speak French?   _____

Check your answers

1	Does she live in South America?	Yes, she does.
2	Does she like it there?	Yes, she does.
3	Does the man speak Spanish?	No, he doesn't.
4	Does he speak French?	Yes, he does.
5	Does he live in South America?	No, he doesn't.
6	Do they work together?	No, they don't.

7 and 8 Yes, I do, OR No, I don't.

How do you pronounce it?

Intonation of questions with *what?*, *where?* etc.

Example from *The Story*:

The woman asks 'Where are you <u>from</u>?'

→ Read the questions below.
→ Listen to these mini-dialogues on Recording 2, part 1. Pay special attention to the important word in the question – the syllable with stress.

In questions with *what? where?* etc. the voice:

a goes **up** on the syllable with stress or ↗
b goes **down** on the syllable with stress. ↘

→ Choose **a** or **b**. The answer is the same for all the questions.

Recording 2, part 1

1	What's your <u>name</u>?	Monica.
2	Where are you <u>from</u>?	New York.
3	Where does he <u>work</u>?	In a school.
4	When do they arr<u>ive</u>?	At 5 o'clock.
5	Who can <u>drive</u>?	I can.
6	Which one's <u>yours</u>?	That one.
7	Why aren't they <u>here</u>?	Their train's late.
8	How's your <u>mother</u>?	She's fine.
9	Whose is <u>this</u>?	I don't know. It's not mine.

☑ **Check your answer**

b   The voice goes down. ⌒➘
    Many learners of English go up with questions.
    Questions with question words (*what*, *when*, etc.) go down. ⌒➘

→ Now listen again and repeat the questions.
→ Pay special attention to the fall on the syllable with stress.

Plurals with an extra syllable – *languages*

Example from *The Story*:

The woman says 'Do you speak any foreign languages?'
And 'I really like languages.'

★ Sometimes plural nouns have an extra syllable.

   For example, *language* has two syllables (lang-uage) and *languages*
   has three syllables (lang-uag-es). (A syllable is part of a word with a
   vowel sound.)

★ The pronunciation of the extra syllable is 'is' / ɪz /.

→ Look at the pictures below and opposite and listen to Recording 2, part 2.
→ Write the number of syllables you hear in the boxes.

🎧 *Recording 2, part 2*

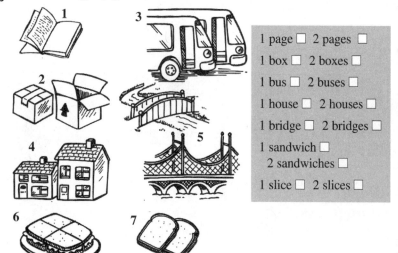

1 page ☐   2 pages ☐
1 box ☐   2 boxes ☐
1 bus ☐   2 buses ☐
1 house ☐   2 houses ☐
1 bridge ☐   2 bridges ☐
1 sandwich ☐
  2 sandwiches ☐
1 slice ☐   2 slices ☐

1 piece ☐	2 pieces ☐
1 dishes ☐	2 dishes ☐
1 glass ☐	2 glasses ☐
1 orange juice ☐	
2 orange juices ☐	
1 kiss ☐	2 kisses ☐

Check your answers

1 page (1) pages (2) **2** box (1) boxes (2) **3** bus (1) buses (2) **4** house (1) houses (2) **5** bridge (1) bridges (2) **6** sandwich (2) sandwiches (3) **7** slice (1) slices (2) **8** piece (1) pieces (2) **9** dish (1) dishes (2) **10** glass (1) glasses (2) **11** orange juice (3) orange juices (4) **12** kiss (1) kisses (2)

Q How do I know when there's an extra syllable?

A After the letters 's', 'ss', 'sh', 'ch', 'ge', 'se', 'ce', 'x' there's an extra final syllable.

Q Why these letters?

A Because after these letters it's difficult to pronounce the 's' without an extra vowel in the middle.

→ Now listen to Recording 2, part 2 again and repeat the words.

Grammar and communication 2

Ability – *can*

Examples from *The Story*:

The woman asks about languages. He says, 'I can speak a bit of French.' She's interested. She says, 'Can you?'

Meaning

★ Here, *can* is for ability.

Form – *can*

Affirmative		
I You He/she/it We They	can	eat fish

Negative		
I You He/she/it We they	can't	eat fish

Questions, short answers and question tags						
Can	I you he/she/it we they	eat fish?	Yes, No,	I you he/she/it we they	can, can't can't, can	I? you? he/she/it? we? they?

! **Common mistakes – *can***

'He can speak French.'
Not 'He can to speak French.'

'Can you speak English?'
Not 'Can you to speak English?'
Or 'Do you can speak English?'

Ability, *can*

→ Complete the questions and short answers.

1   The man _____/ _____ French but he _____/_____ Spanish.
2   _____the woman _____ Spanish? Yes, _____/_____.
3   _____they both_____ English? Yes, they can.
4   About you: I _____ /_____ some English.

Check your answers (Recording 3)

1 The man can speak French but he can't speak Spanish.
2 Can the woman speak Spanish? Yes, she can.
3 Can they both speak English? Yes, they can.
4 I can speak some English.

How do you pronounce it?

Can

★ *Can, can't* has two different vowel sounds.

→ Listen to Recording 3 above. Can you hear two different vowel sounds?

→ Then read **1** and **2** below to check your answers.

1 reduced *a* / ə / (*can* is not the important word in the sentence):
   a The man can speak French.
   b Can the woman speak Spanish?
   c Can they both speak English?
   d I can speak some English.

2 full and negative *a* / ɑe / (*can* is the important word):
   a Yes, she can.
   b He can't speak Spanish.

Q *Why is this pronunciation important?*

A The vowel in full *can* and negative *can't* are similar. Often people don't pronounce the 't'.

→ Now listen to Recording 3 again and repeat the sentences.
→ Pay special attention to *can/can't*.

Grammar and communication 3

Expressing interest – echo questions

→ Look at these examples from *The Story* and answer the questions.

1   The woman says,   'I'm from the U.S. too.'
    The man is interested. He says,   'Really?'

2   The woman says,   'I live in South America.'
    The man is interested. He says,   'Oh, do you?'

3   The man says,   'I can speak a bit of French.'
    The woman is interested. She says, 'Oh, can you?'

                                      'I live in South America.'
                                      'Oh, really?'

Another possibility for **2** and **3** above: 'I can speak a bit of French.'
                                               'Oh, really?'

→ Answer these questions.

1   It is always possible to use *really*.   Yes/No
2   We use short question forms to express interest.   Yes/No

☑ **Check your answers**

1   Yes. You can use *really* with all tenses. It doesn't change.
2   Yes. Use **auxiliary** (*do*, *can* etc.) + subject. These are **echo questions**.

How do you pronounce it?

Intonation – expressing interest, echo questions

★ To express interest, intonation is important.
★ A big fall and a little rise in the voice expresses interest.
★ A small fall and no rise in the voice expresses little or no interest.

a very interested   **b** not interested

→ Listen to Recording 4.
→ Write 'I' for 'interested or 'NI' for 'not interested' in the boxes.

Recording 4

Examples:

1	**a**	Really?	*NI*	**b** Really?	*I*
2	**a**	Do you?		**b** Do you?	
3	**a**	Can't she?		**b** Can't she?	
4	**a**	Is it?		**b** Is it?	
5	**a**	Does he?		**b** Does he?	
6	**a**	Aren't you?		**b** Aren't you?	

Check your answers

2	**a**	Interested	**b**	Not interested
3	**a**	Interested	**b**	Not interested
4	**a**	Not interested	**b**	Interested
5	**a**	Interested	**b**	Not interested
6	**a**	Not interested	**b**	Interested

Expressing interest, making conversation – echo questions

→ Express interest. Choose the correct question from box 1 on page 66.
→ Continue the conversation. Choose from box 2.

Example: His new song is really good.   ***Is it?   What's it called?***

1 I can play the guitar.	_____	_____
2 My brother's new job's very interesting.	_____	_____
3 My father lives in Mississippi.	_____	_____
4 My children don't like ice cream.	_____	_____
5 I'm thirsty.	_____	_____
6 Sue's not here today.	_____	_____
7 I like this cold weather.	_____	_____
8 Jessica can't drive.	_____	_____
9 I don't drink coffee.	_____	_____
10 I'm not very well.	_____	_____

Box 1

Are you?	Oh, can you?
Don't you?	Isn't she?
Do you?	Does he?
Can't she?	Aren't you?
Don't they?	Is it?

Box 2

What's the matter?
So, how does she get to work?
What does he do?
I prefer the summer myself.
What sort of music do you play?
Isn't that her, over there?
I have about five cups a day.
Whereabouts?
Would you like something to drink?
It's very popular in my house.

 Check your answers (Recording 5)

1 A I can play the guitar.
  B Oh, can you? What sort of music do you play?
2 A My brother's new job's very interesting.
  B Is it? What does he do?
3 A My father lives in Mississippi.
  B Does he? Whereabouts?
4 A My children don't like ice-cream.
  B Don't they? It's very popular in my house.
5 A I'm thirsty.
  B Are you? Would you like something to drink?
6 A Sue's not here today.
  B Isn't she? Look, isn't that her over there?
7 A I like this cold weather.
  B Do you? I prefer the summer myself.
8 A Jessica can't drive.
  B Can't she? So, how does she get to work?
9 A I don't drink coffee.
  B Don't you? I have about five cups a day.
10 A I'm not very well.
   B Aren't you? What's the matter?

→ Now listen to these mini-dialogues on Recording 5 and respond. Remember to show your interest with your intonation.

Very interested   Not very interested

Example: Can you?   Can you?

How do you pronounce it?

Countries – stress

→ Look at the names of the countries in the box.
→ Look at the stress patterns below the box, for example, (●o).
→ Listen to Recording 6.
→ Write the countries under the correct stress pattern.

Recording 6

the United States		Italy	Portugal	Egypt
China	Australia	Mexico	England	Poland
Brazil	Germany	Japan		

a ● o   **b** o ●   **c** ● o o

Example: *Egypt*   _____   _____

_____   _____   _____

_____   _____   _____

d o ● o o   **e** o o o o ●

_____   _____

✓ Check your answers

a ● o   **b** o ●   **c** ● o o
   Egypt   Brazil   Mexico
   China   Japan   Italy
   England   Portugal
   Poland   Germany

d o ● o o   **e** o o o o ●
   Australia   The United States

What's the right word?

Countries, nationalities and languages

→ Match these countries, nationalities and languages.
→ Write your answers in the spaces below.
→ Use your dictionary to help you, if necessary.

Example: a   Country   **a**   Spain
                  Nationality **2**   Spanish
                  Language   **B**   Spanish

Country	**Nationality**	**Language**
a Spain	1 Polish	**A** English
b Japan	2 Spanish	**B** Spanish
c the United States	3 Mexican	**C** Polish
d Italy	4 Portuguese	**D** German
e Portugal	5 Australian	**E** Chinese
f Egypt	6 Brazilian	**F** Portuguese
g China	7 American	**G** Japanese
h Australia	8 English	**H** Arabic
i Mexico	9 Italian	**I** French
j England	10 Egyptian	**J** Italian
k Poland	11 Japanese	
l Brazil	12 Chinese	
m Germany	13 French	
n France	14 German	

a _2B___   b _____   c _____   d _____   e _____
f _____   g _____   h _____   i _____   j _____
k _____   l _____   m _____   n _____

✓ **Check your answers**

a 2 B   **b** 11 G   **c** 7 A   **d** 9 J   **e** 4 F   **f** 10 H   **g** 12 E   **h** 5 A   **i** 3 B
j 8 A   **k** I C   **l** 6 F   **m** 14 D   **n** 13 1

How do you pronounce it?

Languages – stress

→ Look at the groups of languages in Recording 7 on page 69.
→ Listen to the recording.
→ <u>Underline</u> the syllable with stress.

Recording 7

English	Japanese	Italian	Arabic
Spanish	Chinese		
Polish	Portuguese		
German			

✓ Check your answers

English	Japane<u>se</u>	It<u>a</u>lian	<u>A</u>rabic
Sp<u>a</u>nish	Chin<u>ese</u>		
P<u>o</u>lish	Portug<u>uese</u>		
G<u>er</u>man			

Nationalities and languages

→ Write the name of your country and three more – not those on the list above.

→ Write the nationality and language for each one.

→ <u>Underline</u> the stress on all the words.

→ Use your dictionary if necessary.

Country	Nationality	Language
1		
2		
3		
4		

→ Check your answers in a dictionary.

Stress is marked (ˈ) at the beginning of the stressed syllable in the phonetics in dictionaries. For example, *Swedish* in the dictionary is

Swedish / ˈswiːdɪʃ /.

Countries and languages

Q *In Recording 1 the woman says, 'Where are you from?' Can I say 'Where do you come from?'*

A Yes, both are correct and common. The meaning is the same.

Q *Can I say 'Do you speak English?'*
and   'Can you speak English?'

A Yes, both are correct and common.

> **i**   **Culture – ability, responses**
>
> ■ English speakers don't usually say *I can... very well.*
>   More common expressions are:
>   *I can... but not very well* and *I can... not too badly.*

→ Look at the symbols in Recording 8, for example (+) and the
  expressions below.
→ Listen and repeat the answers.

Recording 8

1	A Do you speak Polish?	(–)	B	No, not at all.
2	A Do you speak Japanese?	(+)	B	Yes, but not very well.
3	A Can you speak Russian?	(++)	B	Yes, not too badly.
4	A Do you speak Italian?	(+++)	B	Yes, actually it's my native language.

Ability, can, responses

Situation You can speak two foreign languages.

→ Read the questions below and look at the response symbols.
→ Copy the right response phrase from the exercise above.
→ Listen to Recording 9.
→ **a** Write the language you hear.
  b Read your response.

1 Can you speak_____?   **You** (-)_____
2 And do you speak_____?   **You** (++)_____
3 How about _____?   **You** (+)_____
4 And what is your native language? **You** _____.

Check your answers (Recording 9)

1	Can you speak Arabic?	No, not at all.
2	And do you speak Italian?	Yes, not too badly.
3	How about Japanese?	Yes, but not very well.
4	And what's your native language?	Yours _____

What can you do? How well? A little? Not too badly?

→ Write about the topics below or prepare to tell a friend.
→ Use your dictionary to help you if necessary.

1 Transportation – for example, can you ride a bike, drive a car, drive a bus

_____

2 In the house – for example, cook

_____

3 Sport – for example, swim

_____

4 Hobbies – for example, play chess

_____

5 Music – for example, play the guitar, sing

_____

6 Languages

_____

What would you say?

Situation 1 In the street

Someone speaks to you in a language you can't speak.

_____

Situation 2 You are in a language class

At the end of the class another student takes your dictionary by mistake.

_____

Possible answers

1 I'm sorry but I don't understand.   2 Excuse me, that's my dictionary.
Advanced alternative: Excuse me, I think that dictionary's mine.

Review

How do you say it in your language?

→ Here are some examples of the important points in this topic.
→ Translate the sentences into your language.
→ Remember – translate the idea, not the words.

1 Where are you from?

_____

2 I'm from…

_____

3 Oh, really?

_____

4 How about you?

_____

5 **A** Can you speak German?   **B** Yes, but not very well.

_____

6 **A** Do you like it here?   **B** Not very much, actually.

_____

7 He lives in Paris.   **B** Does he? That's interesting.

_____

Join the conversation

→ Look at the text of Recording 1, _The Story_, again.
→ Listen to Recording 10.
→ Say the **woman's** words in the spaces.

TEST 3

Which one is right?

→ Choose the correct sentence **a** or **b**.

1 Ability
   a He can swim.
   b He can to swim.

2 **a** I'm not very good in math.
   b I'm not very good at math.

3 Present simple – everyday activities.
  a Do he drive to work?
  b Does he drive to work?

4 Echo questions – making conversation.
  I'm not an English student.   **a** Are you?
                                     b Aren't you?

5 He lives next door.   **a** Does he?
                                     b Is he?

Write a dialogue

Situation You are at a friend's house. You meet Claudia there. She isn't from your country.

You
1 Ask Claudia where she's from   **Claudia**
                                     2 Respond. Ask the same question

3 Reply
                                     4 Express interest and make
                                         conversation

5 Ask about languages – which?
                                     6 Respond

7 Express interest and make
    conversation.

Check your answers

Which one is right?

1 a **2** b **3** b **4** b **5** a

Dialogue: model answers

1 You   Where are you from?
2 Claudia   I'm from Italy. And you?
3 You   I'm [your nationality]
4 Claudia   Are you? That's interesting.
5 You   Which languages do you speak?
6 Claudia   Italian, of course, some English and a little Chinese.
7 You   Chinese? Really? Isn't it difficult? Can you write it too?

4 | TALKING ABOUT YOUR DAILY LIFE

Grammar and communication
- Jobs and *a/an* – the article
- Using prepositions *in*, *for*, *to*
- Asking *Do you like it?* – saying *yes* and *no*
- Likes and dislikes – verbs + *ing* – the gerund

Vocabulary
- Jobs and work

Pronunciation
- Stress and reduced forms – *do/don't*, *does/doesn't*
- Stress for emphasis
- Intonation – Single words/short phrases

The two passengers continue their conversation. They talk about their work ...

Understanding the important information

→ Cover the text of Recording 1, *The Story*.
→ Read the questions below.
→ Listen to the recording and answer the questions.

1 What's the man's job?

_____

2 What does the woman do?

_____

Recording 1 (and 6) – The Story

Woman	What do you do?
Man	I work in computers. And you? – what's your job?
Woman	I'm a teacher.
Man	You're not an English teacher by any chance, are you?
Woman	Yes, I am, actually. I teach in a school in Uruguay.
Man	Really? Whereabouts?
Woman	In a town about 75 miles from the capital. I teach in an International School.
Man	Do you? Do you like your job?
Woman	Yes, I really enjoy teaching and the students are lovely. What about you? What sort of work do you do in computers?
Man	Well, I'm in marketing. I work for a big company, so I travel a lot as part of my job. In fact, I'm on my way home now from a Computer Fair in Argentina.
Woman	And do you enjoy working in marketing?
Man	It's O.K., but I'm not very enthusiastic about all the traveling.

✓ Check your answers

1 He works in marketing computers. **2** She teaches English.

Understanding more

→ Cover the text of Recording 1 again.
→ Read the sentences on page 76.
→ Listen to the recording and check ✓ all the correct answers.

1   The woman

　　☐ **a**   lives in Tokyo.
　　☐ **b**   works in South America.
　　☐ **c**   teaches in an International School.
　　☐ **d**   doesn't like her job.

2   The man

　　☐ **a**   lives in Argentina.
　　☐ **b**   is on a business trip.
　　☐ **c**   works for a small company.
　　☐ **d**   likes his job.
　　☐ **e**   really enjoys the travelling.

✓ **Check your answers**

1   The woman
　　b   works in South America.
　　c   teaches in an International School.

2   The man
　　b   is on a business trip.
　　d   likes his job.

What do they say?

→ Read the sentences below.
→ Listen to Recording 1 again and try to complete the words.
→ Then read the text of the recording to help you, if necessary.

1 Talking about jobs

　　a   The woman asks, 'What / _ _ / you / _ _?'
　　　　　The man answers, ' I / w _ _ _ / _ _ / computers.'
　　b   The man asks, 'W _ _ _ 's / y _ _ _ / j _ _?'
　　　　　The woman answers, 'I' _ / _ / teacher.'
　　c   The woman asks for more information. She says,
　　　　　'W _ _ _ / s _ _ _ / of / w _ _ _ / do you do in computers?'
　　　　　The man answers,
　　　　　'I ' _ / _ _ / m _ _ _ _ _ _ _ g.'
　　d   The man talks about his company.
　　　　　He says, ' I work / _ _ _ / a big company.'

2 Likes and dislikes

a   The man asks, 'D _ / y _ _ / like / your / _ _ _ ?'
    She answers, 'Yes, I / really/ e _ _ _ y / t _ _ ch _ _ g.'

b   She asks,
    'D _ / you / e _ _ _ y / w _ _ k _ _ g / _ n / marketing?
    He answers, '_ _ ' _ / O.K.'

c   He doesn't like the traveling very much. He says,
    I'm n _ _ / v _ _ _ / enthusiastic /_ _ _ _ t / all the traveling.'

✓ Check your answers

1   Talking about jobs

a   'What do you do?'
    'I work in computers.'

b   'What's your job?'
    'I'm a teacher.'

c   'What sort of work do you
    do in computers?'
    'I'm in marketing.'

d   'I work for a big company.'

2   Likes and dislikes

a   'Do you like your job?'
    'Yes, I really enjoy teaching.'

b   'Do you enjoy working in
    marketing?'
    'It's O.K.'

c   'I'm not very enthusiastic about
    all the traveling'.

Find the words and phrases

→ Read the questions below.
→ Read the text of Recording 1 again and find the answers.

1   The man thinks the woman is an English teacher. He wants to check
    and make conversation.
    He says, 'You're / _ _ _ / an English teacher, b _ / _ _ _ / c _ _ _ _ _ /,
    / _ _ _ / you?

2   The woman says she teaches in an International School.
    He asks where. He says 'W _ _ _ _ _ _ _ _ _ s?'

3   The woman talks about her job. Then she asks the man about his job.
    She doesn't ask, 'How about you?'
    Instead she asks, ' _ _ _ _ about you?'

4   It's the end of the Computer Fair in Argentina. Where is the man going?
    He says, 'I_/ f _ _ _,/ I'm / o _ / m _ / w _ _ / h _ _ _ / now/ f _ _ _ /
    a Computer Fair in Argentina.'

☑ Check your answers

1   You're not an English teacher, by any chance, are you?
     ★ The phrase 'by any chance' makes the question less direct.
2   Whereabouts?
3   What about you?
     ★ 'What about you?' and 'How about you?' mean the same.
4   In fact, I'm on my way home now from a fair in Argentina.
     ★ 'In fact' is very similar to 'actually'. (See Topic 3.) 'In fact' can be
        more formal.

Using these words and phrases

1 Where? and whereabouts?

Q *What's the difference between 'where?' and 'whereabouts?'.*

A The meaning is the same.
     Where is more direct and specific.
     Example: 'I can't find my keys? Where are they?'

     Whereabouts is common because it is less *direct*.

     It is especially common when it is the only word in the question.
     Example: A 'Paul works in the U.S.'
                    B 'Does he? Whereabouts?'

Whereabouts

→ Complete these conversations.
→ Choose **a–f** from the box on page 79.

1   **A** I live in Denver.
     B _____ ?

2   **A** We go to Florida on our vacations.
     B _____ ?

3   **A** My parents are in Georgia.
     B _____ ?

4   **A** I travel to Cadaques a lot.
     B _____ ?

5 A This is the name of the hotel.
   B _____ ?

6 A Whereabouts do you work?
   B _____ .

---

  a Really? Whereabouts are they?
  b Do you? Whereabouts?
  c I know what it's called but whereabouts is it?
  d In the center of town, actually.
  e That's nice. Whereabouts do you go?
  f That's interesting but whereabouts is it?

Check your answers

1 b **2** e **3** a **4** f **5** c **6** d

2 On the way ...

→ Look at the pictures below and complete the sentences.

Are you on your way to the fair?

No I'm ___/___/way back.

They'___/___/___/ ___ to school.

___'s / on / ___ /
___ / home. **3**

He'___ / ___ / **4**
___ / ___ / to
work.

We'__ / on / ___ / way
/___ / the / ___ . **5**

___ / ___
my / ___ /
there right
now.

6

✔ **Check your answers**

1 No, I'm on my way back. **2** They're on their way to school. **3** She's on her way home. **4** He's on his way to work. **5** We're on our way to the airport. **6** I'm on my way there right now.

Grammar summary – *on the way…*		
On the way	there back	No *to* with these words
	to school to work	No *the* with these places
	to the aiport	

How do you pronounce it?

Do/don't

★ The letter *o* in *do* has two pronunciations, one full / u /and one reduced / ə /.

★ The pronunciation of 'o' in *don't* is different from the two pronunciations of 'o' in *do*.

→ Look at the mini-dialogue below. Study the three different vowel sounds.

A Do you <u>drive</u>?	Reduced *do* / ə / (*do* is not the important word)
B Yes, I <u>do</u>.	Full *do* / u / (*do* is the important word)
C Oh! I <u>don't</u>.	Negative *don't* / o / (The negative doesn't change.)

★ The vowel in *does* has two pronunciations, one full / ʌ /, one reduced / ə /.

★ The vowel in *doesn't* / ʌ / is the same as in full *does* / ʌ /.

→ Look at the mini-dialogue below. Study the two different vowel sounds.

A Does David <u>drive</u>?	Reduced *does* / ə / (*does* is not the important word)
B Yes, he <u>does</u>.	Full *does* / ʌ / (*does* is the important word)
C No, David <u>doesn't</u> <u>drive</u>.	Negative *doesn't* / ʌ / (The same vowel as full *does*.)

→ Listen to Recording 2, part 1 below and repeat.

→ Pay special attention to the vowels in *do*, *don't*, *does*, *doesn't*.

Recording 2, part 1, do/don't, does/doesn't

1 <u>Wha</u>t do you <u>do</u>?	reduced / ə /, full / u /
2 <u>Where</u> do you <u>live</u>?	reduced / ə /
3 <u>How</u> do you <u>know</u>?	reduced / ə /
4 I <u>don't</u> know.	negative / o /
5 <u>Yes</u>, you <u>do</u>.	full / u /
6 **A** Does your <u>father</u> like <u>golf</u>?	reduced / ə /
7 **B** <u>Yes</u>, he <u>does</u> **C** <u>No</u>, he <u>doesn't</u>.	full and negative / ʌ /

Q *Why are these differences important?*

A If you know that some words can be very short, with reduced vowels, you can understand more when people speak.

If you use proper stress and reduced vowels when you speak, people can understand you better.

Stress for emphasis

In *The Story*, the woman asks the man about his job.
She says, 'What do you do?'
The man answers. Then he asks 'What's your job?'

★ Stress is on the important information words in a sentence.
For example, A asks: 'What's your name?'
The important information word is 'name'.
B answers and asks the same question. 'What's your name?' This time, 'name' isn't important – we know the conversation is about 'names'. This time 'your' is important.

→ Read the seven half-dialogues below. The person answers a question and then asks the same question. Underline the stressed word in the questions.

1 I'm fine thanks. How are you?
2 I'm Carol. And you? What's your name?
3 I live in Miami. Where do you live?
4 My birthday's in April. When's yours?
5 I don't smoke. Do you?
6 I'd like some coffee. How about you? Would you like a drink?
7 I live with my parents. Do you live with yours?

☑ **Check your answers *(Recording 2, part 2)***

🎧
1 I'm fine, thanks. How are you?
2 I'm Carol. And you? What's your name?
3 I live in Miami. Where do you live?
4 My birthday's in April. When's yours?
5 I don't smoke. Do you?
6 I'd like some coffee. Would you like a drink?
7 I live with my parents. Do you live with yours?

→ Listen again and repeat the answers and questions.
→ Pay special attention to the stress in the questions.

Intonation and meaning – single words and short phrases

★ One way to express feelings in English is through intonation.

Example from *The Story:*

'It's **O.K.**' is positive.   'It's O.K.' is not very positive.

★ To sound positive, start high and finish low.
★ Flat intonation expresses that you are not very happy or interested.

Intonation summary

POSITIVE	= HIGH START	+	BIG FALL
NOT VERY POSITIVIE	= LOW START	+	SMALL FALL

→ Listen to Recording 2, part 5 on page 84.
→ For each question, one response is positive and one response is not very positive.
→ Write 'P' for 'positive' or 'NP' for 'not very positive' in the boxes.

🎧 *Recording 2, part 3*

1 Can you help me?
   a O.K. ☐
   b O.K. ☐

2 How are things?
   a All right. ☐
   b All right. ☐

3 Is that nice?
   a It's not bad. ☐
   b It's not bad. ☐

4 Are you happy about it?
   a Yeah. ☐
   b Yeah. ☐

5 Is this alright?
   a Yes, it's fine. ☐
   b Yes, it's fine. ☐

6 Do you agree?
   a Of course. ☐
   b Of course. ☐

7 Do you like it?
   a Yes. ☐
   b Yes. ☐

✅ Check your answers

1 a P
   b NP

2 a P
   b NP

3 a NP
   b P

4 a NP
   b P

5 a P
   b NP

6 a NP
   b P

7 a NP
   b P

★ *Yeah* is informal for *Yes*.

→ This time listen and repeat the responses. Can you hear the difference? Can you use intonation to sound positive?

What's the right word?

Jobs

→ Look at the pictures and the letters.
→ Write the correct word for each job.
→ Use your dictionary if necessary.

1 ITAX VREDIR

2 TAWREI

3 ROTCOD

4 TPSIERECONTI

5 CIMECAHN

6 STEDNIT

7 TACRO

8 AESLSRELKC

9 UROT DUEGI

10 REDSSREAIHR

11 AVRTEL GTAEN

12 EIRSHCA

13 TDUSENT

✓ Check your answers

1 Taxi driver **2** Waiter **3** Doctor **4** Receptionist **5** Mechanic **6** Dentist
7 Actor **8** Salesclerk **9** Tour guide **10** Hairdresser **11** Travel agent
12 Cashier **13** Student

Grammar and communication 1

Jobs – *a, an*

Example from *The Story*:
  The man asks, 'What's your job?'
  The woman says, 'I'm a teacher.'

! Common mistake

  'She's a teacher.'✓
  (Not 'She's teacher.')

Grammar summary – Jobs		
She's He's	a an	travel agent actor
Subject + verb *be*	**indefinite article**	**job**
Plurals Compare He's They're	a **X**	doctor (+ article *a*) doctors (no article)

Jobs

→ Look again at the pictures on page 85. Some people have name labels, for example, the waiter is Dan.

→ Complete the answers and questions below and on page 87.

  Example: 'What does Dan do?' **You *'He's a waiter.'***

1 What does Dan do? _____

2 What's Pat's job? _____

3 What does Carl do? _____

4 What's Kate's job? _____

5 Now you ask: Jo ?_____ She's a tour guide.

6 You ask again: Jim? _____ He's a travel agent.

Check your answers *(Recording 3)*

1 What does Dan do? He's a waiter.

2 What's Pat's job? He's a hotel receptionist.

3 What does Carl do? He's a mechanic.

4 What's Kate's job? She's a sales clerk.

5 What does Jo do? OR What's Jo's job? She's a tour guide.

6 What's Jim's job? OR What does Jim do? He's a travel agent.

→ Listen to Recording 3 and repeat the questions and answers.

Grammar and communication 2

Using prepositions

work in

Example from *The Story*: 'I'm **in** marketing.'

→ Correct A in the conversations below. Use the words in the box at the end.

→ Use your dictionary if necessary.

Example: David designs airplanes.

    A You're a dentist, aren't you, David?

    B No, *I'm in engineering*, actually.

1 Jack is a member of congress.

    A Jack works in publishing.

    B No, he's _____

2 Brenda works for Bank of America.

    A Brenda's in education.

    B No, she's _____

3 Paul is the director of a language school.

    A Paul works in banking.

    B No, not Paul. He's_____

4   Matt draws pictures for books.

   A   Matt works in administration.

   B   Are you sure? I think he works _____

---

*publishing   education   banking
engineering   politics*

✓ **Check you answers**

1 in politics. **2** in banking. **3** in education. **4** in publishing.

work for

Example from *The Story*: 'I work **for** a big company.'

→ Write the words in the correct order.

1   for/Sue/Kodak/works.

   _____

2   does/for/brother/which/your/company/work?

   _____

3   who/know/she/for/works/do/you?

   _____

✓ **Check your answers**

1   Sue works for Kodak.

2   Which company does your brother work for?

3   Do you know who she works for?

★   In spoken English you can finish a question or sentence with a preposition.

★   In written English we sometimes avoid this.

Grammar and communication 3

Asking *Do you like it?*

Examples from *The Story*:

The woman says: 'I really enjoy teaching.'

Then she asks: 'Do you enjoy working in marketing?'
The man says: 'It's O.K. but I'm not very enthusiastic about all the traveling.'

→ Read the phrases and look at the symbols below.
→ Listen to Recording 4 and repeat the phrases.

★ To answer only *yes* or *no* to the question *Do you like...?* can sound rude. Use one of these phrases instead.

Recording 4

'I really enjoy it.' (++)

'I like it.'   (+)

'I don't mind it.' (+/-)

'I'm not very enthusiastic about it, actually.' (-)

'Actually, I don't like it at all.' (- -)

★ With *actually*, the negative isn't so direct.
★ This is the other common use of the word *actually*.

Do you like it? – responses

→ Look at the questions and symbols (for example ++) below.
→ Listen to Recording 5 and respond.

Example: You are the woman in *The Story*.
Question: Do you like being a teacher?
You answer: (++) *Yes, I really enjoy it.*

These are from the vocabulary exercise earlier in this topic (page 87).

1 Dan, do you enjoy being a waiter? (+) Yes,_____
2 Pat, do you like working in reception? (-) No,_____
3 Carl, how do you like your job? (++) _____
4 Kate, do you enjoy working in a shop? (+/-) _____
5 Jo, what's it like being a tour guide? (- -)_____
6 Do you like working in travel, Jim? (+) Yes, _____

☑ **Check your answers** *(Recording 5)*

1 'Yes, I quite like it.'
2 'No, I'm not very enthusiastic about it, actually.'
3 'I really enjoy it.'
4 'I don't mind it.'
5 'Actually, I don't like it at all.'
6 'Yes, I quite like it.'

Grammar and communication 4

Likes and dislikes – verb + *ing*/gerund

Examples from *The Story*:

'I really enjoy teaching.'
'I'm not very enthusiastic about all the traveling.'

After *enjoy*, *like*, *not mind* and *be keen on* the verb ends in *ing*. This is the **gerund**.

enjoy + verb/'*ing*'   *like* + verb/'*ing*',
mind + verb/'*ing*'   *be enthusiastic about* + verb/'*ing*'

→ Read this interview with a schoolgirl, Sophie.
→ <u>Underline</u> all the verbs + gerunds.

Interviewer So, tell us about what you like doing and don't like doing, Sophie.

Sophie Well, I really enjoy going out with my friends on the weekend. I like inviting them home, too. I don't mind doing my homework – I know that's important, but I'm not very enthusiastic about helping my Mom with the housework.

☑ **Check your answers**

Interviewer Like doing… don't like doing…
Sophie enjoy going out… like inviting… don't mind doing… not very enthusiastic about helping

Likes and dislikes

→ Complete these mini-dialogues using *enjoy, like, don't mind, not enthusiastic about.*
→ Use the verbs in the box below.

1 **A** What sort of thing do you like _____ in the evening?

    B Well, actually, I enjoy _____ 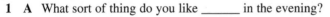 and I like _____ too.

2 **A** Jack, can you help us with some housework on Saturday?

    B O.K. I don't mind _____ but I'm not very enthusiastic about _____

3 **A** Do you like _____ ?

    B Yes I really enjoy_____

4 **A** That new film is showing at the movies.

    B Actually, 'I'm _____ out tonight. I'm very tired.'

5 **A** I'm sorry but the dentist can't see you for another half an hour.

    B That's O.K. I _____

---

vacuum	*cook*	*go*	*do*	*watch T.V.*	*make*
	wait	*iron*	*read*		

Check your answers

1 **A** doing.
    B watching T.V, reading
2 **B** vacuuming, ironing
3 **A** cooking
    B making cakes
4 **B** not very enthusiastic about going
5 **B** don't mind waiting

What's the right word or phrase?

Work

→ Match **1–12** with **a–l**.
→ First try without a dictionary. Then use your dictionary if necessary.

1	Hannah works in the house for her family.	☐ **a**	She works full-time.
2	Kate is 70.	☐ **b**	She's unemployed.
3	Dawn hasn't got a job.	☐ **c**	She's a colleague.
4	Sue works from 10–2.	☐ **d**	She works a lot of overtime.
5	Twenty people work for Julie.	☐ **e**	She's a housewife.
6	May works 50 hours a week.	☐ **f**	She's a manager.
7	Denise works from 9–5.	☐ **g**	She works part-time.
8	Myra is a student doctor at the hospital.	☐ **h**	She works freelance.
9	Chris's office is in her house.	☐ **i**	She's retired.
10	Sheila works in the same office. as her sister.	☐ **j**	She works on different shifts.
11	Lena works on short contracts for different companies.	☐ **k**	She works from home.
12	Lucy goes to the University.	☐ **l**	She's a student.

✓ **Check your answers**

1 e, **2** i **3** b **4** g **5** f **6** d **7** a **8** j **9** k **10** c **11** h **12** l

How about you? – work

→ Write or prepare to tell a friend about your job/studies.
   What do you do/study?
→ Give some extra information about your job/studies.
→ Use some of the expressions in the vocabulary exercise above.
   How much do you enjoy your job/studies?

_____

_____

_____

_____

$\boxed{i}$ **Culture – work**

- In the U.S., usual office hours are 9.00 or 9.30 a.m.–5.00 or 5.30 p.m., Monday to Friday.
- The average working week is 35 hours.
- People usually have one hour for lunch between 12 and 2 o'clock.
- Three weeks per year is the average holiday.
- The company deducts some money from the salary before they pay it:
  – A percentage for income tax.
  – A percentage for Social Security.
- It is not polite to ask people their salary.

→ Write or prepare to tell a friend about work in your country. Give information on the points above.
Use the phrases in the text to help you.

_____

_____

_____

What would you say?

1 You and John work for the same company. John leaves and goes to work for another company. Someone telephones and asks you, 'Can I speak to John, please?'

_____

2 You work in a shop that is open seven days a week. You work on Saturdays and Wednesdays. It's the end of the day on Saturday. A colleague asks you, 'Are you in tomorrow?'

Possible answers

1 'I'm sorry but John doesn't work here any more.'
2 'No, I'm not in again until Wednesday.'
★ Here 'to be in' means 'to be here, at work'.

Review

How do you say it in your language?

→ Here are some examples of the important points in this topic.
→ Translate the sentences into your language in the spaces.
→ Remember – translate the idea, not the words.

1 What do you do?   I'm a… _____

2 Do you like cooking?   _____
   Yes, I really enjoy it.   _____
   Yes, I like it.   _____
   It's O.K.   _____
   I'm not very enthusiastic about _____
   it, actually.
   Actually, I don't like it at all. _____

3 I don't mind waiting.   _____

4 I'm on my way home.   _____

Join the conversation

→ Look at the text of Recording 1 (page 75) – *The Story*, again.
→ Listen to Recording 6.
→ Read the **man's** words.

TEST 4

Which one is right?

Choose **a** or **b**.

1 **a** What work does your brother?
   b What does your brother do?

2 **a** Like you your job?
   b Do you like your job?

3 **a** We're on our way there now.
   b We go to there now.

4 **a** Are you enjoy to travel?
   b Do you enjoy traveling?

5 **a** What sort of company does he work for?
   b For which sort of company he works?

6 a We can't use the car but I don't mind to walk.
   b We can't use the car but I don't mind walking.

Choose the correct stress
7 My brother's a mechanic.   **a** What does <u>your</u> brother do?
                                 b What does your <u>bro</u>ther do?

Write your part of the dialogue

Situation You are at a party. You are in the middle of a conversation with a person you don't know.

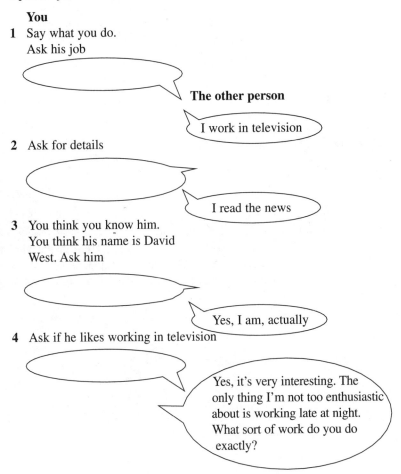

You
1 Say what you do.
Ask his job

The other person

I work in television

2 Ask for details

I read the news

3 You think you know him.
You think his name is David
West. Ask him

Yes, I am, actually

4 Ask if he likes working in television

Yes, it's very interesting. The only thing I'm not too enthusiastic about is working late at night. What sort of work do you do exactly?

5 Respond

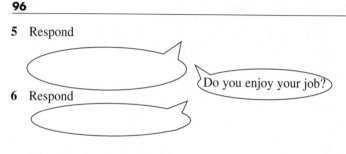

Do you enjoy your job?

6 Respond

His wine glass is empty. Offer more

7

Yes, please. That would be nice

✓ **Check your answers**

Which one is right?

1 b **2** b **3** a **4** b **5** a **6** b **7** a

Dialogue: model answers

1 I'm a… What do you do? OR What's your job?
2 What sort of work do you do in television?
3 I think I know you. You're David West, aren't you?
4 Do you like working in television?
5 I … [details about you]
6 I really enjoy it OR I like it OR I don't mind it OR I'm not very enthusiastic about it actually OR Actually I don't like it at all.
7 Would you like some more wine? OR Would you like another glass of wine?

5 GIVING EXPLANATIONS

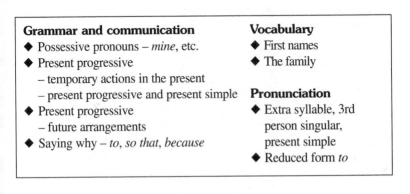

Grammar and communication
- Possessive pronouns – *mine*, etc.
- Present progressive
  - temporary actions in the present
  - present progressive and present simple
- Present progressive
  - future arrangements
- Saying why – *to*, *so that*, *because*

Vocabulary
- First names
- The family

Pronunciation
- Extra syllable, 3rd person singular, present simple
- Reduced form *to*

The conversation on the plane continues... They exchange names, talk about their families and the reasons for their trips

Understanding the important information

→ Read the sentences below.
→ Listen to Recording 1, *The Story*.
→ Circle *Yes* for the things they talk about.
→ Circle *No* for the things they don't talk about.

They talk about

a	their names	Yes/No
b	where he lives	Yes/No
c	his family	Yes/No
d	the reason for her trip	Yes/No
e	her mother	Yes/No
f	her father	Yes/No

Recording 1 (and 5) – The Story

Woman	What's your name?
Man	Oliver. And yours?
Woman	My name's Tasha. It's short for Natasha, a Russian name. My mother's Russian. So, whereabouts in the U.S. do you live, Oliver?
Man	I live in Canada, actually, in Toronto, but I'm staying in Denver for a couple of weeks, because of my job. And you? Are you on vacation?
Woman	Yes, I'm going to Colorado to see some friends of mine. They live near Denver.
Man	Oh, I see. And your family?
Woman	My father's working in London at the moment – until next June. He works abroad quite a lot. It's nice because my mother organizes her work so that she can travel with him. Even if they aren't at home, I go to Denver every year because I need to see other relatives and friends.

✓ **Check your answers**

a yes **b** yes **c** no **d** yes **e** yes **f** yes

Understanding more

→ Cover the text of Recording 1, *The Story*.
→ Read the questions below.
→ Listen to the recording and circle ⬭ the right answer.

1 His name is <u>Oliver/Leo</u>.
2 Her name is <u>Sasha/Tasha</u>.
3 Her name is from <u>Greece/Russia</u>.
4 Her <u>mother/father</u> is from the same country.
5 The man lives in <u>Toronto/Windsor</u>.
6 But for the next 2/3 weeks his work is in <u>Denver/Reno</u>.
7 She's on her way to visit <u>her family/some friends</u>.
8 They live <u>in/near</u> Denver.
9 Her parents are in <u>South Africa/England</u>, for another <u>2 years/6 months</u>.
10 When her parents aren't in Denver <u>she goes/doesn't go</u> home.

11 When she goes to Denver she visits her friends and <u>museums/</u>
<u>her family</u>.

✓ **Check your answers**

1 Oliver **2** Tasha **3** Russia **4** mother **5** Toronto **6** 2 weeks … Denver
7 some friends **8** near **9** England… 6 months **10** goes **11** her family

What do they say?

→ Cover the text of Recording 1, *The Story* again.
→ Read the sentences below.
→ Listen to the recording and try to complete the sentences.
→ Then read the text of the recording to help you, if necessary.

1 The woman asks the man his name.
   He says, 'Oliver.' Then he asks the same question 'A _ _ / y _ _ _ _ ?'

2 **a** Oliver has work in Denver for two weeks.
      He says, 'I' _ / s _ _ _ _ _ _ / in Denver for a couple of weeks.'
   b He says why.
      'B _ _ _ _ _ _ / o _ / my job.'

3 Oliver asks Tasha, 'Are you on vacation?'
   She says, 'Yes,/ I' _ / g _ _ _ _ / t _ / Colorado/ t _ / see some friends /
   o _ / m _ _ _ .'

4 Tasha's parents aren't in Denver now.
   She says, 'My / f _ _ _ _ _'s / w _ _ _ _ _ g / in London at
   the moment.'

5 Tasha's mother likes traveling with her father but she works.
   Tasha says, 'My mother organizes her work s_ / t _ _ t / s _ _ / c _ _
   travel with him.'

6 Why does Tasha go to Denver every year? She says,
   'B _ _ _ _ _ e / I / n _ _ _ / t _ / see other relatives and friends.'

✓ **Check your answers**

1 And yours? **2 a** I'm staying in Denver for a couple of weeks. **b** Because of
my job. **3** Yes, I'm going to Colorado to see some friends (of mine). **4** My
father's working in London at the moment. **5** My mother organizes her
work so that she can travel with him. **6** Because I need to see other
relatives and friends.

Find the words and phrases

→ Read the sentences below.
→ Read the text of Recording 1 on page 98 and complete the words.

1 Tasha is the short name. Natasha is the long name.
Tasha is s _ _ _ t / f _ _ Natasha.

2 Tasha says, 'My mother's Russian.' Then she starts a new topic.
She says, ' _ _ / whereabouts in the U.S. do you live, Oliver?'

3 Tasha asks, 'Whereabouts in the U.S. do you live, Oliver?'
Oliver doesn't live in the U.S., he lives in Canada.
He says, 'I live in Canada /, a _ _ _ _ _ _ _ /.'

4 Oliver's going to Denver. How long for? Two weeks.
He says, 'f_ _ / a / c _ _ _ _ e / o _ / weeks.'

5 Is Tasha working? No, she's _ _ vacation.

6 Tasha says, 'I'm going to Colorado to see some friends. They live near
Denver.'
Oliver responds with another question.
He says, 'O _, / I / s _ _. And your family?'

7 Tasha's father works in other countries. He works a _ _ _ _ _ .

8 Does Tasha's father work in other countries all the time?
Not all the time but q _ _ _ e / _ / l _ _ of the time.

9 Tasha goes to Denver when her parents are there and when her
parents aren't there. She goes to Denver e _ _ _ / i _ her parents
aren't there.

10 How often does Tasha go to Denver? E _ _ _ _ / y _ _ r.

✓ **Check your answers**

1 Tasha is short **for** Natasha. (preposition!)
2 So, whereabouts in the U.S. do you live, Oliver?
3 I live in Canada, actually.
4 I'm staying in Denver **for** a couple of weeks. (preposition!)
5 She's **on** vacation. (Not: 'in vacation'). (preposition!)
6 Oh, I see.
7 He works abroad.
8 Not all the time but quite a lot of the time.

9 She goes to Denver even if her parents aren't there.

10 Every year. (Not: every ~~years~~).

| i | **Culture – first names** |

- It is common to have one first name, one middle name and one family name.
  Example:

Victoria	Ann	Smith
First	Middle	Family name or surname

- First names and middle names often come from other members of the family.
- It is very common to shorten first names, e.g. Victoria → Vicky.
- If a first name has a short form, it can be more formal to use the long form. e.g. Michael can be more formal than Mike.
- When we write a name, we usually start with the first name, e.g. Collette Dickenson. 'Collette' is the first name, 'Dickenson' is the family name. On official papers and documents, the family name usually comes first.
- At work it is very common to use first names.
- You can give your child the name you like. There is no official list.

Find the right first name

Example from *The Story*:
'Tasha is short for Natasha.'

→ Look at the names on page 102 and in the box.
→ Match the short and long names.

Girls		**Boys**	
1	Jo _____	1	Pat _____
2	Alex _____	2	Chris _____
3	Liz _____	3	Nick _____
4	Sam _____	4	Ricky _____
5	Kate _____	5	Sam _____
6	Ros _____	6	Joey _____
7	Chris _____	7	Mike _____
8	Nicky _____	8	Alex _____
9	Pat _____	9	Tom _____
10	Di _____	10	Dan _____

Girls		**Boys**	
Patricia	Christine	Nicholas	Samuel
Joanna	Rosalyn	Michael	Daniel
Alexandra	Elizabeth	Richard	Thomas
Nicola	Catherine	Alexander	Christopher
Samantha	Diana	Patrick	Joseph

✓ Check your answers

Girls	**Boys**
1 Jo/Joanna	Pat/Patrick
2 Alex/Alexandra	Chris/Christopher
3 Liz/Elizabeth	Nick/Nicholas
4 Sam/Samantha	Ricky/Richard
5 Kate/Catherine	Sam/Samuel
6 Ros/Rosalyn	Joey/Joseph
7 Chris/Christine	Mike/Michael
8 Nicky/Nicola	Alex/Alexander
9 Pat/Patricia	Tom/Thomas
10 Di/Diana	Dan/Daniel

As you can see, some short names are the same for both men and women.

→ How many examples of this can you find in the lists? Write them here.

_____

Asking someone about their name

→ Put these words in the right order:

for/name/what/your/'s/short? _____

✓ Check your answers

Four. Alex, Sam, Chris and Pat are short names for both boys and girls.
What's your name short for?

About you: first names

→ Write answers to these questions or prepare to tell a friend.

Is your first name short for another name?_____

Does another member of the family have the same name?_____

Where does your name come from?_____

Is it common or unusual in your country?_____

What does your first name mean?_____

Using these words and phrases

1 *So*

Example from *The Story*:

Tasha My mother's Russian. So, whereabouts in the U.S. do you live, Oliver?

★ We can use *so* to change the topic
In the conversation above, Tasha talks about her mother. Then she asks Oliver where he lives. *So* starts the new topic

★ *So* is not essential.

So, to start a new topic

Situation John and Jean live in Miami. They have a party. Two guests have a conversation.

→ Read the conversation on page 104. The topic changes three times.

→ Write *so* where the topic changes.

Jo	My name's Jo and yours?
Sam	Sam.
Jo	Where do you come from Sam?
Sam	I'm from New York. I work in a bookshop there.
Jo	Do you like it?
Sam	Yes, I really enjoy it, actually. I love books. Do you know this town well?
Jo	Quite well. I come here on vacation from time to time. How about you? Where do you go for vacations?
Sam	I like going to Florida for vacations – I love Miami and I know Atlanta and Key West and a few other places. How do you know John and Jean?
Jo	John's my brother.
Sam	Oh, right.

✓ **Check your answers**

Jo	My name's Jo and yours?
Sam	Sam.
Jo	(So,) where do you come from Sam?
Sam	I'm from New York. I work in a bookshop there.
Jo	Do you like it?
Sam	Yes, I really enjoy it, actually. I love books. (So,) do you know this town well?
Jo	Quite well. I come here on vacation from time to time. How about you? Where do you go for vacations?
Sam	I like going to Florida for vacations – I love Miami and I know Atlanta and Key West and a few other places. (So,) how do you know John and Jean?
Jo	John's my brother.
Sam	Oh, right.

2 Correcting people – *actually*

Example from *The Story*:

Tasha: 'So, whereabouts in the U.S. do you live, Oliver?'
Oliver doesn't live in the U.S. He lives in Canada.
He says: 'I live in Canada, **actually**.'

He doesn't say the wrong information, 'I don't live in the U.S.' This can sound rude. He says 'I live in Canada, actually.' He says the correct information + *actually*.

With *actually* the correction is less direct.

★ *Actually* goes at the beginning or the end of the correction,
  Example: 'Actually, I live in Canada' OR 'I live in Canada, actually.'

→ Read the short dialogues below.
→ Correct the 'mistakes'.

Recording 2

Example:	**A**	Good morning, Jo.	**B**	***My name's Sam, actually.*** (Your name's Sam)
1	**A**	So, what's it like working for Sony?	**B**	_____ (You work for Panasonic)
2	**A**	Excuse me … here's your bag.	**B**	_____ (The bag isn't yours)
3	**A**	Would you like some wine?	**B**	_____ (You don't drink alcohol)
4	**A**	Please take me home.	**B**	_____ (You can't drive)
5	**A**	So, whereabouts in France are you from?	**B**	_____ (You're from Italy)
6	**A**	Peter's really nice, isn't he?	**B**	_____ (You don't know Peter)
7	**A**	(On the phone) Sue?	**B**	_____ (You're Sue's mother)
8	**A**	Lovely, isn't it?	**B**	_____ (You're not very enthusiastic about it)
9	**A**	What sort of work does your husband do?	**B**	_____ (You're not married)

✓ Check your answers

1 (Actually), I work for Panasonic, (actually).
2 (Actually), it's not mine, (actually).
3 (Actually), I don't drink alcohol, (actually).
4 (Actually), I can't drive, (actually).
5 (Actually), I'm from Italy, (actually).

6 (Actually), I don't know him, (actually).
7 (Actually) I'm her mother, (actually).
8 (Actually) I'm not very keen on it, (actually).
9 (Actually) I'm not married, (actually).

→ Listen to Recording 2 and say the responses.

3 *Abroad*

Example from *The Story*:
Tasha's father works abroad.

★ *Abroad* has no preposition and no **article** ('the').

It isn't correct to say:
'He works ~~in the~~ abroad.'
'He goes ~~to~~ abroad for his vacation.'

→ Complete these answers with *abroad* and information about Oliver and Tasha from the recording.

1 Is Tasha's mother in the U.S.?
No, _____

2 Does Tasha live in the U.S.?
No, she_____

3 Oliver _____ a lot as part of his job.

4 Tasha's father _____ quite a lot.

5 What sort of vacations do you like?
I enjoy (travel) _____

✓ **Check your answers**

1 No, she's abroad. **2** No, she lives abroad. **3** Oliver travels abroad a lot as part of his job. **4** Tasha's father works abroad quite a lot. **5** I enjoy traveling abroad.

How do you pronounce it?

He, she, it and *who?* forms of present simple

🎧 *Recording 3, part 1*

Example from *The Story*:   My mother organizes her work.

→ Read the question below.
→ Listen to the sentence on the recording and choose **a** or **b**.

The verb *organize* has three syllables – or-gan-ize.

'Organizes' has $\left.\begin{array}{l}\textbf{a} \text{ three}\\\textbf{b} \text{ four}\end{array}\right\}$ syllables?

✔️ Check your answer

b 'organizes' has four syllables - or-gan-iz-es. / ˈɔrgənaɪzɪz /
   Remember, a syllable is part of a word with a vowel sound.

★ Some verbs add an extra syllable / ɪz / after *he* and *she*, *it* and *who?*

→ Listen to Recording 3, part 2 and repeat these verbs.

🎧 *Recording 3, part 2*

close	fin-ish	re-lax	watch	dance
clos-es	fin-ish-es	re-lax-es	watch-es	danc-es

Pronunciation – 3rd person singular, present simple

Situation Kate and Joey are married. Joey has a shop and his wife works in a supermarket. Who does what in their house?

→ Read Joey's sentences on page 108.
→ Complete the verbs and write the number of syllables in the parentheses ( ). All the verbs here change.
→ Practice the extra syllable. Read the verbs aloud as you write.

My wife and I

Example: I close (1) my shop at 6:00 but Kate's supermarket *closes* (2) at 9:00.

I finish ( ) work early but she _____ ( ) late.

At home I wash ( ) the dishes and she _____ ( ) the clothes.

I fix ( ) the car and she _____ ( ) things in the house.

I relax ( ) in the bath but she _____ ( ) with a book.

I watch ( ) sports on T.V. but Kate _____ ( ) news programs.

I dance ( ) a bit but my wife _____ ( ) well.

I use ( ) soap but my wife _____ ( ) shower gel.

I change ( ) the baby in the morning and Kate _____ ( ) her at night.

I sneeze ( ) when I'm ill but she _____ ( ) every morning.

I organize( ) the money and she _____ ( ) the vacations.

I kiss ( ) my wife and my wife _____ ( ) me.

✓ Check your answers *(Recording 3, part 3)*

I close (1)...the supermarket closes (2)
I finish (2)...she finishes (3)
I wash (1)...she washes (2)
I fix (1)...she fixes (2)
I relax (2)...she relaxes (3)
I watch (1)...Kate watches (2)
I dance (1)...my wife dances (2)
I use (1)...my wife uses (2)
I change (1)...Kate changes (2)
I sneeze (1)...she sneezes (2)
I organize (3)...she organizes (4)
I kiss (1) my wife and my wife kisses (2) me.

→ Listen to the answers above on Recording 3, part 3 and repeat.
→ Pay special attention to the extra syllable for *she*.

Asking *who?* – pronunciation 3rd person singular '-*es*'

Who does these things? Kate or Joey?

→ Complete the questions with one word only.

Who _____( ) the dishes?	Joey.
Who _____ ( ) work at 9:00?	Kate does.
Who _____ ( ) sport on T.V.?	Joey does.
Who _____( ) things?	They both do.

✓ Check your answers

		Note
1	Who washes the dishes?	Not: ~~Who does wash the dishes?~~
2	Who finishes work at 9.00	When *who* is the subject, no *do*.
3	Who watches sports on T.V.?	
4	Who fixes things?	

❓ When do we add an extra syllable for 'he, she, it' and question 'who'?

When it's difficult to say the 's' without adding an extra vowel sound. An extra vowel sound creates an extra syllable (It's the same reason as for the plural nouns in Topic 3.)

→ Look at the summary below.

Pronunciation and spelling summary

3rd person singular

★ For *he, she, it* and *who* add an extra syllable to verbs ending in:

- se	-ce	-ge	- ze	-ss	-sh	-tch	-x
close	dance	change	sneeze	kiss	wash	watch	relax
use					finish		fix
			organize				
				Here, the spelling changes too. Add 'es'			

→ Look at the verbs below.
→ Which ones change with *he, she, it* and question *who*?

touch	cross	read	think	want	drink
fax	pass	manage	pronounce	wish	

☑ **Check your answers**

Touch, cross, fax, pass, manage, pronounce, wish.
All these words have an extra final syllable in 3rd person singular.
The syllable is / ɪz /.

What's the right word?

The family: close relatives

Who's who in this family?

→ Look at the family diagram on page 111 and the vocabulary in the boxes.
→ Complete the sentences on page 112.
→ Use your dictionary if necessary.

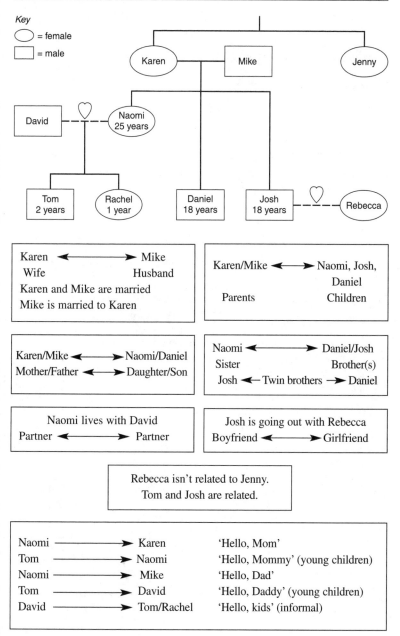

Key
◯ = female
▢ = male

Karen — Mike — Jenny

David — ♡ — Naomi 25 years

Tom 2 years — Rachel 1 year — Daniel 18 years — Josh 18 years — ♡ — Rebecca

Karen ◄──────► Mike
Wife   Husband
Karen and Mike are married
Mike is married to Karen

Karen/Mike ◄──────► Naomi, Josh, Daniel
Parents   Children

Karen/Mike ◄──────► Naomi/Daniel
Mother/Father ◄──────► Daughter/Son

Naomi ◄──────► Daniel/Josh
Sister   Brother(s)
Josh ◄── Twin brothers ──► Daniel

Naomi lives with David
Partner ◄──────► Partner

Josh is going out with Rebecca
Boyfriend ◄──────► Girlfriend

Rebecca isn't related to Jenny.
Tom and Josh are related.

Naomi ──────► Karen   'Hello, Mom'
Tom ──────► Naomi   'Hello, Mommy' (young children)
Naomi ──────► Mike   'Hello, Dad'
Tom ──────► David   'Hello, Daddy' (young children)
David ──────► Tom/Rachel   'Hello, kids' (informal)

→ Now complete these sentences with the vocabulary from the diagram and boxes above.

1 🔔 Mike: Could I speak to Karen, please? It's her _____ here.'

2 🔔 This is Karen, Josh's mother. Is my _____ there, please?'

3 I'm Naomi, Daniel's sister. Is my _____ here, please?

4 **A** Who's David? **B** Naomi's _____ .

5 **A** Josh, are you _____/_____ to Mike? **B** Yes, he's my dad.

6 Mike: Naomi's a lovely _____ .

7 Mike: I'm married to Karen now. Sue's my first _____ .

8 Naomi: Daniel's my _____ .

9 Josh is Daniel's _____/_____. They look exactly alike.

10 Josh is in love with his _____. He wants to marry her. He asks her, 'Will you marry me?'

11 When David goes to work, little Tom says, 'Bye, bye _____.'

12 **A** Naomi, is Daniel a _____ of yours? **B** Yes, he's my brother.'

13 'We always give our _____ flowers on Mother's Day.'
*Mother's Day is usually in May in the U.S.

14 🔔 It's Daniel here, Naomi's brother. Can I leave a message for my _____, please?'

15 a Naomi and David have got two _____.
b When Naomi takes them out, she says 'Come on _____ . We're going out.'

16 🔔 Daniel: I need to talk to Mom. Naomi: Mom isn't here but _____ is. Shall I get him?'

17 Tom is in a shop. He can't find Naomi. He says, 'Where's my _____?'

18 Naomi and Josh are _____ and _____.

19 A Who's Karen _____/_____? **B** Mike

20 A Who's Rebecca _____/_____/_____? **B** Her _____'s name's Josh.

✓ **Check your answers**

1 husband **2** son **3** brother **4** partner **5** related to (preposition! Not: ~~related with~~') **6** daughter **7** wife **8** brother **9** twin brother **10** girlfriend **11** Daddy **12** relative **13** Mom **14** sister **15 a** children **b** kids

*It is rude to use the singular in this way. Instead we use the name e.g. 'Come on David', not '~~Come on kid~~'.

16 Dad **17** Mommy **18** brother and sister **19** married to (preposition! Not: ~~married with~~') **20** going out with/boyfriend

Family relationships

Possessive *'s* contraction of *is* and *has*

A sentence can have more than one possessive **'s**.
→ Look at the examples below.

1 Who**'s** Karen? Mike**'s** wife (Not: ~~The wife of Mike~~)
     is   possessive 's

2 Karen**'s** daughter**'s** name**'s** Naomi. (Not: ~~The name of the daughter of~~
     possessive ' s   is   ~~Karen is Naomi~~)

3 What**'s** David**'s** son**'s** name? (Not: ~~What's the name of the son of~~
     is   possessive 's   ~~David~~)

OR What**'s** the name of David**'s** son?
     is   possessive 's

4 Daniel has a friend, Jack.
   Who**'s** Jack? A friend of Daniel**'s**. (Not: ~~A friend of Daniel.~~)
     is   possessive 's

1 A Who's Josh? **B** M____'_ / s_____
2 A Who'_ Mike? **B** K____'_ / h_____
3 Daniel' __/m____'_/n_____'_/ Karen.
4 Josh'_/ f_____'s/ n_____'_/ Mike.
5 Mike'_ / d_____'_ / n ____' _ Naomi.
6 A: What'__/ K___n'_ / d_____'_ / n____? **B:** Naomi.
7 A: Who'_ Daniel? A f _____ / o__/ J ____'_.

✓ **Check your answers**

1 Mike's son. **2** Karen's husband. **3** Daniel's mother's name's Karen.
4 Josh's father's name's Mike. **5** Mike's daughter's name's Naomi. **6** What's
Karen's daugher's name? **7** Who's Daniel? A friend of Jack's.

Write about you and your family

→ Choose the right information below to make a paragraph about you and your family.

→ Delete, circle, complete or tick the right answers about you.

→ Use your dictionary if necessary.

For example: I'm ⎰ married
             ⎱ ~~not married~~

My   husband's
        wife's   name's Mary/John
        partner's
        girlfriend's
        boyfriend's

I've got 1
          2   children ✓
          3

About you

My name's _____
My family and friends call me _____
I'm ⎰ married
    ⎱ not married
I've got a ⎰ partner
       ⎨ girlfriend
       ⎩ boyfriend

About your partner

      My ⎧ husband's
         ⎪ wife's   name's _____
         ⎨ partner's
         ⎪ girlfriend's
         ⎩ boyfriend's

OR
I haven't got a partner/girlfriend/boyfriend
OR
I'm too young to have a girlfriend/boyfriend

About your brothers and sisters

I've got 1 brother His name's _____

2 brothers Their names are _____ and _____

3 brothers Their names are _____,_____ and _____

4 etc. brothers Their names are _____

_____ and _____

I've got 1 sister Her name's _____

2 sisters Their names are _____ and _____

3 sisters Their names are _____,_____ and_____

4 etc. sisters Their names are _____

_____ and _____

OR

I haven't got any brothers or sisters. I'm an only child

About your parents

Both my parents are alive. They live in _____

{ Both my parents are alive but they aren't together.
My mother lives in _____ and my father lives in _____

My mother's alive but my father's dead. She lives in _____
My father's alive but my mother's dead. He lives in _____
Both my parents are dead

About your children

I haven't got any children
I've got one child, a son. His name's
I've got one child, a daughter. Her name's _____
I've got two, three, four etc. children. Their names are _____
_____ and _____

Grammar and communication 1

Possessive pronouns – *mine*, etc.

Examples from *The Story*:

1 The woman asks the man his name.
He says, 'Oliver.' Then he asks the same question.
He says, 'And **yours**?'

2 Why is Tasha going to Denver?
   She says, 'To see some friends of mine.'

★ 'They're friends of mine' is more common than 'they're my friends.'

→ Use the possessive pronouns in the box to complete the table below.

Subject	Possessive adjective	Possessive pronoun
I ———————→	my ———————————→	_____
he ———————→	his ———————————→	_____
she ——————→	her ———————————→	_____
you ——————→	your ——————————→	_____
we ———————→	our ———————————→	_____
they ——————→	their —————————→	_____

ours	*mine*	*theirs*	*his*	*yours*	*hers*

✔ **Check your answers**

Subject	Possessive adjective	Possessive pronoun
I	my	mine
he	his	his
she	her	hers
you	your	yours
we	our	ours
they	their	theirs

Possessive pronouns

→ Complete the sentences below with the correct possessive pronoun.

1 **A** My birthday's in April. When's _____?   **B** In November.
2 We're seeing friends of _____ for dinner tomorrow.
3 **A** Does David know Jack?   **B** Yes, Jack's a friend of _____
4 That isn't their car. _____ is blue.
5 **A** Is Jo a classmate of _____?   **B** Yes, we're in the same English class.

6 The family is going on holiday.
   a Which bag is yours?   That big one's _____
   b And John's?   The red one's _____
   c Where's Mary's?   _____ is this black one.
   d How about Kay's and Mike's? _____ are in the car.
   e And we can take _____.   Come on, let's go.

Check your answers

1 yours **2** ours **3** his **4** theirs **5** yours **6 a** mine **b** his **c** hers **d** theirs **e** ours

Grammar and communication 2

Present progressive – temporary actions

Example from *The Story*:

1 Tasha's parents aren't in the U.S. now.
   She says, '**My father's working** in London until June.'
                        is

   The name of the tense is the **Present Progressive**.
   What's the meaning and form?

→ Choose the right answers.

Meaning

1 Here the present progressive is for **a** the past.

                                          b the present.

                                          c the future.

2 The action is **a** permanent.

                    b temporary.

Form

1 The verb has **a** one word.

                    b two words.

2 The present of 'be' **a** is   ⎫
                          b isn't ⎬ part of this tense

Check your answers

Meaning 1 b the present **2 b** temporary.
Form   1 b two words **2 a** The present of 'be' is part of this tense.

★ Here the **present progressive** is for **a temporary action** in the **present**.

Present progressive – form

→ Complete the table on page 118 with the correct part of the verb *be*.
→ Write the contractions in the brackets, for example I am (I'm).

Affirmative ('yes')		Negative ('no')	
I _ _ ('m)		I _ _ not ('m)	
He She _ _ It ('_)	working.	He She _ _ not It ('_) OR _ _ n't	working.
You We _ _ _ They ('_ _)		You _ _ _ not We ('_ _) They OR _ _ _ n't	

Questions		Question tags – to make conversation Echo questions – to express interest	
		Positive	**Negative**
_ _ I		_ _ I?	aren't I?

_ _   he
     she
     it
	working?	_ _ she?
		     it?
			he?
			 _ _ n't she?
			     it?

you
 _ _ _ we
     they
		you?
		 _ _ _ we?
		     they?
			you?
			 _ _ _ n't we?
			     they?

Check your answers

Affirmative ('yes')		Negative ('no')	
I am ('m)		I am not ('m)	
he she is it ('s) you we are they ('re)	working	he she is not it ('s) OR isn't you are not we ('re) they OR aren't	working

Questions		Question tags – to make conversation	
		Echo questions – to express interest	
		Positive	**Negative**
Am I		am I?	aren't I?

Is   he
      she
      it
	working?	he?
		is she?
		      it?
			isn't he?
			          she?
			          it?

Are   you
      we
      they
		you?
		are we?
		      they?
			aren't you?
			          we?
			          they?

More questions! Present progressive – form

→ Answer *Yes/No* to these questions

1 The main verb is always with 'ing'.	Yes/No
2 To make questions, you use auxiliary *do*.	Yes/No
3 To ask a question, you change the word order.	Yes/No
4 In questions the verb *be* is before the person.	Yes/No
5 The negative can have two forms.	Yes/No
6 The 'I' form of the negative question tag is irregular.	Yes/No

Check your answers

1 Yes **2** No **3** Yes **4** Yes **5** Yes **6** Yes (aren't I?)

Temporary actions in the present – present progressive

What's happening at home?

Situation Mark arrives home. He's talking to his brother, Dave. They've got one sister, Sharon and a brother, Jamie.

→ Complete the conversation. Use the correct parts of the present progressive and appropriate verbs.

Mark	Where's Dad?
Dave	He'_/_____ the car. This water's for him.
Mark	And Mom?
Dave	She's in the kitchen – _____ a cake for your birthday.
Mark	What' __ Jamie _____?
Dave	_____ T.V in his room.
Mark	__/__?

Mark	_____ Sharon _____ her homework?
Dave	Of course she __'__. She's upstairs with some friends. They'_/ l_____/ to music.
Mark	They a____'t /l_____/__ my new CD, a___/ they?

[Mark goes to Sharon's room]

Mark	Sharon, what / __/you/ l_____/ t__?
Sharon	Your new CD. It's great! I'__ really _____ it!
Mark	A____/y____? Now come on. Give it back to me.
Sharon	Sorry! Here you are.

✓ Check your answers

Mark	Where's Dad?
Dave	He's washing the car. This water's for him.
Mark	And Mom?
Dave	She's in the kitchen – making a cake for your birthday.
Mark	What's Jamie doing?
Dave	Watching T.V in his room.
Mark	Is he?

Mark	Is Sharon doing her homework?
Dave	Of course she isn't. She's upstairs with some friends. They're listening to music.
Mark	They aren't listening to my new CD, are they?

[Mark runs up to Sharon's room]

Mark   Sharon, what are you listening to?
Sharon   Your new CD. It's great! I'm really enjoying it!
Mark   Are you? Now come on. Give it back to me.
Sharon   Sorry! Here you are.

In the conversation above, what's the difference between the two answers below.

Mark   What's Jamie doing?
a Dave **He's watching** T.V.
b Dave **Watching** T.V.

Both are correct and common.

a is always appropriate. *b* is more informal.

In the story, why is it:

'My father's living in London until June?'
present progressive

Can I also say, 'My father lives in London?'
present simple?

This is a very important question. The grammar in both sentences is correct. They mean different things.

With the **present progressive**, ('My father's living') the situation is **temporary**.

With the **present simple**, ('My father lives'), the speaker thinks the situation is **permanent**. So, 'My father lives in London until June' is wrong. ✗

Situation *It's 3:00. Where's Sharon?*

Is it correct to say, 'She's sleeping?'

This answer is not wrong but it's not common. 'She's asleep' is more common.

It's the same with questions and the negative.

'Is she asleep?' is more common than 'Is she sleeping?'.
'She isn't asleep' is more common than 'She isn't sleeping'.

Present simple or present progressive?

→ Circle the correct verb form. Choose present simple for permanent situations. Choose present progressive for temporary situations.

1 Your teacher's ill, so today <u>I teach/I'm teaching</u> your class.
2 Are you in a hotel? No, <u>I stay/I'm staying</u> with friends.
3 My son <u>lives/is living</u> with me until his new apartment is ready.
4 Now, come on Joseph, <u>you are/you're being</u> very naughty today. Stop that and sit down. Usually <u>you are/you are being</u> a very good boy.
5 Normally, <u>I work/I'm working</u> hard but this month I don't/ I'm not. – it's very quiet.
6 <u>Does your daughter live/Is your daughter living</u> at home? Yes, she's only 14.

☑ Check your answers

1 I'm teaching. **2** I'm staying. **3** Is living. **4** You're being…. You are.
5 I work…..I'm not. **6** Does your daughter live?

Present progressive – future arrangements

Example from *The Story*:

Oliver is on a plane on his way to Denver.
He says, 'I'm **staying** in Denver for a couple of weeks.'

Meaning

→ Answer these questions. For **1, 2** and **4** find the right answer. For **3** answer 'Yes' or 'No'.

1 Here, this tense is for an action in the

(a) Past   **(b) Present**   **(c) Future**

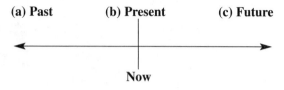

Now

2 The decision to stay in Denver is

(a) In the past   **(b) In the present**   **(c) In the future**

Now

3 a The plan is for Oliver to spend two weeks in Denver. Yes/No
   b Action to arrange the time in Denver is in the past. Yes/No

4 The arrangement is **a** personal **b** part of a timetable?

Check your answers

1 c future **2 a** in the past **3 a** yes – planned **b** yes – arranged **4 a** personal

★ Here the **present progressive** is for **personal future arrangements**.

→ Complete this conversation between two friends.

A What __/you ____ this evening?
B I' __/_____ to the movies with Don. Would you like to come with us?
A No, thanks, Jim'_ / _____ in a minute. We' _/_____ out for a drink.
B Which bar ____/you/____/ __?
A The one by the river.

Check your answers

A What are you doing this evening?
B I'm going to the movies with Don. Would you like to come with us?
A No, thanks. Jim's arriving in a minute. We're going out for a drink.
B Which bar are you going to?   **A** The one by the river.

Example:
   'I'm going to the movies this evening.'

Can I also say, 'I go to the movies this evening'? ✗

No. This is a personal arrangement in the future. The present progressive is the only correct tense.
(The present simple is only used for the future to talk about timetables, schedules and itineraries – see Topic 8.)

Present and future actions

→ Read the sentences below. They are all in the present progressive.
→ Which sentences refer to an action in the present?
→ Which sentences refer to a personal future arrangement?
→ Write 'present' or 'future'.

1 I'm doing it right now!   _____
2 I'm leaving soon.   _____
3 Is he arriving on Friday?   _____

4 I'm busy talking on the phone at the moment. _____

5 I'm seeing him in the morning _____

6 The telephone's ringing – Can someone please answer it? _____

7 I'm having dinner with him tomorrow evening. _____

8 They're taking a vacation at the end of the contract. _____

9 You're not meeting John after work, are you? _____

10 **A** Mommy, I can't sleep.

    B I'm coming in a minute, darling. _____

☑ **Check your answers**

1 Present **2** Future **3** Future **4** Present **5** Future **6** Present **7** Future **8** Future
9 Future **10** Future

Future arrangements – present progressive

→ Read the mini-dialogue below about arrangements for next weekend.

→ Underline the personal future arrangements.

A So, what are you doing next weekend?

B Well, on Saturday morning <u>I'm visiting</u> a friend. Then, in the evening we're having dinner in the new pizza restaurant. On Sunday my parents <u>are coming</u> for the day.

☑ **Check your answers**

A So, what <u>are you doing</u> next weekend?

B Well, on Saturday morning <u>I'm visiting</u> a friend. Then, in the evening <u>we're having</u> dinner in the new pizza restaurant. On Sunday my parents <u>are coming</u> for the day.

Find the mistakes with the verbs

→ There are five mistakes in this mini-dialogue. Write the correct dialogue below.

A Do you come to class tomorrow? **B** No, I won't.

A Why you can't come? **B** Because tomorrow comes my mother from Germany. I go to the airport to meet her.

A _____ **B** _____

A _____ **B** _____

Check your answers

A Are you coming to class tomorrow? **B** No, I'm not.

A Why can't you come? **B** Because tomorrow my mother is coming from Germany. I'm going to the airport to meet her.

→ What are you doing next weekend? Write or prepare to tell a friend.

→ List a minimum of three things about your arrangements for next weekend.

_____

_____

_____

Grammar and communication 3

Saying why - *to, so that, because*

Examples from *The Story*:

1 Tasha: 'I'm going to Denver **to see** some friends.'

2 Tasha: 'My mother organizes her work **so that** she can travel with my father.'

3 Why does Tasha go to Denver every year?
She says, '**because** I need to see other relatives and friends.'

4 Why is Oliver staying in Denver for 2 weeks?
Because of his job.

Summary – Saying why
A Why is Tasha traveling to Denver?
To
B Because she wants to/likes to/needs to } visit friends and family.
So (that) she can
A Why is Oliver staying in Denver?
B Because of his job (because of noun +)

Answers to 'Why?'

→ Why is Tasha traveling to Denver?
→ Write *because*, *because of* or *so (that) she can*.

a .... buy new books for her job.
b .... her friends and relatives.
c .... it's her country.
d .... take a vacation.

✓ Check your answers

a So that she can buy new books for her job.
b Because of her friends and relatives.
c Because it's her country.
d So that she can take a vacation.

! Common mistake – Saying why

Example from *The Story*:

> Tasha says 'I'm going to Denver **to see** some friends.'
> This is **the infinitive of purpose**. In other words, it answers the question *Why?* or *What for?*

Not: 'I'm going to Denver ~~for~~ to see some friends.'
Not: 'I'm going to Denver ~~for seeing~~ some friends.'

How do you pronounce it?

Infinitive of purpose – *to* + verb

→ Look at the words with stress in the phrase below.
'... to <u>see</u> some <u>friends</u>.'

The pronunciation of *to* is reduced / tə /. The important word in the phrase 'to see' is *see*.

→ Complete sentences **1–8** with an expression from the box below.

> **Example**: We go to France ***to buy nice wine***.

1 I'm phoning _____
2 I go to the coffee shop _____
3 I need some change _____
4 I'm going to the kitchen _____

5 You call 911 _____
6 I swim _____
7 She's in Italy _____
8 I'd like to go to Denver _____

to learn Italian   to relax and keep fit

to make a phone call

to have some tea

to tell you about the party

to get an ambulance   ~~to buy nice wine~~

to talk to my friends and have a snack   to visit the museums

Check your answers (Recording 4)

1 I'm phoning to tell you about the party.
2 I go to the coffee shop to talk to my friends and have a snack.
3 I need some change to make a phone call.
4 I'm going to the kitchen to have some tea.
5 You call 911 to get an ambulance.
6 I swim to relax and keep fit.
7 She's in Italy to learn Italian.
8 I'd like to go to Denver to visit the museums.

→ Listen to the sentences above on Recording 4 and repeat them.
→ Pay special attention to reduced form of *to* / tə /. The stress is on the verb after *to*.

Saying why

→ Read the questionnaire below and tick ✓ the right answers for you.

Why are you learning English?

☐ Because I like it. It's a hobby.
☐ Because I need it for my job.
☐ Because I need it for my studies.
☐ Because I want to visit the United States.

☐ So I can travel independently.
☐ So I can understand and talk to my colleagues and/or visitors.
☐ So I can get a better job.
☐ To pass exams.
☐ Because I want to understand the words of songs in English.
☐ Because I like to watch films in English.
☐ To help my children with their English studies.
☐ Because there is an English-speaking person in my family.

What are your main reasons? _____

Why are you using this *Teach Yourself* book?

☐ To improve and practice my English in general.
☐ To learn how to communicate better in English.
☐ To understand speakers of English when they talk.
☐ To improve my pronunciation.
☐ To improve my vocabulary.
☐ To improve my grammar.
☐ To find out more about American life and customs.
☐ Because I can't go to classes.
☐ Because I study on my own.

What are your main reasons? _____

What would you say?

1 You are next in line in a shop. The salesclerk asks 'Who's next? The person behind you says 'Me'.

_____

2 The phone rings. Your brother answers it. You're in your room. Your brother calls you and says 'It's for you'.

_____

Possible answers

1 'I think it's my turn, actually' OR 'Excuse me, I think I'm next.'
2 (I'm) coming.'

Review

How do you say it in your language?

→ Here are some examples of the important points in this topic.
→ Translate the sentences below into your language in the spaces.
→ Remember – translate the idea, not the words.

1 Here's my car. Where's yours?

2 Maria's a friend of mine.

3 I'm studying English because of my job.

4 I listen to the tape or CD to improve my pronunciation.

5 I'm working tomorrow.

6 **A** Where's Pat?   **B** She's taking a bath.

7 I don't work so that I can be with my children.

Join the conversation

→ Look at the text of Recording 1 (page 98), *The Story*, again.
→ Listen to Recording 5.
→ Read the **woman's** words in the spaces.

TEST 5

Which one is right?

Choose **a** or **b**.

1 Where's Sue?   **a** She's in vacation.
                  b She's on vacation.

2 **a** Do you go out this evening?
   b Are you going out this evening?

3 I go to the movies a lot **a** because of I like new films.
b because I like new films.

4 I'm working hard **a** so as to can travel **a** abroad.
b so that I can travel   **b** in the abroad.

5 Why are you calling David?   **a** To invite him to the party.
b For to invite him to the party.

6 We go there **a** all the weekends.
b every weekend.

7 I like playing tennis **a** even if it's raining.
b if even it's raining.

8 **a** I don't wait any more. I leave right now.
b I'm not waiting any more. I'm leaving right now.

9 **a** Susan is the girlfriend of Paul and Paul's a friend of me.
b Susan is Paul's girlfriend and Paul's a friend of mine.

10 a She's a friend of Peter.
b She's a friend of Peter's.

For **11** and **12** choose the appropriate answer.

11 You live at number 2, don't you?   **a** No.
b Actually, my house is number 3.

12 I'm a friend of your brother's.   **a** Oh, right.
b Yes.

Write a dialogue

Situation You are in a new English class in the U.S. You meet another student. She is not the same nationality as you.

You

1 You say your name
You ask her name

Gloria

2 I'm Gloria

3 You ask why she's studying English

4 Because of my job.

She asks you the same question

5 You answer (work/tourism)

You ask about her arrangements
for after the class

6 She answers (library/homework)
She asks you the same question

7 You answer (lunch/cafeteria)

✓ **Check your answers**

Which one is right?

1 b **2** b **3** b **4** b a **5** a **6** b **7** a **8** b **9** b **10** b **11** b **12** a

Dialogue: model answers

1	**You**	Hello, My name's …. What's yours?
2	**Gloria**	I'm Gloria.
3	**You**	Why are you studying English?
4	**Gloria**	Because of my job. How about you?
5	**You**	I'm studying English because I want to work in tourism in my country. What are you doing after the class?
6	**Gloria**	I'm going to the library to do my homework. And you?
7	**You**	I'm having lunch in the cafeteria.

6 STAYING IN CONTACT

Grammar and communication
◆ Future plans – *going to*
◆ Making arrangements: possibilities, suggestions and offers
◆ Telephone language
◆ Asking for things (2)

Vocabulary
◆ Numbers
◆ The alphabet

Pronunciation
◆ Using stress to correct mistakes

Tasha and Oliver continue their conversation... They exchange personal details and plan future contact.

Understanding the important information

→ Read the sentences below and on page 134.
→ Listen to Recording 1 and answer *Yes* or *No*.

1 Oliver would like to see Tasha again.   Yes/No
2 Tasha would like to see Oliver again.   Yes/No

3 He gives her his contact details.   Yes/No
4 She gives him her contact details.   Yes/No
5 They arrange a meeting.   Yes/No
6 They arrange a telephone call.   Yes/No
7 They're arriving in Denver soon.   Yes/No

Recording 1 (and 16) – The Story

Oliver	As I'm working in Denver for two weeks, we could … we could meet for a drink one evening, if you like.
Tasha	Yes, that would be nice.
Oliver	I don't know where I'm staying but you can phone me at the office, and we can arrange something. Shall I give you my number?
Tasha	O.K. Where's my appointment book?

Tasha opens her bag and gets her appointment book.

Tasha	What's your surname?
Oliver	Rees.
Tasha	Is that R double E, C, E?
Oliver	No, its R, double E, S actually, and the telephone number of the Denver office is 404-555-1212.
Tasha	404…?
Oliver	555-1212. You can get me on extension 159, I think it is. Yes, 159. If you have access to e-mail, my e-mail address is orees@fastpost.com.
Tasha	I can give you the telephone number of my friend's house, too.
Oliver	Why not? Then I can call you. Just a minute.

Oliver opens his appointment book.

Tasha	My last name's Harrison by the way. Tasha Harrison.
Oliver	Harrison, 'H', Tasha Harrison. And your friend's number is…?
Tasha	404-555-9866.
Oliver	404-555-5866.
Tasha	No, it's 404-555-9866… Yes, that's it.
Oliver	When would you like me to call, during the day or in the evening?

Tasha	I don't mind. I'm going to visit relatives and do other things but I'm going to spend time at home with my friends, too. So, any time's all right with me, really. I'm on vacation!
Oliver	Good, I'll telephone you some time next week, Tasha, if that's O.K.
Tasha	Yes, I'll look forward to it.
Oliver	Oh, look, the 'Fasten your seat belts' sign is on. We're landing in a minute.

Check your answers

1 Yes   **2** Yes   **3** Yes   **4** Yes   **5** No   **6** Yes   **7** Yes

Understanding more

→ Cover the text of Recording 1, *The Story*.

→ Read the questions below.

→ For **1** and **5** listen and tick ALL the correct answers.

→ For **2**, **3** and **4** complete the information where possible.

1 Oliver talks about   **a** dinner
                            b a drink   } next week.
                            c the movies

2 Oliver's details   **a** his family name _____
                            b the name of his hotel _____
                            c his home telephone number _____
                            d his office telephone number _____
                            e his e-mail address _____

3 Tasha's details   **a** her family name _____
                            b her friend's name _____
                            c her friend's address _____
                            d her friend's telephone number _____
                            e her e-mail address _____

4 Tasha's plans for her vacation   **a** _____
                                              b _____
                                              c _____

5 Who's phoning who and when?

    a Oliver's phoning Tasha
    b Tasha's phoning Oliver
    c next weekend
    d next week
    e during the day
    f in the evening

☑ **Check your answers**

1 b. **2 a** Rees **b** X. **c** X. **d** 404-555-1212. **e** orees@fastpost.com. **3 a** Harrison.
b X. **c** X. **d** 404-555-9866. **e** X. **4 a** visit relatives. **b** do other things. **c** spend
time with her friends. **5 a d e f**.

What do they say?

→ Read the sentences below.
→ Listen to Recording 1 again and try to complete the words.
→ Then read the text of the recording on page 134 to help you if necessary.

1 a   Oliver would like to see Tasha again.
      He suggests a drink. He says, 'We c _ _ _ d meet for a drink…'.
  b   Tasha responds. 'Yes, t_ _ t / w _ _ _ d / be / n _ _ e.'

2 a   Oliver talks about possible contact.
      He says, 'I don't know where I'm staying but you / c _ _ / phone
      me at the office and we / _ _ _ / arrange something.'

  b   Tasha also talks about possible contact.
      She says, 'I / _ _ _ / give you the telephone number of my
      friend's house.'

3   Oliver offers to give Tasha his telephone number.
      He says, 'S _ _ _ _ / _ / give you my number?'

4 a   Oliver offers to phone Tasha next week.
      He says, 'I' _ _ / telephone you some time next week.'
  b   Tasha feels positive about it.
      She says, 'I' _ _ / l _ _ k / f _ _ w _ _ d / t _ / i _ .'

5 a   Oliver asks Tasha for a time.
      He says, 'When w _ _ _ _ / you / l _ _ _ / m _ / t _ / call?'

6 Tasha talks about her plans for her holiday.
She says, 'I' _ / g _ _ _ _ / t _ / v _ _ _ t / relatives and do other
things but I'm / g _ _ _ _ / t _ / s _ _ _ _ / time at home with my
friends, too.'

Check your answers

1 a 'We could meet for a drink …'
 b 'Yes, that would be nice.'
2 a 'You can phone me … and we can arrange something.'
 b 'I can give you…'
3 a 'Shall I give you…?'
4 a 'I'll telephone you…'
 b 'I'll look forward to it.'
5 a 'When would you like me to call?'
6 'I'm going to visit relatives and do other things but I'm going to spend
 time at home with my friends, too.'

What's the right word?

Numbers 1–10

→ Write the numbers next to the words. Use your dictionary if necessary.

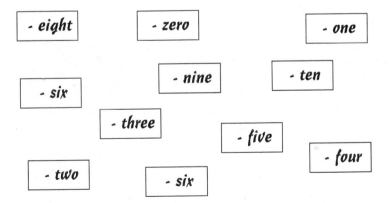

- eight   - zero   - one

- six   - nine   - ten

- three   - five

- two   - six   - four

Check your answers

0 – zero; 1 – one; 2 – two; 3 – three; 4 – four; 5 – five; 6 – six; 7 – seven; 8 – eight; 9 – nine; 10 – ten

→ Practice saying the numbers backwards as fast as possible: ten, nine, etc.
→ Practice counting in twos.
→ What are the *even* numbers? 2, 4, etc.
→ What are the *odd* numbers? 1, 3, etc.

How do they say it?

Telephone numbers

→ Read the sentences below.
→ Listen to the telephone numbers on Recording 2 and choose **a** or **b**

1 For '0' they say **a** zero
　　　　　　　　b O (the name of the letter).
2 For 404 they say **a** four – zero – four
　　　　　　　　b four – oh – four
3 When two numbers are the same, for example '66', they say
　a 'two sixes' or **b** 'six–six'.

Check your answers

1 **b** (**a** is also correct but it is more formal.) **2 a 3 b**

Recording 2

> **Oliver** …and the telephone number of the office is 404-555-1212.
> **Oliver** And your friend's number is…?
> **Tasha** 404-555-9866

Find the words and phrases

→ Read the sentences below.
→ Read text of Recording 1 again (page 134) and complete the words.

1 Oliver would like to meet Tasha for a drink. Does he say exactly when?
　No. He says, 'We could meet o _ _ / e _ _ _ _ _ g.'

2 a Oliver checks it is alright with Tasha. He says,
'We could meet for a drink......, i _ / y _ _ / l _ _ _ .'

b Later he checks that a phone call is alright.
He says, ' i _ / t _ _ _ ' s / _ . _ .'

3 He doesn't know the telephone number of his hotel. He says,
'You can phone me /_ _ / t _ _ / o _ _ _ _ _.'

4 Is the meeting fixed? No.
Oliver says, 'You can phone me... and we can a _ _ _ _ _ _ /
s _ _ _ _ _ _ _ g.'

5 People often write names and telephone numbers in the special
pages in their a _ _ _ _ _ _ _ _ _ _ / b _ _ ks.

6 S _ _ _ _ _ _ means the same as family name.

7 404-555-1212 isn't Oliver's direct number. His telephone is
e _ _ _ _ _ _ _ n 159.

8 Tasha hasn't got a computer in Denver but perhaps her friends
have got e-mail. Oliver says, 'If you h _ _ _ / a _ _ _ _ s / t _ /
e-mail.'

9 Oliver gives Tasha his phone number and she gives him her
number t _ _ .

10 Oliver needs time to find his appointment book. He says 'J _ _ _ /
a minute.'

11 Does he need Tasha's surname? Yes. Has he got it? No. Tasha
gives him this information. She says 'My last name's Harrison,
b_ / t _ _ / w _ _.'

12 a Does Tasha choose 'day' or 'evening' for the phone call?
No. She says, 'I / d _ _ ' _ / m _ _ d.'

b Oliver can phone in the day and he can phone in the evening. He
can phone / a _ _ / t _ _ _.

13 Tasha accepts Oliver's suggestion. Oliver starts his promise to
call her next week with the phrase, 'G _ _ _.'

14 Which day is Oliver calling Tasha? We don't know exactly. He
says 'S _ _ _ / t _ _ _ / next week.'

15 This is a 'fasten your seatbelts' / s _ _ _.
Is it _ _? Yes. Why? Because they're
arriving soon.

16 Planes take off and l _ _ _.

17 Verb *get*.
  a Why does Tasha open her bag? – to *get* her appointment book.
  b Oliver says, 'You can *get* me on extension 159.'

Which one means *contact*, which one means *take*?

✓ Check your answers

1 We could meet one evening. **2 a** We could meet for a drink, if you like.
b If that's O.K. **3** at the office (preposition!) **4** You can phone me and we can
arrange something. **5** appointment book **6** surname **7** extension **8** If you have
access to e-mail. (electronic mail) **9** too **10** Just a minute. **11** My last name's
Harrison, by the way. **12 a** I don't mind. **b** any time **13** Good. **14** Some time
next week. **15 a** sign **b** on (preposition!) **16** land **17 a** take **b** contact

Using these words and phrases

1 *Some time* and *any time*

For example, 'I'm going home **some time** next week.'

Some time means:

a I'm going next week.
b The time of the trip is fixed.
c I don't know the time OR I don't remember the time.

Any time means: **a** the time isn't fixed.
                          b The person can choose the time.

For example, 'You can call me *any time* tomorrow.'
The person can call at 9, or 10, or 11, etc. – when they like.

Another example: 'We can meet *at any time* between 11 and 1.'
The person can choose a time between 11 and 1.

→Complete these sentences with *some time* or *any time*:

1 When's John coming back from Australia?
_____tomorrow, I think.
2 When can I use the computer?
_____ you like.
3 When can we visit him in the hospital?
_____ between 10 a.m. and 9 p.m.
4 When's your appointment at the dentist's?
_____ next Wednesday.

Check your answers

1 Some time tomorrow. **2** Any time you like. **3** Any time between 10 a.m.
and 9 p.m. **4** Some time next Wednesday.

2 By the way

We know that indirect language is very common in English. *By the way* is
another example.

In the story, Oliver opens his appointment book to write Tasha's telephone
number. He needs her surname. Before he asks, she gives him the extra
information. She says, 'My last name's Harrison, *by the way*.'

★ Without *by the way* the sentence or question is:
  – correct
  – communicative
  – direct.
★ With *by the way* the sentence or question is:
  – correct
  – communicative
  – indirect.

When do I use this expression?
★ Use *by the way* to
  a give extra information

b introduce a new topic in an indirect way
   (*so* on page 103 is more direct)
c introduce a difficult topic.

★ *By the way* can go at the beginning or the end of the sentence.

By the way

→ What would you say in these situations?

1 Your colleague's talking to you about her husband. You want to know her husband's job. Ask her.

_____

2 You're talking to a friend. You can't remember her boyfriend's name.

_____

3 Your colleague's baby is very ill. He is in the hospital.
   You're talking to your colleague. Ask about the baby.

_____

4 You buy a new computer.
   You're at work, talking to your colleagues. Tell them.

_____

5 You're at a friend's house. Your friend is having a party tomorrow.
   You would like your new girlfriend to come to the party. Ask your friend.

_____

6 Your friend, Mary, is thinking about a trip to England.
   You want to know her decision.

_____

7 Your friend promises to give you the telephone number of a new friend. It's a week later. Ask for the number.

_____

8 You invite a new friend to dinner. You want to cook fish. You're talking to him on the phone. Check that he likes fish.

_____

9 A colleague is having a meeting with a new client. You join the meeting and introduce yourself.

_____

✓ **Check your answers**

1 By the way, what does your husband do*? **2** By the way, what's your boyfriend's name*? **3** By the way, how's your baby*? **4** By the way, I've got a new computer* **5** By the way, is it O.K. if my new girlfriend comes to the party*? **6** By the way, are you going to Denver*? **7** By the way, have you got X's phone number*? **8** By the way, do you like fish*? **9** Hello, *my name's X, by the way.

* *By the way* can go here, too.

How do you pronounce it?

Using stress to correct mistakes

★ In English we often use stress to correct mistakes.
   How do you correct, for example, a wrong telephone number in your language? Some languages use extra words. For example, 'No, it's not 3 it's 2'.

→ Listen to this example from *The Story* on Recording 3, part 1.

Recording 3, part 1

Oliver	And your friend's number is…?
Tasha	404-555-9866.
Oliver	404-555-5866
Tasha	No, 404-555-9866.

★ To correct a person, we stress the right number(s).

→ Read the four mini-dialogues below and on page 144.
→ Underline the different number in **B** – the number(s) where there is a mistake.

Recording 3, part 2

1 A Is this 305-636-3409?
   B Sorry, this is 305-636-3490.

2 A I'm calling 1-800-742-1141.
   B Sorry, you've got the wrong number. This is 1-800-752-1141.

3 A Good morning. Kodak.
  B I'm trying to get 556-1313.
  A Sorry, this is 0313.

4 A Hello! Vicky!
  B Sorry, there's no-one called Vicky here.
  A Isn't that 555-1414?
  B No, I'm afraid it's not. This is 555-0414.

✓ **Check your answers**

1 0212. **2** 752. **3** 0313. **4** 0414.

→ Now listen to the four mini-dialogues above on Recording 3, part 2 and correct the mistakes.

Correcting other 'mistakes'

Where are the 'mistakes' in the mini-dialogues below? Some of the 'mistakes' are only a difference of opinion.

→ Underline the 'corrections', the syllable with stress in **B**.

🎧 *Recording 3, part 3*

1 A I'd like to meet your girlfriend.
  B Julie? She's my sister.

2 A The meeting's on Thursday.
  B I think it's on Wednesday.

3 A He's a good singer.
  B He's a fantastic singer.

4 A We need some sandwiches.
  B We need lots of sandwiches.

5 A The dictionary's not on the desk.
  B No, it's under the desk, on the floor.

6 A I can phone you tomorrow.
  B No, it's my turn, I'll call you.

Check your answers

1 <u>sis</u>ter **2** <u>Wed</u>nesday **3** fan<u>tas</u>tic **4** <u>lots</u> **5** <u>un</u>der, <u>floor</u>, **6** <u>my</u>, <u>I'll</u>, <u>you</u>

→ Now, listen to the dialogues on Recording 3, part 3 and correct the mistakes, using stress.

Grammar and communication 1

Future plans – *going to*

Example from *The Story*:

Tasha talks about her vacation plans.

She says, '**I'm going to** visit relatives and do other things but **I'm going to** spend time at home with my friends, too.'

The name of this **tense** is the '*going to*' future.

Meaning

Here, *going to* is for future plans.

Form

The form is the verb *go* in present progressive + *to* + verb.

→ Make mini-dialogues. Match sentences **1–9** with the correct sentence or question (**a–i**) from the box on page 146.

1 A _____
   B Because he's not at home.
2 A _____
   B After the news.
3 A _____
   B Oh, is he? Who to?
4 A _____
   B Is he? I hope he passes.
5 A _____
   B Are you? That's nice.
6 A _____
   B Oh, just a sandwich, I think.

7 **A** _____

   B Yes, I think they are.

8 **A** _____

   B I can, if you like.

9 **A** _____?

   B Aren't you? Why not?

---

a I'm going to visit my parents next week.
b Are your friends going to buy that house?
c He's going to take his driving test soon.
d We aren't going to invite them.
e What are you going to have for lunch?
f Why aren't you going to call him?
g Who's going to make some coffee?
h When are you going to turn the T.V. off?
i He's going to get married.

☑ **Check your answers**

1 f 2 h 3 i 4 c 5 a 6 e 7 b 8 g 9 d

Grammar and communication 2

Making arrangements: possibilities, suggestions and offers

Examples from *The Story*:

'**We could** meet for a drink one evening.'
'**You can** phone me at the office.'
'**I'll call** you some time next week.'
'**Shall I** give you my number?'
'**When would you like me to** call you?'

★ Here, *can, could, I'll, shall I? would you like me to?* are all similar in meaning.

Situation Your friend is ill, in the hospital. You want to visit him/her. You are talking to his/her partner.

Summary – Possibilities, suggestions, offers	
I can I could } I'll	go to the hospital tomorrow.
Shall I Would you like me to }	go to the hospital tomorrow?

★ All these expressions are correct and appropriate.

★ *Could* is a little less direct than the others.

★ *Shall I?* and *Would you like me to?* are questions. Here, *I can*, *I could* and *I'll* aren't questions but they need a response.

★ To say *yes* you can use an echo question. (Echo questions are in Topic 2.)

★ *Can you? Could you?* and *Would you?* are echo questions for the expressions above.

★ The offer and the echo question can have different verbs.

Examples: 1 A I'll do that for you.
        B Can you?
      2 A I could ask him.
        B Would you?

Can I say 'It's possible for me to (go to the hospital tomorrow)' for offers?

The grammar is correct.

Students of English often say *It's possible, Is it possible? It isn't possible.* It is more common to say *I can, I could, I'll, shall I?* or *Would you like me to?* for offers.

Possibilities, suggestions and offers

Situation Debbie is my neighbor. She's got four young children.
I arrive at her house.

→ Read the conversation below and answer these two questions.

1 Debbie is **a** fine
              b not very well

2 I offer to do four things for her. Write them below with her answers:
                – a check mark for *yes* ✓
                – an ✗ for *no*

a Take _____ Answer ☐ **c** _____ Answer ☐
b _____ Answer ☐ **d** _____ Answer ☐

🎧 *Recording 4*

Me	Hi! Debbie. Isn't it cold today? How are you?
Debbie	Not very well at all actually, and it's nearly time for school.
Me	I can take the children to school for you if you like.
Debbie	Really? Are you sure?
Me	Yes, of course.
Debbie	That's very kind of you. I feel really terrible!
Me	Right, now you just go and sit down and I'll make you a cup of tea. Shall I call the doctor?
Debbie	Could you? Thanks.
Me	Where can I find the number?
Debbie	In the little book by the phone. Could you ask for an appointment as soon as possible, please?
Me	No problem. How about dinner this evening? Would you like me to cook for you all? The children could eat at my house.
Debbie	Thanks for the offer, but it's all right. My husband doesn't mind cooking, actually.

✓ Check your answers

1b. 2a Take the children to school – yes. **b** Make a cup of tea – yes. **c** Phone a doctor – yes. **d** Cook dinner – no.

★ 'Really? Are you sure?' It is polite to inquire about an offer of help before you say yes.

★ 'Not very well at all, actually' is more common than 'I'm ill'.

→ Read the sentences below. Find the exact words in the dialogue on p.148.

1 I offer to take the children to school.   Debbie says Yes.
   I say _____   She says _____

2 I offer to make a cup of tea.
   I say _____

3 I offer to call the doctor.   Debbie says Yes.
   I say _____   She says _____

4 I need help to find the number.
   I ask _____

5 I offer to cook dinner.
   I say _____

6 I suggest the children eat at my house.   Debbie says No.
   I say _____   She says _____

Check your answers

1 I can take the children to school for you if you like. Debbie says yes. She says, ' That's very kind of you.' **2** I'll make you a cup of tea. **3** Shall I call the doctor? Debbie says yes. She says, 'Could you?' **4** Where can I find the number? **5** Would you like me to cook? **6** The children could eat at my house. Debbie says no. She says 'Thanks for the offer, but it's all right.'

→ Now listen to the dialogue on Recording 4 and repeat it.

Common mistake – offers and suggestions

'Would you like me to make some tea?'
(Not: 'Would you like that I make some tea?'

would like	🧍	to + verb
Would you like	us	to help you?
When would you like	Richard	to do the job?
I'd like	the children	to come with us.

Possibilities, suggestions and offers

Situation   You are on the phone to your friend. Your friend is bored.

→ Read the conversation and complete with the correct phrase.

Your friend	I'm bored.
You	_____(1) go to the movies (?)
Your friend	That's a good idea. _____(2) go to the ABC(?) They've got nine screens there.
You	Why not? I've got the car tonight. _____(3) pick you up on the way(?)
Your friend	_____?(4) Great! Thanks!
Your friend	Do you know what time the films start there?
You	I've got no idea. _____(5) call and ask(?)
Your friend	Don't worry, I think it's usually about 8 o'clock.
You	Fine. _____(6) get to your house around seven(?) Is that O.K.?
Your friend	Yes, an hour is plenty of time to get there, decide which film to see and buy the tickets.
You	See you later, then. Bye.
Your friend	Bye!

☑ **Check your answers**

1   We can ⎫
    We could ⎬ go to the movies.
    Shall we ⎭   go to the movies?

2   We can ⎫
    We could ⎬ go to the ABC.
    Shall we ⎭   go to the ABC?

3 I can
  I could } pick you up on the way.
  I'll

  Shall I
  Would you like me to } pick you up on the way?

4 Can
  Could } you?
  Would

5 I can
  could } call and ask.
  I'll

  Shall I
  Would you like me to } call and ask?

6 I can
  I could } get to your house around seven.
  I'll

  Shall I
  Would you like me to } get to your house around seven?

→ Now look at these responses from the dialogue above. Do they mean *yes* or *no*?

→ Write a check mark ✓ or an ✗ in the boxes.

Suggestions/offers	**Responses**
1 We could go to the movies.	That's a good idea. ☐
2 Shall we go to the ABC?	Why not? ☐
3 Shall I pick you up on the way?	Can you? or Could you? or Would you? ☐
4 I'll call and ask (the times).	Don't worry. ☐

Check your answers

1 ✓ 2 ✓ 3 ✓ 4 ✗

Here's a summary of all the responses from the three conversations about offers and suggestions in this topic. (Recording 1 and 5 and the dialogue above.)

Summary – Saying *Yes* and *No* to offers and suggestions	
Yes That's very kind of you (Yes), That's a good idea (Yes), Why not? (Yes), that would be nice O.K. Could you? Can you? Would you?	**No** Thanks (for the offer), but it's all right Don't worry

You can see from these expressions that

★ It is very common to say *yes* without the word 'yes'.
★ It is very common to say *no* without the word 'no'.
★ These are more examples of indirect language.

What's the right word

> **i**
>
> **Culture – surnames/family names/last names**
>
> **Q** *How do I answer the question, 'What's your name?'*
>
> **A** In an informal situation give your first name.
> In a more formal situation give your first name and then your last name.
> In official situations give your last name.
>
> ■ Nowadays, at work most people are informal – they use first names.
> ■ When women get married they usually change their name to their husband's surname, for example, Brenda Dickens marries Jack Green. Her new name is Brenda Green or Mrs. Green.

- Nowadays, some women don't change their surname.
- What are the most common family names? Here are some from the telephone book: Baker, Smith, Walker, Jones, Miller, Brown, Ward, Campbell, Wilson, O'Brien, Harris, Evans, Fisher, Hall, Dickinson, King, Woods, Lee, Green, Young, Taylor, Thomas, Matthews, Palmer, West, White.
- A very common name for a man is John Jones and for a woman Mary Smith.
- Some surnames are male first names + 's'.
  For example,
  First name: Edward; family name: Edward<u>s</u>.

→Look at the two lists below. They are the same except for the 's' at the end of the surname.

First names	Surnames
William	Williams
Daniel	Daniels
Peter	Peters
Richard	Richards
Steven	Stevens
Hugh	Hughes
Matthew	Matthews
Edward	Edwards

First names and surnames

Which name is it, the first name or surname?

→Recording 5 on page 154 has eight mini-dialogues – one for each pair of names above.
→Listen and tick the 'first name' or the 'surname' in the boxes above.

Check your answers *(Recording 5)*

1   Hello, my name's **Williams**.
2 A What's your name? **B Daniel**.
3   Hi! I'm **Peter**.
4 A And your name is…? **B Richards**.
5 A Could I have your name, please sir? **B** Yes, it's **Stevens**.
6   Is that **Hugh**?
7   Her father's name's **Matthews**.
8   No, **Edwards** is his last name.

Names in your country

→ Read the questions below.
→ Either write your answers or prepare to tell a friend.

How many names do people usually have in your country?

_____

Which names do people use more at work, first names or family names?

_____

What happens to a woman's name when she gets married?

_____

What are the most common family names in your country?

_____

In your language have you got special words or names for people who are special to you? Give some examples.

_____

Do you have special titles for older people?

_____

| i | **British culture – special telephone services** |

→ Cover the text of Recording 6.
→ Read the information below.
→ Listen to the recording and complete the numbers for Britain.

International phone calls	And in your country?
The international code for the U.S. is ____	_____

Special services
- Emergency – fire ⎫
  police ⎬ This number
  ambulance ⎭ is free   _____
                                         _____
                                         _____
- **Operator** National _____   _____
  International _____   _____
- **Directory inquiries**
  National _____   _____
  International _____   _____

Check your answers *(Recording 6)*

To phone a number in the U.S. from abroad, the international code is 1.
For emergency services – fire, police or ambulance – dial 911. This is a
free number.
Operator services are at 0.
To ask for a telephone number call 411.

→ What are these numbers in your country? Complete the list on the
right above.

Grammar and communication 3

Using the telephone

What do these **telephone sounds** mean?

→ Read the sentences below.
→ Listen to Recording 7 and match **1–6** with **a–e**.

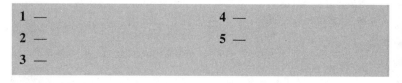

🎧 *Recording 7*

1 —	4 —
2 —	5 —
3 —	

a It's busy. Try again later.
b That means you've got a line. You can dial now.
c **A** What's happening? **B** The computer is dialing the number.
d Wrong number? Dial it again.
e It's ringing. Someone'll answer it in a minute.

☑ **Check your answers**

1 c 2 b 3 e 4 a 5 d

Hello! – Telephone language

★   We say 'This is', (Not: 'I̶ ̶a̶m̶…')
              'Is this?' (Not: 'A̶r̶e̶ ̶y̶o̶u̶…?')

{   'Speaking' (Not: 'Yes, I̶ ̶a̶m̶ ̶X̶')
    'John speaking'
    'It's John speaking'
    'This is John' (Not: 'I̶ ̶a̶m̶ ̶J̶o̶h̶n̶')
    'John'

→ Listen to the two mini-dialogues on Recording 8.

⅃ *Recording 8*

[Ring ring]
Rachel   555-1212. Hello?
Richard Can I speak to Rachel, please?
Rachel   Speaking.

[Ring ring]
Rachel   Hello?
Matt   This is Matt. Is this Rachel?
Rachel   Yes, it's me.

→ Complete these dialogues with the phrases above.

1
Tom

Hi, _____ Tom. _____ Andrea?

Vicky

Hello, Tom. No, _____ Vicky. Hang on a minute and
I'll call her. Andrea, _____ Tom on the phone for you.

2
Peter

Hello. Is David there, please?

David

_____

☑ **Check your answers**

1 **Tom** Hi, This is Tom. Is that Andrea?
  Vicky Hello, Tom. No, this is Vicky … Andrea, it's Tom on the phone for you.
2 Speaking *or* This is David *or* This is David speaking.

Asking for numbers on the telephone

Situation You need the codes for the different parts of the U.S. and Canada. You can look in the telephone directory to find them (for free). You can call the operator at 0, zero (usually free). You can call Directory Assistance at 411 (usually for a small fee).

→ Cover the text of Recording 9.
→ Look at the map below.
→ Read the names of the towns.
→ Listen to the recording and write the code number under the name of the town.

Detroit

Baltimore

Plymouth

Washington

Otis•

Phoenix•   Atlanta•

                                     Orlando

Austin•

                              •
Key West• •Miami
                305

Recording 9

Example: Operator	Directory Assistance. What city, please?
Caller	Hello, yes. Could I have the area code for Miami, Florida, please?
Operator	Yes, the area code for Miami is 305.
Caller	Thank you. Goodbye.

1 Operator	Directory Assistance, Lynn speaking. What city, please?
Caller	Yes, could you tell me the area code for Phoenix, please?
Operator	Yes, the area code for Phoenix is 480.
Caller	Thanks. Bye.
2 Operator	Directory Assistance. What city, please?
Caller	Hello. I'd like the area code for Washington, DC, please.
Operator	Washington – that's 202.
Caller	Many thanks. Goodbye.
3 Operator	Directory Assistance, Nick speaking. Can I help you?
Caller	Yes, can you give me the area code for Orlando, please?
Operator	Orlando – yes, that's 407.
Caller	Thanks very much. Bye.
4 Operator	Directory Assistance. What city, please?
Caller	Hello. Could I have the area code for Austin, Texas, please?
Operator	Yes, Austin's 512.
5 Operator	Directory Assistance, Diane speaking. What city, please?
Caller	Hello, yes. What's the area code for Otis, Kansas, please?
Operator	One second please. Yes, that's 785.
6 Operator	Directory Assistance. What city, please?
Caller	Hello. Can you give me the code for Plymouth, Michigan, please?
Operator	Sorry, which town?
Caller	Plymouth, Michigan, please.
Operator	The code for Plymouth is 734.

Check your answers

1 Phoenix – 480 **2** Washington, DC – 202 **3** Orlando – 407 **4** Austin, Texas – 512 **5** Otis, Kansas – 785 **6** Plymouth, Michigan – 734.

Grammar and communication 4

Asking for things

→ Read the text of Recording 9 on page 159.
→ Find five expressions to ask for things.
→ Write them below.

a C _ _ _ _ / I / h _ _ _ ...?

b C _ _ _ _ / y _ _ / t _ _ _ / me...?

c I ' _ / l _ _ _ ...

d C _ _ / y _ _ / g _ _ _ / m _...?

e W _ _ _ ' _ / t _ _ / area code for...?

☑ **Check your answers**

a Could I have...? **b** Could you tell me...? **c** I'd like... **d** Can you give me...?
e What's the area code for...?

Asking for telephone numbers

→ Look again at the map on page 158.
→ Cover the text of Recording 10 below.
→ You need the area codes for the other four places on the map, (1) Atlanta,
   (2) Detroit and (3) Baltimore and (4) Key West.
→ Listen and use the questions above to ask for the codes.
→ Write the codes on the map.

☑ **Check your answers (Recording 10)**

1	**Operator**	Directory Assistance. What city, please?
	You	_____.
	Operator	Yes, the area codes for Atlanta are 770, 404, 678.
2	**Operator**	Directory Assistance. Mandy speaking. What city, please?
	You	_____.
	Operator	The area code for Detroit is 313.
3	**Operator**	Directory Assistance. For what city?
	You	_____.
	Operator	The area codes for Baltimore are 443 and 410.

4 **Operator**	Directory Assistance. For what city?
You	_____ .
Operator	The code for Key West is 305.

How do you pronounce it?

Do you know your ABCs (alphabet) in English?

? *How many letters are there in the alphabet?*

A 26.

? *How many sounds are there in English?*

A 44

? *How many vowels are there in the alphabet?*

A Five, 'a', 'e', 'i', 'o', 'u'. But there are 16 vowel sounds in English.

? *How many consonants are there in the alphabet?*

A 21. But there are 24 consonant sounds in English.

★ English spelling doesn't always help with the pronunciation. (This is why I always suggest you listen to the recordings several times before you read the words. Listening to English before you read it always helps with good pronunciation.)

★ In English one pronunciation can have different spellings and different meanings.

For example   *no* and *know*
                       see and *sea*
                       right and *write*
                       meet and *meat*

★ Because English sounds can have different spellings, it is very common to ask for spellings of words, especially names and addresses.

→ Look at the columns of letters below.
The names of the letters in each column start or end with the same sound.
→ Listen to Recording 11, part 1 and repeat the names of the letters. You will hear each letter twice.

Recording 11, part 1

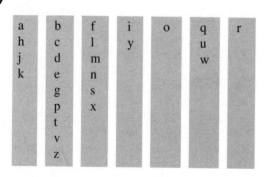

a	b	f	i	o	q	r
h	c	l	y		u	
j	d	m			w	
k	e	n				
	g	s				
	p	x				
	t					
	v					
	z					

Can you say the names of the letters?

→ Listen to the first letter from each column on Recording 11, part 2.
→ Say the others with the same vowel sound.

Spelling

Situation: I teach a class of people who want to be English teachers. Here is my class list. Some names are missing. The spelling of some names is wrong.

→ Listen to Recording 12 and write or correct the surnames.

CLASS LIST

1 Lesley_____
2 Denise Varnish
3 Matt Hanant
4 Anne _____
5 Simon _____
6 John Pierson
7 Joan _____
8 Liz Thomson-Smith

Recording 12

Me	So, could you tell me your surnames, please? Lesley, What's your surname?
Lesley	Crowley.
Me	How do you spell that, Lesley?
Lesley	C – R – O – W – L – E –Y.
Me	And yours, Denise?
Denise	My family name's Farnish.
Me	Is that with an 'F' or a 'V'?
Denise	With an 'F'. F – A – R – N – I – S – H.
Me	And how about you, Matt? What's your last name?
Matt	Hannant. That's H – A double N – A – N – T.
Me	Anne, your surname is…?
Anne	Johnson, spelt J – O – H – N – S – O – N.
Me	Simon, yours next, please.
Simon	Lawrence.
Me	How do you spell it?
Simon	L – A – W – R – E – N – C – E.
Me	And John? I've got Pierson here. Is that right?
John	Yes. P – E – A – R – S – O – N.
Me	Oh, I've got P – I – E.
John	No, it's P – E – A at the beginning.
Me	And Joan – How about you? What's your last name?

Joan	Rawlings. R – A – W – L – I – N – G – S.
Me	And the last one is Liz, please.
Liz	My surname's Thompson-Smith.
Me	Is that Thompson with a 'P' or without?
Liz	With a 'P' and 'Smith' at the end.
Me	Thanks very much everybody. Now let's start the lesson.

☑ **Check your answers**

1 Lesley Crowley 2 Denise Farnish 3 Matt Hannant 4 Anne Johnson 5 Simon Lawrence 6 John Pearson 7 Joan Rawlings 8 Liz Thompson-Smith

→ What's the question?

The answer is S – M – I – T – H.
The question is _____?

(Answer: 'How do you spell it?' (Not: 'How do you write it?') ☹

How do you spell it?

It is easy to confuse some letters, for example 's' and 'f' or 'p' and 'b', especially on the telephone. To make the difference, we say, for example, 'F for 'Foxtrot' or 'S for Sierra'. Some people use other common words or names for this, for example, A for 'apple'.

On page 165 is the International Phonetic Alphabet (NATO Alphabet).

→ Look at this example:

Operator	What name is it, please?
Caller	Eva Rach.
Operator	Is that R – A – **T** for Tango?
Caller	No, it's R – A– **C** for Charlie – H.

→ Listen to Recording 13 and repeat the letters and words.

Recording 13

A – Alpha	N – November
B – Bravo	O – Oscar
C – Charlie	P – Papa
D – Delta	Q – Quebec
E – Echo	R – Romeo
F – Foxtrot	S – Sierra
G – Golf	T – Tango
H – Hotel	U – Uniform
I – India	V – Victor
J – Juliet	W – Whisky
K – Kilo	X – X-Ray
L – Lima	Y – Yankee
M – Mike	Z – Zulu

→ Help to spell aloud this Japanese surname correctly

S A K O T A

It's 'S' for _____
'A' _____
_____
_____
_____
_____

Check your answers

'S' for Sierra
'A' for Alpha
'K' for Kilo
'O' for Oscar
'T' for Tango
'A' for Alpha

Which letter is it?

Example from the class list exercise on page 163:

A My name's 'Farnish'
B Is that with an 'F' or a 'V'?
A With an 'F'.

→ Look at the pairs of names below.
→ Listen to Recording 14 and choose the correct spelling **a** or **b**.

1	**a** Hallis	**b**	Harris
2	**a** Fraser	**b**	Frazer
3	**a** Stephens	**b**	Stevens
4	**a** Simms	**b**	Sims
5	**a** Stupps	**b**	Stubbs
6	**a** Initial 'F'	**b**	Initial 'S'

🎧 *Recording 14*

1
A My name's Hallis.
B Double 'R' is that?
A No, double 'L', H – A – double L – I – S.

2
A The name's Frazer.
B Do you spell that with an 'S' or a 'Z'?
A With a 'Z'.

3
A My name's Stevens.
B Is that with a 'PH' or a 'V'?
A With a 'V'.

4
A My name's Simms.
B Is that one 'M' or two?
A S - I - double M - S.

5
A Her name's Helen Stubbs.
B Is that 'P' for Papa or 'B' for Bravo?
A Double 'B' for Bravo.

6
A   What's your initial?
B   'S'.
A   Is that 'F' for Foxtrot or 'S' for Sierra?
B   'S' for Sierra.

Check your answers

1 a 2 b 3 b 4 a 5 b 6 b

Spelling vowels

Many learners of English have problems with the names of English vowels (a,e,i,o,u). Here's some practice.

→ Listen to Recording 15 and complete the spelling of these surnames.

1 P _ P _ R
2 S N _ _ T H _
3 S M _ _ T _ N
4 T _ Y L _ R
5 S H _ R _ D _ N
6 R _ _ D _ R
7 S _ M _ _ L S

Check your answers *(Recording 15)*

1 Piper, that's P–I–P–E–R.
2 My name's Snaithe, spelt S–N–A–I–T–H–E.
3 Yes, it's Smeaton, S–M–E–A–T–O–N.
4 And my surname is Taylor, T–A–Y–L–O–R.
5 The family name's Sheridon, S–H–E–R–I–D–O–N.
6 And the second name is Reeder, that's spelt R–E–E–D–E–R.
7 Samuels, S–A–M–U–E–L–S.

Spelling your name aloud and giving your contact details

→ Practice spelling your names and address aloud – clarify difficult letters.

→ Practice saying the numbers aloud.

First name_____

Middle name(s) _____

Surname(s) _____

Telephone number (home) _____(work)_____(mobile) _____

E-mail address_____

Address _____

Passport number _____

What would you say?

1 You telephone a friend in Canada from your country. You get a wrong number.

_____

2 You are on the telephone. The line is very bad. You can't hear the other person.

_____

Possible answers

1 I'm very sorry. It's the wrong number.

Advanced alternative: Sorry to disturb you. I think I've got the wrong number.

2 I'm sorry, this line's terrible. I can't hear you.

Advanced alternative: I'm sorry, this line's terrible. Could you speak up a bit, please?

Review

How do you say it in your language?

Here are some examples of the important points in this topic.

→ Translate the sentences below into your language.

→ Remember – translate the idea, not the words.

1 a We could go out for a pizza tonight. **b** That's a good idea!

2 a I'll make reservations for tomorrow. **b** I'll look forward to it.

3 a Shall I make some coffee? **b** Yes, please.

4 a Can I help you? **b** It's very kind of you, thank you, but it's all right.

5 By the way, how's your mother today – is she better?

6 I'm going to buy a car tomorrow.

Join the conversation

→ Look at the text of Recording 1 (page 134), *The Story*, again.
→ Listen to Recording 16.
→ Read **Oliver's** words in the spaces.

TEST 6

Which one is right?

→ Choose **a** or **b**.

1 Three and five is
   a nine
   b eight.

2 'surname', 'family name' and 'last name' mean
   a the same
   b something different.

3 You ask someone to wait. You say,
   a 'A moment'
   b 'Just a minute, please.'

4   Beer or wine?
   a   I don't mind.
   b   It is not matter.

5   I can't speak to Peter. His number is
   a   occupied.
   b   busy.

6   I can't use the machine. It's
   a   out of operation.
   b   out of order.

7   On the telephone
   a   Here speaks Jane.   **a**   Is that Peter?
   b   This is Jane.   **b**   Are you Peter?

8   **a**   Please, it is possible I speak with Jenny?
      b   Could I speak to Jenny, please?

9   Your telephone number is in my
   a   appointment book.
   b   agenda.

10 The shop is open 24 hours a day. You can go shopping
   a   all the times.
   b   at any time.

11 **a**   Would you like that I go with you?
      b   Would you like me to go with you?

12 Shall I ask him?
   a   Yes, you shall.   **b**   Yes, please.

13 Shall we go out for a drink after work?
   a   Sorry, I go out with my wife to a family dinner.
   b   Sorry, I'm going out with my wife to a family dinner.

14 **a**   Why he is going to sell the house?
      b   Why is he going to sell the house?

Which one is better?

15 Would you like me to translate that for you? I speak Japanese.
   a   Yes, I would.
   b   Thanks.

16 Shall I do that?
   a   No.
   b   I'm alright, thanks.

Which ones are right?

17 I'll do that for you, shall I?
   a   Can you? Thanks.
   b   Could you? Thanks.
   c   Would you? Thanks.

Write a dialogue

Situation You are on the phone to your friend.

1   You   **Your friend**
                                     What can we do this evening?

Suggest a Chinese meal and
a video at his house.

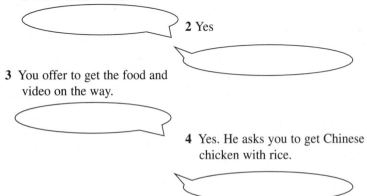

2 Yes

3 You offer to get the food and
    video on the way.

4 Yes. He asks you to get Chinese
    chicken with rice.

5 You say yes.
You offer to get some beer.

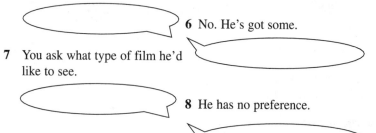

6 No. He's got some.

7 You ask what type of film he'd like to see.

8 He has no preference.

☑ **Check your answers**

1 b **2** a **3** b **4** a **5** b **6** b **7** b a **8** b **9** a **10** b **11** b **12** b **13** b **14** b **15** b **16** b **17** a, b, c

Dialogue: model answers

1 You	We could have some Chinese food and watch a video at your house.
2 Your friend	Yeah, why not?
3 You	Shall I get the food and the video on the way?
4 Your friend	That would be good. Could you get me some Chinese chicken with rice, please?
5 You	No problem. I could get some beer, too.
6 Your friend	No, don't worry about that. I've got some.
7 You	What sort of film would you like to see?
8 Your friend	I don't mind.

7 | TRAVELING AND HANDLING MONEY

Grammar and communication
◆ Inviting people to do things
◆ Suggesting doing something together
  – *let's*
◆ Asking people to do things
◆ Asking for help – indirect questions

Vocabulary
◆ Numbers (2)
◆ Money
◆ Travel

Pronunciation
◆ Pronouncing
  groups of words –
  linking

The plane is arriving at the Denver International Airport

Understanding the important information

Situation The pilot of the plane talks to all the passengers. He makes an announcement.

→ Cover the text of Recording 1, *The Story* on page 174.
→ Read the sentence above it.
→ Listen to the recording and choose ALL the correct answers.

The captain talks about

    a seat belts
    b passports
    c the time
    d the arrival time
    e the temperature
    f the weather

🎧 *Recording 1 – The Story*

> **Pilot** Good morning, ladies and gentlemen. This is your captain speaking again. In a few moments, we will begin our descent into Denver International Airport. Please return to your seats and fasten your seatbelt. If you would like to adjust your watches, the time in Denver is now 6:50 in the morning and the temperature on the ground is –2 degrees centigrade, that's 29 degrees Fahrenheit. Our estimated time of arrival is 7:15. That's a quarter past seven on the ground in Denver. The forecast for today is cold … but bright … .

☑ **Check your answers**

a c d e f

Understanding more

→ Cover the text of Recording 1, *The Story*.
→ Read the questions below.
→ Listen and choose **a** or **b**.

1 The time in Denver is now   **a** six fifteen (6:15) **b** six fifty (6:50).
2 The temperature is   **a** 2 degrees centigrade **b** -2 degrees centigrade.
3 They're landing at   **a** seven fifteen (7:15) **b** seven fifty (7:50).

☑ **Check your answers**

1 b 2 b 3 a
*In the U.S. we measure temperature in Fahrenheit. 0°C = 32°F.

How do they say it?

Pronouncing groups of words – Linking words

★ When we speak, we often join a word to the next word.
★ This happens when one sound is a consonant and the other a vowel.
★ Two examples from the story above are, 'ladies and', 'this is'.
★ Sometimes the last **letter** isn't a consonant. It's the last sound that's important, for example, 'time in Denver' – the last **sound** in 'time' is /m/.

→ Read the phrases below. They are from *The Story* on page 174.
→ Listen to these phrases on Recording 2 and repeat them.
→ Pay special attention to linking the words marked.

Recording 2

Ladies and gentlemen

This is your Captain speaking again

In a few moments

The time in Denver is now 6:50

That's a quarter past seven on the ground in Denver

What's the right word?

Numbers to 100

→ Complete this table with the numbers on page 176.

1 one	11_____		
2 two	12_____	20_____	
3 three	13 *thirteen*	30 _____	
4 four	14 _____	40_____	
5 five	15 _____	50 _____	
6 six	16 _____	60 _____	
7 seven	17 _____	70 *seventy*	
8 eight	18 _____	80 _____	
9 nine	19 _____	90 _____	100 *a hundred*

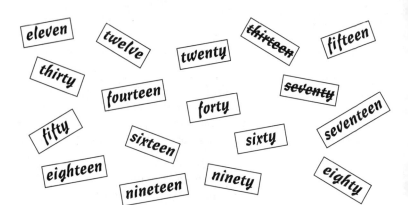

 Check your answers

1 one	11 eleven	
2 two ⟶	12 twelve ⟶	20 twenty
3 three	13 thirteen	30 thirty
4 four	14 fourteen	40 forty
5 five	15 fifteen	50 fifty
6 six	16 sixteen	60 sixty
7 seven	17 seventeen	70 seventy
8 eight	18 eighteen	80 eighty
9 nine	19 nineteen	90 ninety 100 a hundred

→ Write these numbers in figures.

ninety-nine ___	twelve ___	forty-three ___	thirty-one ___
eleven ___	seventy-six ___	eighty-five ___	twenty-two ___
sixty-four ___	fifty-seven ___	seventeen___	a hundred ___

 Check your answers

Ninety-nine – 99; Twelve – 12; Forty-three – 43; Thirty-one – 31; Eleven – 11; Seventy-six – 76; Eighty-five – 85; Twenty-two – 22; Sixty-four – 64; Fifty-seven – 57; Seventeen – 17; A hundred – 100

→ Write these numbers in words.

Example: 72 – *Seventy-two*

18_____	59_____	13 _____
93 _____	15 _____	21 _____
86 _____	16 _____	45 _____
19 _____	37 _____	12 _____
14 _____	68 _____	100 _____

✓ **Check your answers**

18 eighteen	59 fifty-nine	13 thirteen
93 ninety-three	15 fifteen	21 twenty-one
86 eighty-six	16 sixteen	45 forty-five
19 nineteen	37 thirty-seven	12 twelve
14 fourteen	68 sixty-eight	100 a hundred

→ Now try some mental math. Say the totals aloud when you do them.

1 Eleven and five and seventeen and forty-two is _____
You say, 'Eleven and five is sixteen, and seventeen is… and forty-two is…

2 Nine and six and twenty-three and eighteen is _____

3 Four and twelve and two and fourteen is _____

✓ **Check your answers**

1 Eleven and five is sixteen, and seventeen is thirty three and forty-two is seventy-five. **2** Nine and six is fifteen, and twenty-three is thirty-eight and eighteen is fifty-six. **3** Four and twelve is sixteen, and two is eighteen and fourteen is thirty-two.

→ Say these numbers aloud as quickly as possible.

a Say the **even** numbers up to twenty – two, four, six, etc…

b Say the **odd** numbers up to twenty – one, three, five, etc…

c Count in 5s up to 50. Five, ten, etc…

d Count in 3s up to 36. Three, six, etc…

e Can you say the 'eight times table' in English?
One eight is eight
Two eights are sixteen
Three eights are …

✓ **Check your answers**

a Two, four, six, eight, ten, twelve, fourteen, sixteen, eighteen, twenty

b One, three, five, seven, nine, eleven, thirteen, fifteen, seventeen, nineteen

c Five, ten, fifteen, twenty, twenty-five, thirty, thirty-five, forty, forty-five fifty

d Three, six, nine, twelve, fifteen, eighteen, twenty-one, twenty-four, twenty-seven, thirty, thirty-three, thirty-six

e One eight is eight
Three eights are twenty-four
Five eights are forty
Seven eights are fifty-six
Nine eights are seventy-two

Two eights are sixteen
Four eights are thirty-two
Six eights are forty-eight
Eight eights are sixty-four
Ten eights are eighty

Math talk

→ Write the totals below in figures.
Use the numbers and signs in the box to help you.

a Twenty plus ten equals thirty 20_____10_____30

b Twelve minus one is eleven _____

c Four multiplied by six equals twenty-four_____

d Twenty-seven divided by three is nine_____

4	12	30	11	3	10	27	6	1	24	9	20
		+	–		×	÷		=			

✓ **Check your answers**

a $20 + 10 = 30$. **b** $12 - 1 = 11$. **c** $4 \times 6 = 24$. **d** $27 \div 3 = 9$.

Q *How do you say this?* $3 \times 6 = 18$.

A There are 3 ways
a three sixes are
b three times six is
c three multiplied by six equals
(more formal/technical)
} eighteen

Find the words and phrases

→ Read the sentences below.
→ Read the text of Recording 1 (page 174), *The Story*, and find the correct words and phrases.

1 The pilot wants to talk to all the people on the plane.
He says 'Good morning, l _ _ _ _ s / and g _ _ _ l e _ _ n.'

2 Does he say 'I am your captain?' No, he uses telephone language. He says, 'T _ _ _ / _ _ / your captain.'

3 We don't call the pilot 'Pilot Smith', we say 'C _ _ _ _ _ _ Smith'.

4 The pilot invites the passengers to change the time on their watches. He says 'I_ / y _ _ / w _ _ _ _ / l _ k _ / t _ / adjust your watches, the time in Denver is…'

5 Does the pilot know the exact time they are arriving in Denver? No, he says, 'Our e _ _ _ _ _ _ _ d / time / o _ / a _ r _ _ _ l / is 7:15.'

6 What television program is immediately after the news? Usually it's the weather f _ _ _ _ _ _ _ where they talk about the weather for the rest of today, tomorrow, etc.

Check your answers

1 ladies and gentlemen. *These words are often on public toilet signs.
2 This is. **3** captain. **4** If you would like to adjust your watches. **5** estimated time of arrival. **6** forecast.

Grammar and communication 1

Inviting people to do things

Example from *The Story*:

The pilot invites the passengers to change the times on their watches.
He says, '**If you would like to** adjust your watches…'

★ We use *if you would like to* for two situations:
1 to invite people
2 to ask and tell people to do things in a polite, indirect way.

For example:
1 'We're having a small dinner party on Saturday. If you would like to join us…' Meaning: I'm inviting you to the dinner party.

2   'If you would like to take a seat for a moment...' Meaning: Please sit
     down and wait.

★   When you are asking someone to do something, it is common not to
     finish the sentence.

For example:

Situation At the reception of a small hotel.

Receptionist: 'If you would like to follow me, please...' (and s/he doesn't
say 'I can show you to your room' – the meaning is clear from the
situation. She doesn't need to finish the sentence.)

★   This expression is particularly common in formal and new situations.

Asking someone to do something

Where can you hear these 'invitations'?

→ Read the 'invitations' below and choose the place. You can use each
  place more than once.

| office | dentist's | shop |

| school | dinner party |

1   If you would like to come back for your watch some time later this
     afternoon... around 4 ...
2   If you would like to sit there, Kevin, next to my husband ...

3 I've got your son here. I'm afraid he's not very well so if you would like to come and pick him up …

4 I'm sorry but Mr. Smith isn't here this afternoon. If you would like to give me your name and number …

5 If you would like to come with me to the cash desk …

6 If you would like to go into the waiting room …

7 If you would like to go in, the manager can see you now …

8 If you would like to just open your mouth and say 'aah'…oh yes …

9 If you would all like to come to the table …

Check your answers

1 shop **2** dinner party **3** school **4** office **5** shop **6** dentist's **7** office **8** dentist's **9** dinner party

What are the possible responses to these 'invitations'? Is it OK to say 'Yes'?

'Yes' alone isn't appropriate. ☹

→ Look at these responses.

1 You can say, 'Thank you'
    'Yes, that's fine'
    'Yes, of course'
    'Yes, I'll' + verb

2 You say nothing and 'do' the action.

3 If you are following someone, you can say, 'After <u>you</u>.'

→ Match these sentences from the exercise above with an appropriate response from the box on page 182.

1 In a shop:

A If you would like to come back for your watch some time later this afternoon… around 4 …

B _____

2 In a school:

A I've got your son here. I'm afraid he's not very well so if you would like to come and pick him up …

B _____

3 In an office:

A I'm sorry but Mr Smith isn't here this afternoon. If you would like to give me your name and telephone number …

B _____

4 In a shop:

A If you would like to come with me to the cash register …

B _____

5 In an office:

A If you would like to go in, the manager can see you now.

B _____

---

  a Thank you

  b Yes, I'll be there as soon as I can

  c Yes, of course, have you got pen and paper, it's 555…

  d Yes, that's fine

  e After you

✓ **Check your answers**

1 d **2** b **3** c **4** e **5** a

Our story continues. Oliver and Tasha get off the plane

→ Look at pictures **1–5** on page 183.
   In Recording 3 on page 184, the conversation between Oliver and Tasha is in five parts, **a–e**. The parts are in the wrong order.

→ Listen and write the correct letter **a–e** under the pictures.

1

2

3

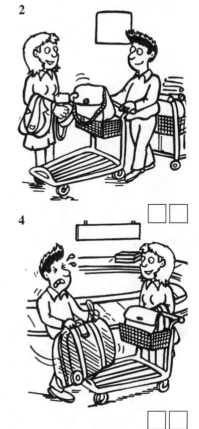

4

5

🎧 *Recording 3 – The Story*

a

Oliver	Well, it's been really nice talking to you, Tasha.
Tasha	Yes, and thanks for the help with the luggage.
Oliver	I'll be in touch next week, then.
Tasha	Yes, bye.
Oliver	Bye.

b

Oliver	Wow, this suitcase is a bit heavy – is that it now?
Tasha	The suitcase, the small bag and my handbag – yes, that's everything.

c

Immigration officer	Thank you madam. Sir, your passport please. Thank you.

d

Oliver	Do you need a luggage cart?
Tasha	That would be a good idea – I've got quite a lot of luggage.
Oliver	They're right over here. Now, let's find the rest of the luggage.

e

Tasha	Would you mind waiting for just a minute, Oliver?
Oliver	Of course not. The suitcases aren't here yet, anyway.
Tasha	Could you look after my luggage cart, oh, and can you take my coat, please?
Oliver	Sure, go ahead.

Tasha asks for help at the information desk.

Airport employee	Can I help you?
Tasha	Yes, could you tell me where the restroom is, please?
Airport employee	Of course, madam. Just over there. Can you see the sign?

Check your answers

1 c **2** d **3** e **4** b **5** a

→ Write the correct words on the signs in the pictures on page 183.

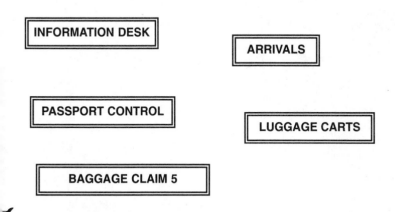

Check your answers

1 Passport Control **2** Luggage carts **3** Information Desk **4** Baggage Claim 5
5 Arrivals.

→ Read the sentences and mini-dialogues below. Where are the people?

→ Write the letters **A** to **F** in the second box, under the correct picture
   (**1–6**) on page 183.

A 'Could you open your bag for me, please?'
   'Yes, of course.'
B 'Hello, Rachel, it's lovely to see you again. How are you?'
C 'Excuse me, I'm from this flight but my suitcase isn't here.'
D 'Have you got a visa?'
   'Yes, it's on the next page.'
E 'I think we need two, don't you? One isn't enough for all this luggage.'
F 'How can I help you, sir?'
   'Where can I exchange some money, please?'

✅ **Check your answers**

1 D   2 E   3 F   4 C   5 A   6 B

Understanding more

→ Read the questions below.
→ Read the text of Recording 3 on page 184 and choose **a** or **b**.

1 a Tasha has 1 piece ⎫ of luggage.
  b   2 pieces ⎭

2 a They agree to ⎰ get in touch.
  b   ⎱ go to dinner.

3   Tasha needs to **a** exchange some money.
                  b go to the restroom.

✅ **Check your answers**

1 b 2 b 3 b

What do they say?

→ Read the sentences below.
→ Read the text of Recording 3 on page 184 and complete the sentences.

1   They get the luggage cart. Oliver suggests they find their suitcases.
He says, 'Now, l _ _ ' _ / find the rest of the luggage.'

2 a Tasha asks Oliver to wait for her. She says,
    'W _ _ _ _ / you / m _ _ _ / w _ _ _ _ _ g/ for just a minute?'
  b Oliver responds, 'Of / c _ _ _ _ e / n _ t .'
  c Tasha asks Oliver to look after her luggage cart and take her coat.
    She says, 'C _ _ _ _ / y _ _ / look after my luggage cart?
    Oh, and / c _ _ / y _ _ / take my coat, p _ _ _ _ _ ?'
  d Oliver responds, /'S _ _ _ -/ g _ / a _ _ _ d.'

3 a The person at the information desk offers Tasha help.
    She says, 'C_ _ / I / h _ _ _ / y _ _ ?'
  b Tasha asks help to find the restroom.
    She asks, 'C _ _ _ _ / y _ _ / t _ _ _ / m _ / where the r _ _ _ _ _ _ _ /,
    i _ / please?'

Check your answers

1 Now let's find the rest of the luggage. **2 a** Would you mind waiting for just a minute? **b** Of course not. **c** Could you look after my luggage cart and can you take my coat, please? **d** Sure. Go ahead. **3 a** Can I help you? **b** Could you tell me where the restroom is please?

★ *Restroom* is the most common term for a public toilet.
★ For men, the door to a restroom usually says *Men* or *Gentlemen*.
★ For women, the door to a restroom usually says *Women* or *Ladies*.
★ We can also say *the mens' room* or *the ladies' room*.

Find the words and phrases

→ Read the questions below.
→ Read the text of Recording 3 again and complete the words and phrases.

1 Oliver has only got one suitcase but Tasha's got q _ _ _ _ / a / l _ _ / of / l _ _ g _ _ e.

2 Are the suitcases on the way? Yes.
Are the suitcases there? No, not y _ _.

3 Tasha asks Oliver to wait. To wait isn't a problem because the suitcases aren't there. Oliver says, 'The suitcases aren't here yet, a _ _ w _ _.

4 How can you ask, 'Is that all (your luggage?)' in two other ways?
'Is that / _ _ /? ' or 'Is that e _ _ _ _ t _ _ _ g?'

5 When you take someone somewhere, you can say, 'It's t _ _ _ / w _ _.'

6 Oliver is happy about meeting Tasha on the plane. He says, 'I_ ' _ / b _ _ n / r _ _ _ _ y / n _ _ e / t _ _ k _ _ g / t _ / you / Tasha.'

7 Tasha thanks Oliver f _ _ the help with her suitcase.

8 He says he'll contact her next week. He says, 'I'_ _ / b _ / i _ / t _ _ _ _ / next week.

9 Verb *get*: In part **e** 'I'll go and *get* one' (luggage cart).
Here, *get* means **a** buy **b** bring one here?

☑ **Check your answers**

1 Tasha's got quite a lot of luggage. **2** No, not yet. **3** The suitcases aren't there, anyway. **4** 'Is that it?' 'Is that everything?' *'Is that it?' is informal, 'Is that everything?' is always appropriate. **5** It's this way. **6** It's been really nice talking *to* you Tasha (Preposition!) **7** Tasha thanks Oliver *for* his help (Preposition!) **8** I'll be *in* touch next week (Preposition!) **9** b.

Q *What are the differences between suitcase, luggage and baggage?*

A Answer:

Meaning

1 This is a suitcase.

2 This is luggage.

3 This is baggage.

Form

Suitcase is countable – one *suitcase* (two syllables), two *suitcases* (three syllables).

Luggage and *baggage* are uncountable/mass words.

Example: Our suitcases and bags are in the car   OR
        Our luggage is in the car.

★ The unit word for *luggage* is *piece*. For example, an airport employee: 'How many pieces of luggage have you got?'

★ We sometimes say *case* for *suitcase*.

→ Complete the sentences below with *(suit)case(s)*, *luggage*, *piece(s)* of *luggage* or *baggage*.

1 People take guitars, boxes, and all sorts of _____ on planes.

2 Passengers can take one small piece of hand-_____ into the plane with them.

3 On flights from the U.S. to Europe you can take two _____ of _____ .

4 Let's go kids! Are your _____ in the car?

Check your answers

1 baggage 2 hand-luggage 3 pieces of luggage 4 (suit)cases (Luggage is wrong here because the verb is plural – *are*)

Grammar and communication 2

Suggesting doing something together – *let's*

Example from *The Story*:

They get the luggage cart. Oliver suggests they find their suitcases. He says, 'Now **let's** find the rest of the luggage.'

Meaning

Who is making a suggestion? Oliver.
Does the suggestion include Oliver? Yes.

★ Use *let's* when the suggestion includes *you*.

Form

Let's + verb

★ The negative is *let's not* + verb.
★ The short answer is, *Yes, let's.*
★ The question tag is *Let's (go), shall we?*

Let's – **summary of responses**	
Positive responses are	O.K./All right
	Yes, why not?
	That's a good idea ☺
	Yes, why don't we?
Possible negative responses are	Do you really want to?
	I'm not too sure ☹
	Perhaps not
	Actually, I'm not too enthusiastic

Situation You live with Chris, a friend of yours.

→ Write suggestions and responses for these situations.

1 It's very hot. You and Chris are sitting on the patio, talking. You're thirsty.
   You _____
   Chris _____ ☺

2 **Situation** You both have a friend, Hilary. Hilary is ill. Suggest you both go and visit her this afternoon.
   You _____, _____?
   Chris _____ ☹

3 Chris turns the T.V. on. There's a football match on. You don't like football and there's a good film on Channel 5.
   You _____the football. Why don't we watch the film on Channel 5 instead?
   Chris_____ ☺

4 You are talking about a vacation. Suggest Mexico.
   You _____Mexico.
   Chris_____ ☺

   Chris suggests inviting Sam (another friend) too.
   Chris _____
   You _____ ☹

5 You are going to a party tonight. You're very tired. You don't want to go.
   You _____to the party. _____ stay here instead.
   Chris Shall we have Chinese food?
   You Yes ____'__!

Check your answers

1 Let's have a drink. **2** Let's go and visit Hilary this afternoon, shall we? **3** Let's not watch the football. Why don't we watch the film on Channel 5 instead? **4** Let's go to Mexico. Let's invite Sam, too. **5** Let's not go to the party. Let's stay here instead. Yes, let's!

Responses

☺ Any response from the ☺ list in the box on page 190.

☹ Any response from the ☹ list in the box on page 190.

Q *What's the difference between 'We could'* ⎫ *(Topic 6)*
                               'We can...' ⎭

and 'Let's' ...?

A Here are two examples:

Situation You're with a friend, talking about this evening.

a 'We could go to the movies.'
b 'Let's go to the movies.'

With **a** *We could...* the movies is a possibility.

With **b** *Let's...* you would like to go to the movies and you would like the other person to go, too.

In summary, *we could* is less direct.

Grammar and communication 3

Asking people to do things

Examples from *The Story*:

1 Tasha asks Oliver to wait for her. She says, '**Would you mind** waiting for just a minute?'
Oliver responds, 'Of course not.'

2 Tasha asks Oliver to look after her cart and take her coat.
She says, '**Could you** look after my luggage cart, oh, and can you take my coat, please?'
Oliver responds, 'Sure. Go ahead.'

Grammar summary – Asking someone to do something		
Request	**Responses – it's O.K.**	**Responses – it isn't O.K.**
Can you + verb…? Could you + verb…?	Sure Of course Of course I can/could Yes, that's no problem	I'm afraid I can't I'm sorry but I can't I'm sorry but + reason
Would you mind + verb/ing?	Of course not Not at all	

★ A response isn't always necessary. The person can 'do' the action without a response.

★ It is very common to say *please* when you ask someone to do something.

★ Answers *Yes, I can, Yes, I could, No, I can't, No, I wouldn't*, etc. alone are not usually appropriate. ☹

★ *Would you mind?* means 'Is it a problem for you to…?'
If it is not a problem, the response is negative, *No, of course not*.

★ When you say *no*, it is common to give a reason.
Example 'Could you cook the dinner tomorrow, please?'
'I'm sorry, I can't. I'm going out to dinner with Julie.'

★ *Could* is less direct than *can*.

★ *Would you mind…?* can be more formal than *can you?/could you?*

Asking someone NOT TO do something	
Would you mind not + *verb* + 'ing'?	<u>Positive response</u> Oh! I'm sorry
	<u>Negative response</u> Is it really a problem?

Asking people to do things – *Can you..? Could you...? Would you mind...?*

→ Read the situations below.
→ Complete the requests.
→ Choose an appropriate response from the box on page 194, where necessary.

1 Someone speaks to you in English but you don't understand. Ask them to say it again.
   You *Ca*_____, please?

2 You are eating with friends. You would like some water. A pitcher is at the other end of the table.
   You *Co*_____

   Your friend _____

3 Your child asks for help with his/her English homework.
   Mom/Dad, ca _____?
   You _____

4 You are a tourist and you have a camera. You want a photo with your friends. You ask another tourist.
   *W*_____?
   The tourist _____

5 The telephone rings. You are just going in the shower. Ask the person to call you back in 10 minutes.
   *Ca*_____ ?
   The caller _____

6 A friend is staying in your house. She smokes in the kitchen. You really don't like it. Ask her not to.
   You *W*_____

   Your friend _____

7 Someone tells you a new word in English. You want to write it but you don't know the spelling.
   You *Co*_____?
   The other person _____

Responses

Of course. What is it?

I'm sorry but I'm going out right now and it's urgent

Oh, sorry!

Not at all – what do I do?

Yes, it's T – H – A…

Yes, here you are

✓ Check your answers

1 Can you say that again, please? *This is more common than 'Can you repeat that, please?' **2** Could you pass the water, please? Yes. Here you are. **3** Mom/Dad, can you help me with my homework? Of course. What is it? **4** Would you mind taking a photo of us, please? Not at all. What do I do? **5** Can you call me back in 10 minutes, please? I'm sorry but I'm going out right now and it's urgent. **6** Would you mind not smoking in the kitchen? Oh, sorry! **7** Could you spell that for me, please? Yes, it's T – H – A…

Asking people to do things – official announcements

Situation On a plane or at an airport.

→ Cover the text of Recording 4.

→ Read the flight attendants' requests and invitations below (**a–h**)

→ Listen to the announcements on Recording 4, (**1–8**).

→ Just try to understand the message – it is not necessary to understand all the words.

→ Match the requests and the announcements, for example **1–f**.

→ Write the number in the box.

a 'Could you please go back to your seat, sir? We're landing soon.' ☐

b 'Would you mind not smoking, please, sir? This is a non-smoking flight.' ☐

c 'I'm sorry, could you please sit down again, madam? The plane is still moving.' ☐

d 'Could you put those bags in the overhead compartments, please?' ☐

e 'Could you please hurry, sir? The aircraft is ready to leave.' ☐

f 'Could you please stay in your seat, sir, and fasten your seatbelt? It's a little bumpy ahead.' □

g 'If you wouldn't mind filling this in, madam…You'll need it at immigration.' □

h 'Please report to the special desk sir, when you get off the plane…' □

Recording 4

1 Passengers are requested to remain in their seats with their seat belts fastened – we are entering an area of turbulence.

2 Passenger Smith, going to Rome, is requested to go immediately to Gate 12 where the flight is now boarding.

3 All transit passengers are requested to report to the transit desk.

4 All passengers are requested to return to their seats. We are beginning our descent.

5 Passengers are requested to put all hand-luggage in the storage space above your heads.

6 All passengers are required to complete a landing card for the immigration authorities.

7 Passengers are requested to remain in their seats until the plane comes to a complete halt.

8 Passengers are respectfully reminded that smoking is not allowed on this flight.

Check your answers

a 4 b 8 c 7 d 5 e 2 f 1 g 6 h 3

★ In hotels, restaurants, airports, shops, etc., the staff say *sir* to a man and *ma'am* to a woman. Clients and customers don't use *sir* or *ma'am* with staff.

★ If we use the family name, we say *Mr.* or *Mrs.* + family name.

Grammar and communication 4

Asking for help – indirect questions

The person at the information desk offers Tasha help.
She says, 'Can I help you?'

Tasha asks for help to find the restroom.
She says, '**Could you tell me** where the restroom is please?'

Direct question   'Where's the ladies' room, please?'
Indirect question 'Could you tell me where the restroom **is**, please?'

★   Both are grammatically correct.
★   *Could you...* is very common because it is indirect.
★   Use *Could you tell me...*
      Can you show me...   } to ask for help.
      Would you mind explaining...
★   In other words, expressions for 'asking for help' and 'asking someone
     to do something' are the same.

! Common mistake – indirect questions – word order

'Can you tell me how much **this is**, please?'   ✓
                                    (subject + verb ✓)

(Not: 'Can you tell me how much ~~is this~~, please?) ✗
                                    (Verb + subject ✗)

★   Word order is important with indirect questions.

Q *Where is the question form in indirect questions?*

A At the beginning.
   Can you...
   Could you...   } is the question. (verb + subject)
   Would you mind...

The question is at the beginning.
The second part of the sentence is not a question. For this reason there is
no question form here.

Grammar summary – Indirect Questions – verb *be*			
Indirect question phrase	**question words**	**subject**	**verb**
Can you tell me Could you tell me Would you mind telling me	where how much when who	it	is?

→ Below are six direct questions asking for help.
→ Ask the questions in a polite (indirect) way.
→ Start with *Excuse me,...*

1 'Where's the coffee bar?'
*Excuse me, ca*_____

2 'Where are the restrooms?'
*Excuse me, co*_____

3 'How much is this?'
*Excuse me, co*_____

4 'How much are these?'
*Excuse me, w*_____

5 'How much is this magazine?'
*Excuse me, ca*_____

6 'How much are these chips?'
*Excuse me, co*_____

✓ Check your answers

1 Excuse me, can you tell me where the coffee shop is, please?
2 Excuse me, could you tell me where the restrooms are, please?
3 Excuse me, could you tell me how much this is, please?
4 Excuse me, would you mind telling me how much these are, please?
5 Excuse me, can you tell me how much this magazine is, please?
6 Excuse me, could you tell me how much these chips are, please?

i | Culture – money

- The currency (unit of money) in the U.S. is the U.S. dollar.
- The dollar sign '$' goes in front of the amount: $10.00, $27.00.
- The dollar is divided into 100 cents. For example, 2,750 cents is $27.50.

Coins

- The common coins are the quarter (25 cents, $.25), the dime (10 cents, $.10), the nickel (5 cents, $.05), and the penny or cent (1 cent, $.01). There is also a 1 dollar coin. This coin is not common. 50-cent pieces are also in circulation.

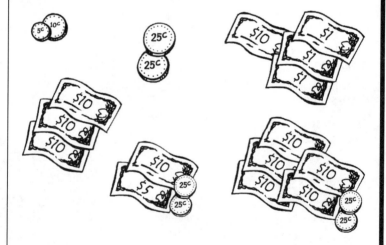

Bills or notes

- The most common notes are $1.00, $5.00, $10.00, $20.00, $50.00 and $100.00 are in circulation. Larger bills exist but are not common. The two-dollar bill is also not common.

Q How do we say, for example, $3.25?

A We can say, 'Three dollars, twenty-five cents' (more formal).

OR 'Three twenty-five'
OR 'Three and a quarter' } less formal

About your country: money

→ Read the questions below.
→ Either write your answers or prepare to tell a friend.

1 What is the currency in your country?

_____

2 What are the coins?

_____

3 What are the notes?

_____

4 How do you write it?

_____

5 How do you say it?

_____

Our story continues. Oliver is in a store in the airport.

Understanding the important information

→ Cover the text of Recording 5.
→ Read the questions below.
→ Listen to Recording 5 and answer the questions.

1 Oliver buys 1, 2, 3, 4, things?
2 Oliver has the right change. Yes/No

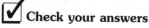 *Recording 5*

Oliver	Excuse me, do you sell *Computing Weekly*?
Seller	Yes, sir, they're here.
Oliver	And a package of mints – have you got Lifesavers?
The seller gets a package of Lifesavers.	
Oliver	$2.86 please, sir.
Oliver	Sorry, I haven't got any change. Is $20.00 all right?
Seller	Yes, no problem. Seventeen dollars, 14 cents change.
Oliver	Thanks.

☑ Check your answers

1 Oliver buys two things. **2** No, Oliver hasn't got the right change.

Understanding more

→ Cover the text of Recording 5 again.
→ Read the sentences below.
→ Listen and choose the correct answer.

1 Oliver buys **a** a newspaper.
　　　　　　　　 b a magazine.

2 He buys **a** a Mars bar
　　　　　　 b a package of Lifesavers
　　　　　　 c a pack of corn chips   } too.
　　　　　　 d a bar of chocolate

3 The total price is **a** $1.86.
                               b $2.68.
                               c $2.86.

4 Oliver gives the man **a** $5.
                               b $10.
                               c $20.

5 The change is **a** $17.40.
                        b $7.14.
                        c $7.40.
                        d $17.14.

6 The change is **a** right.
                             b wrong.

Check your answers

1 b 2 b 3 c 4 c 5 d 6 a

What's the right word?

Snacks

→ Label the pictures. Choose one expression from **Box 1** and one word
   from **Box 2** on page 202.
→ Use your dictionary if necessary.

Example:
a packet of polos

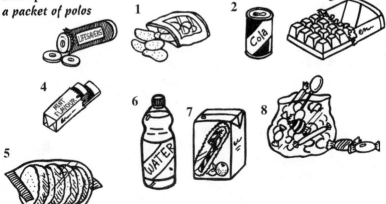

Box 1	
a bar of	a carton of
a can of	a package of
a bottle of	a bag of

Box 2	
water	candy
fruit juice	chips
chocolate	cookies
chewing gum	Coke

☑ **Check your answers** *(Recording 6)*

1 a package of chips
2 a can of Coke
3 a bar of chocolate
4 a package of chewing gum
5 a package of cookies
6 a bottle of water
7 a carton of fruit juice
8 a bag of candy

How do you pronounce it?

Saying groups of words together – linking

→ Look at the link lines and stress on the expressions above.
 The word *of* is weak in all the sentences, so the vowel is *schwa* / ə /.
→ Listen to Recording 6 and repeat the list.
 Pay special attention to
 a stress **b** linking words **c** weak *of*.

i **Culture – snacks**

- Snacks are very common in the U.S.
- Sweet things are very popular, especially sweets and chocolate, for example, Lifesavers (mint sweets) and candy bars.
- Nowadays, salty snacks, for example, corn or potato chips and nuts, are also popular.
- All the snacks in the exercise above are very common.
- People eat snacks at any time of the day.
- At work, a snack with coffee is very usual.
- In the summer, ice cream is a popular snack.

About you: snacks

→ Write answers to the questions below or prepare to tell a friend.

1 What do people eat and drink between meals in your country?

_____

2 Write two lists:
  a snacks you like. _____ _____
  b snacks you don't like. _____ _____

Understanding numbers

Is it 13 or 30?

Look at the stress pattern.

13 thir**teen**	30 **thir**ty
14 four**teen**	40 **for**ty
15 fif**teen**	50 **fif**ty
16 six**teen**	60 **six**ty etc.

Can you hear the difference?

→ Listen to Recording 7 and tick ✓ the correct picture.

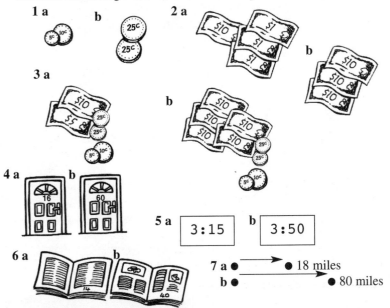

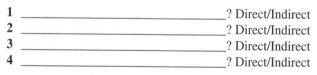

Recording 7

1 **A** Excuse me, how much is this, please?
  B 50 cents.
2 **A** How much does this cost, please?
  B $13.
  A Sorry, is that $13 or $30?
  B $13, sir.
3 **A** Excuse me, could you tell me how much this costs, please?
  B Of course. That's $15.65.
  A Is that one, five or five '0'?
  B One five, fifteen.
4 **A** Where do you live?
  B At number 60.
5 **A** At what time?
  B At 3:15.
6 **A** Where is it?
  B On page 40.
7 **A** How far is it to the town?
  B 18 miles.

Check your answers

1 b 2 a 3 a 4 b 5 a 6 b 7 a

What do they say?

Asking the price

→ Read questions 1–4 of Recording 7 above.
→ Copy below the four questions to ask the price.
→ Choose *direct* or *indirect* for each one.

1 _____? Direct/Indirect
2 _____? Direct/Indirect
3 _____? Direct/Indirect
4 _____? Direct/Indirect

Check your answers

1 Excuse me, how much is this, please? (Direct) **2** How much does this cost, please? (Direct) **3** Do you know how much this is, please? (Indirect) **4** Excuse me, could you tell me how much this costs, please? (Indirect)

→ Listen to Recording 7 again and repeat the questions and answers.

Common mistake – indirect questions

★ The word order in indirect questions is always the same.
The question is at the beginning and the rest is normal word order – subject first, then verb.

'Excuse me, could you tell me how much **this costs**, please?'

(Not: 'Excuse me, could you tell me how much ~~does this cost~~, please?')

★ Use *if* with yes/no indirect questions.
For example: Direct question. 'Does this shop open on Sundays?'
Indirect question. 'Do you know if this shop opens on Sundays?'

Asking for help – indirect questions

→ Which one is correct? Complete the questions with **a**, **b** or **c**.

1 Excuse me, do you know how much _____, please?
   a are these   **b** these are

2 Could you tell me _____, please?
   a where a coffee shop is   **b** where is a coffee shop

3 Do you know when _____ ?
   a starts the film   **b** the film starts

4 Excuse me, can you tell me _____?
   a where this train goes   **b** where does this train go

5 Do you know what _____?
   a does he do?   **b** he does

6 Excuse me, can you tell me _____ to the town center, please?
   a how far is it   **b** how far it is

7 Could you tell me _____ there?
a how do I get   **b** how to get

8 Do you know when _____?
a he is arriving   **b** is he arriving

9 Can you tell me what _____ in English?
a is this   **b** this is

10 Can you tell me _____ to Boston?
a does this train go   **b** if this train goes

11 Could you tell me _____ the right bus for the airport, please?
a if this is   **b** is this

12 Do you know _____ ?
a what means this word
b what this word means
c what does mean this word

This one's difficult for very many learners of English – have you got it right?

✓ **Check your answers**

1 b **2** a **3** b **4** a **5** b **6** b **7** b **8** a **9** b **10** b **11** a **12** b

What would you say?

1 You buy something in a store.
The person gives you the wrong change.

_____

2 You are at the baggage claim at the airport. Your suitcase doesn't come.

_____

Possible answers

1 How much is it again? OR I'm sorry but I don't think this change is right.
I don't think X is right is more common than 'x is wrong'.
I don't think X is right is less direct.
Advanced alternative: I'm sorry but I think there's a mistake here.

2 Excuse me, I don't know where my suitcase is. Could you help me please?

Review

How do you say it in your language?

→ Here are some examples of the important points in this topic.
→ Translate the sentences into your language in the spaces.
→ Remember – translate the idea, not the words.

1 You arrive at a restaurant. The person working there says 'If you would like to follow me… (I'll show you to your table)

---

2 **A** 'What shall we do today?' **B** 'Let's go to my brother's.' **A** 'Fine, why not?'

---

3 **A** 'Shall we walk there?' **B** 'I'm not too keen on that idea. Let's go by car.'

---

4 **A** 'Can I help you?' **B** 'Yes, Could you tell me where the coffee shop is, please?'

---

5 **A** 'I'm sorry I can't go tomorrow. Would you mind changing the meeting to Wednesday?' **B** 'Of course not – that's no problem.'

---

6 At the end of a conversation you say, 'It's been nice talking to you.'

---

7 'Do you need a luggage cart? I'll go and get one.'

Join the conversation

→ Look at the text of Recording 8 on page 208. It's the complete conversation from Recording 3, when Oliver and Tasha get off the plane. Notice the linking.
→ Listen to Recording 8 and read Tasha's words in the spaces.
→ Pay special attention to the linking between the words.

🎧 *Recording 8*

Immigration officer	Thank you madam. Sir, your passport please. Thank you.
Oliver	Do you need a luggage cart?
Tasha	That would be a good idea – I've got quite a lot of luggage.
Oliver	They're right over here.
	Now, let's find the rest of the luggage.
Tasha	Would you mind waiting for just a minute, Oliver?
Oliver	Of course not. The suitcases aren't here yet anyway.
Tasha	Could you look after my luggage cart, oh, and can you take my coat, please?
Oliver	Sure, go ahead.

Tasha asks for help at the information desk.

Airport employee	Can I help you?
Tasha	Yes, could you tell me where the restroom is, please?
Airport employee	Of course, madam. Just over there. Can you see the sign?
Oliver	Wow, this suitcase is a bit heavy – is that it now?
Tasha	The suitcase, the small bag and my handbag – yes that's everything.
Oliver	Well, it's been really nice talking to you, Tasha.
Tasha	Yes and thanks for the help with the luggage.
Oliver	I'll be in touch next week, then.
Tasha	Yes, bye.
Oliver	Bye.

TEST 7

Which one is right?

→ Choose **a** or **b**.

1 Thirty-five and twenty-nine are
   a forty-six.
   b sixty-four.

2 Please go in now, madam…
   a Yes, I would.
   b Thank you.

3 **a** Would you mind to wait, please?
   b Would you mind waiting, please?

4 **a** I'm hungry. Let's have something to eat!
   b I'm hungry. Let's to have something to eat!

5 Could you help me, please?
   a Yes. What do you want?
   b Of course. What would you like me to do?

6 Excuse me, can you tell me where station is, please?
   a Yes, I can.
   b Yes, it's just over there.

7 **a** I'll get a cart for the luggages.
   b I'll get a cart for the luggage.

8 The information desk?
   It's **a** in this way.
        b this way.

9 **a** 'Bye, I'll see you tomorrow.'
   b 'Bye, I see you tomorrow.'

10 Would you mind coming back later? (You can go back later.)
   a Yes.
   b Sure, it's no problem.

11 **a** Can you tell me where are the taxis, please?
   b Can you tell me where the taxis are, please?

12 $24.75. This is
   a dollars twenty four, seventy-five.
   b twenty-four dollars, seventy-five.

Write a dialogue

Situation   Eva is an au-pair with the Lewis family. (She works in the family, helping with the children and the house.) It's the morning and Barbara, Lewis and Eva are talking about the day.

Barbara   **Eva**

1   Barbara asks Eva to take the children to school. She's working this morning.

2 Eva says 'yes'

___ Would you like me to go to supermarket on the way back?

3   Barbara says yes and asks her to buy bread, milk and cartons of fruit juice.

4 Eva responds.

Does Barbara need more things from the store?

5   Barbara says no and asks Eva to take the children to the park after school.

She also asks her to work on Saturday evening.

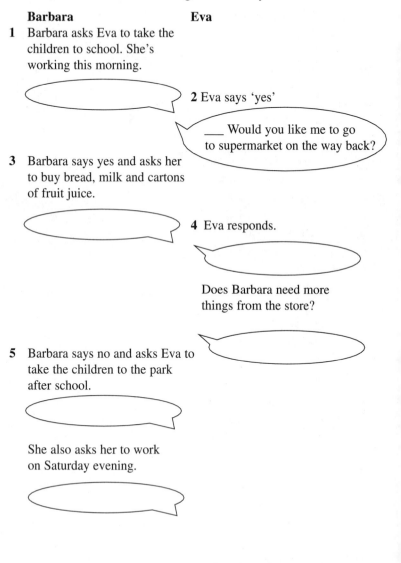

6 Eva can take the children to the park but she can't work on Saturday evening. She's going to a party.

7 It's the afternoon
Eva is in the park with the children. One of the children sees an ice cream stand and suggests they all have some ice cream.

OK. Which one would you like?

Check your answers

1 b 2 b 3 b 4 a 5 b 6 b 7 b 8 b 9 a 10 b 11 b 12 b

Dialogue: model answers

1 Barbara   Could you take the children to school, please? I'm working this morning.

2 Eva   Of course. Would you like me to go to the supermarket on the way back?

3 Barbara   Could you? Can you get some bread, some milk and a few cartons of fruit juice?

4 Eva   Fine. Do you need anything else?

5 Barbara   No, thanks. Could you take the children to the park after school and would you mind working on Saturday evening?

6 Eva   I can take the children to the park but I'm sorry, I can't work on Saturday evening – I'm going to a party.
[In the afternoon]

7 Child   Let's all have some ice cream!

8 | USING PUBLIC TRANSPORTATION

Grammar and communication	Vocabulary
◆ Prepositions at the end of questions	◆ Public transport
◆ Asking for instructions, giving instructions	◆ The time
◆ Asking for and understanding travel information	**Pronunciation**
– the time, timetables, itineraries	◆ Stress – place names

Oliver is at the information desk at the airport. He needs to get into the city.

Understanding the important information

→ Cover the text of Recording 1, *The Story*.
→ Read the question below.
→ Listen to the recording and answer the question.

   How is Oliver going into the city?

♪ *Recording 1 – The Story*

Airport employee	Can I help you?
Oliver	Yes, could you tell me how to get into the city, please?
Airport employee	You can go by taxi, limosine, rental car, or by bus. Where are you going in the city?
Oliver	I need to get to the Denver Tech Center.
Airport employee	Then you can take a skyRide bus. It goes all the way to the Tech Center.
Oliver	skyRide. Good. And where do I get the bus from?
Airport employee	Just over there, sir. You follow the signs that say 'skyRide'.
Oliver	Oh, I see! Do you know when the next bus leaves?
Airport employee	In ten minutes, sir – at 8:05.
Oliver	And how long does it take to get there?
Airport employee	I'm not sure – the best thing is to ask the driver.
Oliver	Many thanks for your help.

Check your answer

By bus

Understanding more

→ Cover the text of Recording 1.
→ Read the questions on page 214.
→ Listen and choose the right answers.

1 Choose ALL the right answers.

The man says Oliver can go by bus, or by

a rental car

b taxi

c subway

d train

(2 – 6 Choose the right answer.)

2 Where exactly in Denver is Oliver going?

a the Denver Tech Center

b a hotel

c RTD Civic Center Station

d the U.S. Mint

3 What's the name of the bus?

a skyRide

b the airport bus

c Denver bus

d Express bus

4 a It's a short walk to the bus.

b The bus is very near.

c The bus goes from the parking lot.

d The bus is downstairs.

5 The next bus leaves

a in an hour

b in half an hour

c in two hours' time

d in ten minutes' time

6 When does the bus arrive in Denver?

a we don't know

b in one hour

c in half an hour

d in ten minutes

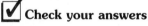 **Check your answers**

1 a and b **2** a **3** a **4** b **5** d **6** a

What do they say?

→ Read the sentences below.
→ Listen to Recording 1 again and try to complete the words.
→ Then read the text on page 213 to help you if necessary.

1 a Oliver doesn't know how to get into the city. He asks for help. He
says, 'C _ _ _ _ / you / t _ _ _ / me / h _ _ / t _ / g _ _ /i _ _ _ / t _ _ /
c _ _ _ , please?'
   b There are four possibilities.
The man says, 'You can go by t _ _ _ / l _ _ _ _ _ _ _ / r _ _ _ _ _ / c _ _,
/ or by b _ _.'

2 a The man asks where exactly in Denver Oliver is going. He says,
'Where are / y _ _ / g _ _ _ _ / in / t _ _ / c _ _ _?'
   b Oliver answers, 'I / n _ _ _ / t _ / g _ _ / to the / D _ _ _ _ _ / T _ _ _ /
C _ _ _ _ _.'

3 a The man suggests taking the skyRide. He says, 'Then y _ _ / c _ _ /
t _ _ _ / a skyRide bus.'

4 a Oliver doesn't know where the buses are. He asks,
'Where / d_ / I / g _ _ / the / b _ _ / f _ _ _?'
   b The man gives Oliver instructions,
'Y _ _ / f _ ll _ _ / the / s _ _ _ _ / t _ _ _ / s _ _ / 'skyRide.'

5   Oliver wants to know how long the journey takes. He asks,
'H _ _ / l _ _ _ / d _ _ _ / it / t _ _ _ / to get / t _ _ _ _?'

Check your answers

1 a Could you tell me how to get into the city, please? (preposition!) **b** You
can go by taxi, limosine, rental car, or by bus. (preposition!) **2 a** Where are
you going in the city? (preposition!) **b** I need to get to the Denver Tech Center.
3 Then you can take a skyRide bus. **4 a** Where do I get the bus from?
(preposition!) **b** You follow the signs that say 'skyRide'. **5** How long does it
take to get there?

How do you pronounce it?

Denver's main streets – stress

1 Broadway
2 Cherokee St.
3 Arapahoe St.
4 Lincoln St.

5 Speer Boulevard
6 Delaware St.
7 16th St.
8 East Colfax Avenue

Example from the story:

The man asks Oliver: 'Which part of the city are you going to?'
Oliver answers: 'I need to get to the <u>Tech</u> Center.'

→ Cover the text of Recording 2 below.
→ Look at the list above with the names of the main streets in Denver.
→ Listen to Recording 2.
→ Repeat the names and <u>underline</u> the stress for each one.

☑ **Check your answers** *(Recording 2)*

1 B<u>roa</u>dway
2 <u>Che</u>rokee St.
3 A<u>ra</u>pahoe St.
4 <u>Lin</u>coln St.
5 Speer <u>Bou</u>levard
6 <u>De</u>laware St.
7 Six<u>teen</u>th St.
8 East Colfax <u>Ave</u>nue

Here are some words for vehicles in the U.S.

bus the large, familiar vehicle that travels on the streets and carries many passesngers.

cable car a kind of single car that runs on tracks and climbs the hills of San Francisco by clamping onto a moving rope or cable.

el an elevated *subway*, part of a *light rail* system that runs on tracks partly or completely above the level of the streets. Found only in the largest cities.

light rail a kind of light train that runs in and out of a city carrying commuters. Found in large cities.

streetcar a *trolley.*

subway a kind of *light rail* train that travels on rails in tunnels beneath the streets. Found only in larger cities.

train a regular heavy train, usually diesel powered, that runs in and out of a city and carries people from more distant cities.

tram a special vehicle for carrying visitors around a park, zoo, or a city. Many of them are open to the weather. Some run on rails.

trolley a kind of single car that usually runs on rails and receives electrical power from overhead wires.

Culture – Getting around in U.S. cities

→ Study the terms on the previous page.
→ Read the statements about vehicles on the previous page and answer
   True or False.

1 A streetcar and a trolley are about the same thing. True/False

2 Cable cars are common all over the U.S.   True/False

3 A subway is a kind of underground train.   True/False

4 A light rail system connects one city to another.   True/False

5 Trains carry people from city to city.   True/False

6 Trams can be cold in the winter time.   True/False

7 A trolley works with electricity.   True/False

8 Cable cars usually work with electricity.   True/False

9 An el usually runs above the level of the street.   True/False

10 A cable car travels on rails.   True/False

11 Trains, trolleys, and cable cars always run on rails. True/False

12 Commuters travel on trams.   True/False

13 You can take a tram to visit a friend.   True/False

14 An el is a special kind of light rail.   True/False

15 American trains usually have diesel   True/False
    engines.

Check your answers

The correct answers are in parentheses ( ).

1 (True) *Streetcar* is an older term. These are not common in most cities.

2 (False) They are only in San Francisco which has many steep hills in the city. People ride the cable cars up the hills.

3 (True) Most subways are completely underground, but some run on the surface for part of their route.

4 (False) Light rail systems are in cities and sometimes connect cities with their suburbs.

5 (True) Real trains are heavy and powerful. They move people and goods.

6 (True) Trams can be open to the weather and can be cold. Sometimes they don't run during the coldest weather.

7 (True) A trolley has arms to contact electric wires that run above its route.

8 (False) Cable cars do not have an engine. They hold onto a cable that is always moving.

9 (True) Real elevated trains exist only in the largest cities. Their tracks are above the level of the street.

10 (True) The cable that moves the car is in the street beneath the car and between the rails.

11 (False) Trolleys *usually* run on rails, but some have wires and travel on the regular road. Their power always comes from overhead wires.

12 (False) Trams do not go where commuters want to go. Trams are for touring and seeing things.

13 (False) Unless your friend lives in a zoo or a city park, trams would not take you where you want to go.

14 (True) An el is usually light because it is high in the air.

15 (True) Some are electric, but most carry their own diesel engines.

He's getting off the bus and she's getting on the bus

Stress – Place and street names

→ Listen to these place and street names on Recording 3. Listen as many times as necessary.

→ Underline the syllable with the most stress in each phrase.

🎧 Recording 3

1 Avenue (1)	**8** Oxford Hotel (2)
2 Boulevard (1)	**9** Oxford Hotel (2)
3 Main Street (1)	**10** Shackleford (1)
4 Maple Street (1)	**11** Market Street (1)
5 Larimer Square (2)	**12** Bus Terminal (1)
6 State Capitol (2)	**13** Skyline Park (2)
7 Amusement Park (1)	**14** Cherry Creek (2)

✓ Check your answers

1 A<u>ve</u>nue **2** <u>Bou</u>levard **3** <u>Main</u> Street **4** <u>Ma</u>ple Street **5** Larimer <u>Square</u> **6** State <u>Cap</u>itol **7** A<u>mu</u>sement Park **8** Oxford Ho<u>tel</u> **9** Civic <u>Cen</u>ter **10** <u>Shack</u>leford **11** <u>Mar</u>ket Street **12** <u>Bus</u> Terminal **13** Skyline <u>Park</u> **14** Cherry <u>Creek</u>

How do you pronounce it?

Stress on place names – addresses

★ English has lots of words for *Road* or *Street*.

→ Listen to Recording 4 and repeat these street names.
→ Underline the syllable with stress.

Park Road	*High Street*	*Eton Avenue*
Buckingham Pike	*Tudor Drive*	*Moor Terrace*
West Trace	*Elm Crescent*	*West Expressway*
River Lane	*Church Grove*	*Esher Place*
Orchard Way	*Maple Court*	*Lansing Highway*

Check your answers (Recording 4)

Abbreviations are in brackets ( ).

Park <u>Road</u> (Rd)	<u>High</u> Street (St)	Eton <u>Av</u>enue (Ave)
Buckingham <u>Pike</u> (Pk)	Tudor <u>Drive</u> (Dr)	Moor <u>Terrace</u> (Terr)
West <u>Trace</u> (Tr)	Elm <u>Crescent</u> (Cres)	West <u>Express</u>way
River <u>Lane</u> (La)	Church <u>Grove</u> (Gr)	Esher <u>Place</u> (Pl)
Orchard <u>Way</u>	Maple <u>Court</u> (Ct)	Lansing <u>High</u>way

★ When we say or write an address, the number is first, before the name of the street, for example, 2 Park Road, 57 Eton Avenue.

Grammar and communication 1

Prepositions at the end of questions

Examples from *The Story:*

1 The man asks Oliver exactly where in Denver he's going
He says, 'Where are you going in the city?' (preposition!)

Affirmative 'I'm going to Denver Tech Center.'

Question 'Which part of Denver are you going to?'

2   Oliver doesn't know where the buses are.
    He asks 'Where do I get the bus **from**?' (preposition!)

Possible answer 'You get the bus from the bus stop outside the terminal.'

★   The grammar is correct with the preposition at the end.

★   Nowadays it is common to put the preposition at the end of the question.

→ Complete these mini-dialogues with the correct question from the box below.

1 A _____? **B** My brother – I call him every week.
2 A _____? **B** This picture. Isn't it attractive?
3 A _____? **B** My girlfriend. It's her birthday today.
4 A _____? **B** My boyfriend. I miss him.
5 A _____? **B** My keys. Do you know where they are?
6 A   There's an urgent e-mail for you. **B** _____?
7 A   I like reading. **B** _____?
8 A   She's married. **B** _____?
9 A   I'm going to that new restaurant this evening. **B** _____?
10 Taxi-driver **A** _____? **B** The station please.
11 A   We could go and see that new film this weekend.
     B _____?
12 A   I'd like to buy a ticket to Paris, please. **B** _____?

---

a Do you know who it's from? **b** Oh, is she? Who to?
c They're nice flowers. Who are they for? **d** Who are you talking to?
e Of course, sir. When for? **f** Are you really? Who are you going with?
g What are you looking at? **h** What's it about?
i Do you? What sort of books are you interested in?
j What are you looking for? **k** Who are you writing to?
l Where to, madam?

✓ **Check your answers**

1 d **2** g **3** c **4** k **5** j **6** a **7** i **8** b **9** f **10** l **11** h **12** e

What's the right word?

Transportation

Look at the following vehicle names.

1 el **2** tram **3** streetcar **4** train **5** subway **6** boat **7** bus **8** taxi **9** cable car **10** trolley

→ Place an X after each one that can run on rails.

→ Place a 0 after each one that does not travel on the surface of the land.

→ Place a Z after each one that does not have an engine of some sort.

→ Place a T after each one that does not run on rails.

→ Place a W after each one that always gets its power from overhead wires.

☑ **Check your answers**

1 X0 2 X 3 XW 4 X 5 X0 6 0T 7 T 8 T 9 XZ 10 XW

Getting around on public transport

→ Read the mini-dialogues and look at the words in the box on page 225.
→ Listen to Recording 5 and complete the dialogues with the correct word(s) from the box.

1

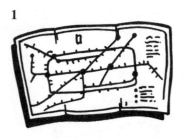

2

3

4

Recording 5

1 **A** I don't know the rail system.
     Could you give me a _____ please?
   B Of course. Here you are.
2 **A** Excuse me, do you know the time of the next train, please?
   B I'm not sure. There's a _____ over there, on the wall.
3 **A** Excuse me, how much is a _____ to Colorado Springs?
   B Is that _____?
   A No, _____ please. I'm coming back this evening.
4 **A** I want to buy a ticket but the _____/_____ is closed.
   B You can get one at the _____ / _____ over there.
5 **A** Which _____ does the train go from, please?
   B Number five, right at the end, over there.
6 **A** What's the _____, please?
   B $7.50.
7 **A** Is this a _____train? **B** No, I'm afraid it stops at all stations.
8 **A** Is this a _____ train? **B** No, sorry, change at the next stop.
9 **A** I'm not sure which track to go to.
   B Let's listen to the _____.
10 **A** We're going on an _____ to Boulder tomorrow.
   B Oh, are you? What time does your bus leave?
11 **A** In a taxi. 'The fare is $4.50. What's a good _____?'
   B 'If you give him $5.00 that's fine.'

---

direct   ticket machine   timetable   fare   ticket   excursion
fast   announcements   tip   one-way ticket   round-trip ticket
map   ticket office

Check your answers

1 map **2** timetable **3** ticket, one-way ticket, round-trip ticket **4** ticket office, ticket machine **5** platform **6** fare **7** fast **8** direct **9** announcements **10** excursion **11** tip

Label the pictures

→ Now label the pictures on page 224.

Check your answers

1 map **2** ticket machine **3** ticket office **4** timetable

! Common mistake

'This is a long travel.' ✗

'This is a long journey.' ✓

Q *What's the difference between 'travel' and 'journey'?*

A *Journey* is a countable noun.
Journey is the time and/or distance from A to B.

For example: 'It's a long journey from England to the U.S.'

Travel can be **a** a verb **b** an uncountable noun

Travel is general movement.
For example: a 'I travel a lot for my job.'
                         b 'Foreign travel is good for a person's education.'

Travel or journey?

→ Complete with *journey* or *travel*.

1 It's a long _____ to get here.
2 He's a _____ agent.
3 Foreign _____ helps people understand other cultures.
4 How long does the _____ take?

Check your answers

1 journey **2** travel **3** travel **4** journey

What's the right word?

Trips

→ Choose the correct phrase from the box to complete the sentences below.
→ Use your dictionary if necessary.

---

change your ticket   get on   buy a ticket   go on the excursion
find out about times and prices   get off   cancel the trip

You would like to go on a bus excursion.

1 First you _____
2 Then you _____
3 If something happens and you can't go, you can either
  a _____ or b _____
4 On the day of the trip you a _____ the coach. When you get there
  you b _____the bus and have a good time!

Check your answers

1 First you find out about times and prices. 2 Then you buy a ticket. 3 You can either change your ticket or cancel the trip. 4 a You get on the bus. b You get off the bus.

Grammar and communication 2

Asking for instructions, giving instructions

1 The man at the information desk says, 'Can I help you?' Oliver says, 'Yes, could you tell me how to get to the Tech center, please?'

2 The man says 'You can take the skyRide bus.'
  Oliver asks, 'Where do I get the bus from?'

Giving instructions

The man answers, 'You **follow** the signs that say 'skyRide'.'

→ Answer these questions about instructions.
    Examples: 'Where do I **get** the bus from?' 'You **follow** the signs…'

Meaning

In the two examples above, *get* and *follow* are   **a** in the past
                                                      b in the present
                                                      c in the future.

Form

The tense is   **a** present simple
                b present progressive
                c future simple.

✓ Check your answers

Meaning c
Form a

★   We can use the present simple to ask for and give instructions.

Asking for instructions

→ Read the seven questions below.
→ How many are correct?

> **Direct questions**
> How do I get downtown?
> How can I get downtown?
> How could I get downtown?

> **Indirect questions**
> Can you tell me how to get downtown?
> Could you tell me how I get downtown?
> Do you know how I can get downtown?
> Do you know how I could get downtown?

✓ Check your answers

All the questions are correct.

What are the differences?

All the questions are appropriate in most situations.
The indirect questions are very common.
Could is the most indirect.

Summary – Instructions

1 Asking for instructions

Direct questions

How	do can could	I get downtown?

Indirect questions

Can		tell	me		I	
	you	show		how	I can	get downtown?
Could					I could	
		explain	to me		to	

Do you know how I	can	get downtown?
	could	

2 Giving instructions – present simple

You go... You follow... You take...

3 For more than one possibility

You can + verb (without 'to') + 'or' + verb (without 'to')

For example: 'You can walk or go by bus.'

Asking for instructions

→ Put the words in the right order to complete the question.

1 Excuse me, _____ the station from here, please?

       to/how/I/do/get

2 Excuse me, _____ a ticket for tomorrow?

       can/where/I/buy

3 Excuse me, _____ excursions to Aspen?

       out/I/how/find/about/could

4 Can you show me _____ a ticket from this machine, please?

        to/how/buy

5 Could you tell me _____ the bus station, please?

        to/get/I/how

6 Do you know _____ this door, please?

        how/open/can/I

7 Do you know _____ my round-trip ticket, please?

        change/I/could/how

✓ Check your answers

1 how do I get to **2** where can I book **3** how could I find out about **4** how to buy **5** how I get to **6** how I can open **7** how I could change

Giving instructions

Example from *The Story*:

Oliver asks: 'Where do I get the bus from?'
The man says: 'You follow the signs that say 'skyRide'.'

★ To give **instructions**, use the **present simple**.

Situation   You are in Europe on vacation. You want to make a trip from London to Paris on the Eurostar train. You ask a friend for instructions.

→ Complete your friend's instructions with the correct verb phrases from the box below.
→ It's not necessary to understand all the words. Just try to get the general idea.

She's going down the escalator.

He's going through
the door.

He's going up the escalator.

When you get to Waterloo, _____(1) the signs to 'Eurostar'. _____(2) the escalator and _____(3) your ticket from the ticket office. Then _____(4) ticket check and security control. After that _____(5) in the departure lounge. When you hear the announcement to board the train_____(6) the right escalator or travelator for your part of the Eurostar platform and _____(7) the train, _____(8) your luggage in the special luggage racks and _____(9) your seat. If you need refreshments during the journey – tea, coffee, something to eat, _____(10) the buffet car.

you go to	you put	you go up	you wait	you go down
you look for	you get on	you go through	you follow	you collect

✓ Check your answers

1 you follow **2** you go down **3** you collect **4** you go through **5** you wait **6** you go up **7** you get on **8** you put **9** you look for/find **10** you go to

Asking for help

→ Correct these questions if necessary. Some of the verbs are wrong.

1 Where I sign? _____

2 Can you tell me what do I write in this card?_____

3 Where pay I, please? _____

4 Can you tell me where I go now, please? _____

5 How do I get a taxi? _____

6 How I open this door? _____

7 Do I write this in English or my language?_____

8 I give a tip or not? _____

✓ Check your answers

1 Where do I sign? **2** Can you tell me what to write/what I write in this card? **3** Where do I pay, please? **4** correct – Can you tell me where I go now, please? **5** correct – How do I get a taxi? **6** How do I open this door? **7** correct – Do I write this in English or my language? **8** Do I give a tip or not?

→ Now match the questions (**1–8**) above with the possible answers (**a–h**) below.

a If you could just wait over there, please sir.

b At the bottom, right here.

c At the cash register over there please.

d Yes, people usually give about 15%.

e 'Happy Birthday' is fine.

f I can call one for you, madam.

g They open automatically when the train stops.

h Either, it doesn't matter.

✓ Check your answers

1 b **2** e **3** c **4** a **5** f **6** g **7** h **8** d

| i | **Culture – an invitation to dinner**
I don't know what to say – I don't know what to do |

Situation Your colleague invites you to his house for dinner.
You don't know about U.S. customs and habits.
You ask a friend to help you.

→ Look at the questions below and then the answers.
→ Write the correct question with the answer.

a What do I say if she offers me more food and I don't want it?

b What do I do if they speak very fast and I don't understand?

c Do I shake hands when I arrive?

d Do I take a present? And if so, what sort of present do I take?

e I don't know his wife's name? What do I call her? Do I call her 'ma'am'?

f What do I say if I want to use the bathroom?

g What do I say when I want to leave?

h The invitation is for seven o'clock. What time do I arrive?

i What do I wear?

j Do I do anything the next day?

k What do I do and say when I leave?

l What time do I leave?

Example:

1 You *What do I wear?*
   Your friend Informal clothes are fine.

2 You _____?
   Your friend A box of chocolates or flowers is the most common type of present. Lots of visitors like to give a little present from their country. That's fine too.

3 You _____?
   Your friend Punctuality's quite important here so it's best to get there within about 10 minutes of the time, but not before the time.

4 You _____?

Your friend Yes, the usual thing is to shake hands and say 'Pleased to meet you' or 'How do you do?' when you meet his wife. _How do you do_ is more formal than _Pleased to meet you._

5 You _____?

Your friend No, we only use that word in shops and places like that. If you call her 'Mrs. Parker' to start with, she'll tell you her first name, I'm sure.

6 You _____?

Your friend You just ask them to speak more slowly.

7 You _____

Your friend You say, 'No thanks. I'm fine.'

8 You _____?

Your friend You just say, 'Is it all right if I use the toilet?'

9 You _____?

Your friend You can say, 'It's getting late. I'd better go now.'

10 You _____?

Your friend Between ten and eleven o'clock is normal.

11 You _____?

Your friend You shake hands again and say, 'Thank you for inviting me – it was a lovely evening.'

12 You _____?

Your friend You can say 'thank you' again to your colleague at work if you like but it's not necessary to write a letter. Some people write a short note or card. This is a

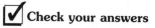

Check your answers

1 i **2** d **3** h **4** c **5** e **6** b **7** a **8** f **9** g **10** l **11** k **12** j

→ Answer these questions about the meaning and form of the verbs in questions **a–l** on page 233.

Meaning

In the exercise, the dinner is **a** in the past
b in the present
c in the future.

Form

The tense in the questions is **a** present simple
b present progressive
c future simple

Check your answers

Meaning c. Form a

★ We use the **present simple** to ask for and give instructions/help with systems. In the exercise above you are asking for help with the cultural systems, in other words, the habits and customs.

What's the difference between, for example, 'What shall I wear?' (Topic 7) *and 'What do I wear?'?*

What shall I (+ verb)…? asks for a suggestion.
What do I (+ verb)….? asks for help with a system. In other words, 'What is the right thing to do/say/wear, etc., in this situation?'

About your country: Invitations

→ Read the questions below.
→ Either write your answers or prepare to tell a friend.

Situation   A colleague invites me to dinner.
Answer my questions about customs and habits in your country.

1 In the U.S. it's common to invite someone home for dinner. Which is more common in your country, an invitation to eat at home or at a restaurant?

_____

2 What do I wear?

_____

3 Do I take a present? If so, what sort of present do I take?

_____

4 The invitation is for seven. Is that a usual time here for a dinner invitation? What time do I arrive?

_____

5 What do I do when I arrive? Do I shake hands with him, with his wife?

_____

6 I don't know his wife's name. What do I call her?

_____

7 What time do I leave?

_____

8 Do I do or say anything the next day?

_____

Our story continues... Oliver is walking towards the skyRide bus. A man talks to him

Understanding the important information

→ Cover the text of Recording 6 on page 237.
→ Read the question below.
→ Listen and choose the correct answer.

What's the time?   **a** 8:00
                           b 7:55
                           c 7:52
                           d 5:28

Recording 6 – The Story

Man Excuse me, can you tell me the time, please?
Oliver Yes, it's five to eight.
Man Many thanks.

Check your answer

b

What do they say?

The time

→ Cover the text of Recording 6 again.
→ Read the questions below.
→ Listen and complete the words.

1 The man asks Oliver the time. He says,
   'Excuse me, c _ _ / y _ _ / t _ _ _ / m _ / t _ _ / t _ _ _ /, please?'
2 Oliver answers,
   'Yes, i _ ' _ / f _ _ _ / t _ / e _ _ _ t.'
3 The man thanks Oliver. He says 'M _ _ _ / t _ _ _ _ _ .'

Check your answers

1 Excuse me, can you tell me the time, please? 2 Yes, it's five to eight. 3 Many thanks.

Grammar and communication 3

Asking for and understanding travel information

Saying the time

→ Read 1–6 on page 238 and draw the hands on these watches.

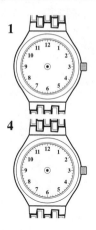
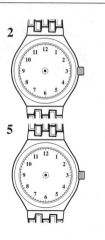
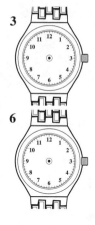

1 Eleven o'clock
2 Three thirty
3 A quarter past four

4 A quarter to six
5 Ten to nine
6 Twenty-five past ten

☑ **Check your answers**

1 11:00   **2** 3:30   **3** 4:15   **4** 5:45   **5** 8:50   **6** 10:25

Timetables

★ There are two ways to say the time. The exercise above is the usual way in spoken English.

★ When we want to be very specific, for example, for a timetable:
   – we might use the twenty-four hour clock
   – we say the exact number of minutes past the hour, even if it's more than 30. For example, '8:43' is 'eight forty-three' and '11:56' is 'eleven fifty-six'.
   – We say 'O' like the name of the letter for zero in timetables.

Timetables

Can you give me times of the trains to …, please?

→ Cover the text of Recording 7.
→ Listen and write down the times you hear.

Times of the trains to go	To come back
1 _____	1 _____
2 _____	2 _____
3 _____	3 _____
4 _____	4 _____

Check your answers

To go

1 6:22 (six twenty-two)
2 7:49 (seven forty-nine)
3 8:13(eight thirteen)
4 9:56 (nine fifty-six)

To come back

1 13:05 (thirteen '0' five)
2 14:50 (fourteen-fifty)
3 15:32 (fifteen thirty-two)
4 16:09 (sixteen '0' nine)

Recording 7

The first train in the morning leaves at 6:22, then there's another at 7:49, one at 8:13, and another at 9:56. To come back you can leave at 13:05, or 14:50, or there are later trains at 15:32 and 16:09.

Frequency – how often do the trains go?

→ Read the expressions in the boxes below.
→ Read the timetables on page 240.
→ Match each timetable (**a,b,c**) with one phrase from **Box 1** (**1,2,3**) and one phrase from **Box 2** (**A,B,C**).
→ Write the number and letter in the boxes after the timetables.

Box 1	Box 2
1 four times an hour	**A** on the hour
2 twice an hour	**B** at five past, twenty past, twenty-five to and ten to the hour
3 every hour	**C** at a quarter past and a quarter to the hour

The timetables

a 6:00, 7:00, 8:00, 9:00, 10:00, 11:00, 12:00 ☐ ☐
b 6:15, 6:45, 7:15, 7:45, 8:15, 8:45, 9:15, 9:45 ☐ ☐
c 6:05, 6:20, 6:35, 6:50, 7:05, 7:20, 7:35, 7:50 ☐ ☐

☑ **Check your answers**

a 3 A Every hour on the hour. **b 2 C** Twice an hour, at a quarter past and quarter to each hour. **c 1 B** Four times an hour, at five past, twenty past, twenty-five to and ten to the hour.

How long from now?

Example from *The Story*: Oliver asks, 'When does the bus leave?'
The employee answers 'In ten minutes'(time) at 8.05.'

In ten minutes' time

→ Make four mini-dialogues. Match the questions (**1–4**) with the correct response (**a–d**).

1 When's the next train?

a In a week('s time). They're in Hong Kong at the moment.

2 When's my Mommy coming?

b In two minutes('time). Come on, let's run!

3 When do they get to Australia?

c In 6 months('time), at the end of my course.

4 When are you going back to your country?

d In a few minutes('time). She's on her way.

☑ **Check your answers**

1 b **2** d **3** a **4** c

How long?

Example from *The Story*:

Oliver wants to know the time the journey takes. He asks, 'How long does **it take** to get there?'

★ To talk about length of time for an activity we use the verb *take*.

★ *It takes* (impersonal subject *it* + verb *take*) + verb with *to*.

→ Complete these mini-dialogues (**1–4**) with (**a–d**).

1 How long does it take to get there?

a No, only a few minutes. It's easy.

2 Does it take a long time to do that?

b I know. Mine's the same.

3 It doesn't take long to walk there.

c About 10 minutes. It's not far.

4 It takes my daughter a long time to get ready in the morning.

d No, it's very near.

Check your answers

1 c **2** a **3** d **4** b

★ To talk about a specific person with the expression *it takes*, we say *it takes* + person + verb with *to*.

For example:

It takes	my daughter	a long time	to get ready.
Or with the pronouns *me, you, him, her, us, them*			
It takes	her	a long time	to get ready.

How long does it take you?

→ Tell me some things about you.

How long does it take you to have breakfast? _____

How long does it take you to get ready in the morning?_____

Does it take you a long time to get to work/school? Is it far?_____

How long does it take your best friend to get to your house from his/her house? _____

How long does it take you to get to the nearest supermarket from your house? _____

Possible answers

You can write short phrases – for example, 'Ten minutes.'
Or 'It takes me/him/her about (10) minutes.'

Does it take you long?

→ Write questions for these answers.

1 _____?
I don't eat much in the mornings, really – about 10 minutes, I suppose.

2 _____?
No time at all – I work from home

3 _____?
I can walk there in about 5 minutes – I go shopping there most days.

4 _____?
School starts at 8:45 and they leave at 8:15 so it's about a half-hour walk.

Check your answers

1 How long does it take you to have breakfast? **2** How long does it take you to get to work? **3** How long does it take you to get to the nearest supermarket? **4** How long does it take the children to walk to school?

Asking and giving the time

→ Look at the clocks below.
→ Cover the text of Recording 8.
→ Listen to the six mini-dialogues asking and giving the time.
→ Write numbers **1–6** below the correct clock(s).

    a   b   c

| **12:58** | **13:00** | **13:04** |

Example: 1_____   _____   _____

Recording 8

1 **A** Dad, what's the time?
   B It's a few minutes to one.

2 **A** Excuse me, could you tell me the time, please?
   B Of course. Er, actually, it's exactly one o'clock.

3 **A** John, have you got the time?
   B Yeah, it's just a few minutes before one.

4 **A** Could you tell me what the time is, please?
   B Yes, it's just after one.

5 **A** Excuse me, can you tell me what time it is, please?
   B I'm sorry, I haven't got a watch but I think it's around one.

6 **A** Do you know what the time is, Sharon?
   B Let me see, it's almost one.

Check your answers

a 1, 3, 5, 6. **b** 2, 5. **c** 4, 5.

Asking the time

On Recording 8 there are five different expressions for asking the time.

→Cover the text of Recording 8.
→Listen again and, this time, complete the questions below.

1 Dad, /_____'_/_____ time?
2 Excuse me,/ c_____/_____/_____/_____/___/time, please?
3 John, / _____ /____ /_____/_____ time?
4 Could/_____/_____/_____/what/_____/_____/_____, please?
5 Excuse me, /_____/_____/_____/_____/_____/ time/ _____/___, please?
6 ____/ you/____/_____/the time/_____, Sharon?

Check your answers

1 Dad, what's the time? **2** Excuse me, could you tell me the time, please?
3 John, have you got the time? **4** Could you tell me what the time is, please?
5 Excuse me, can you tell me what time it is, please? **6** Do you know what the
time is?

There are lots of ways of asking this simple question in English. Look at the summary below.

Summary – Asking the time			
What's Have you got Do you know		the time (please)?	
Could you Can you	tell me	the time (please)?	
	tell me what	the time	is (please)?
		time	it is (please)?
Do you know	what	the time	is (please)?
		time	it is (please)?

★ All the questions are correct and appropriate and common in most situations.

★ The questions in the first group are the most direct.

★ 'Could you tell me ⎫
 'Do you know   ⎬ *what time it is?*' can be formal.

Timetables and Itineraries

Situation Fred Wilson is now in London. He wants to go to Cambridge for the day. He wants to leave London between 9:00 and 10:00 a.m. He phones National Rail Enquiries for some information.

→ Cover the text of Recording 9 on page 245.
→ Look at the timetable below.
→ Listen and complete the timetable.

London King's Cross d	08:24	08:45				10:00	10:25
Cambridge **a**	09:28	09:42				11:09	11:16

d – Departure time   **a** – Arrival time

Recording 9

Information officer	National Rail Enquiries – Can I help you?
You	Yes, I'd like some information about the times of trains from London to Cambridge please.
Information officer	Which day are you thinking of traveling?
You	It's for tomorrow.
Information officer	And what time of day would you like to travel?
You	We'd like to leave London between nine and ten in the morning.
*Information officer	Right. There's one that **leaves** at exactly nine o'clock.
You	What time **does** that get to Cambridge?
Information officer	The nine o'clock **gets** in at twelve minutes past ten. Then there's the nine twenty-four, which **arrives** at ten sixteen, and also a nine fifty-four, which **gets** to Cambridge at ten forty-six.
You	Let me just repeat that to make sure I've got it right. There are three trains. The nine o'clock **arrives** at twelve minutes past ten, the nine twenty-four gets there at sixteen minutes past ten and the nine fifty-four **arrives** in Cambridge at ten forty-six.*
Information officer	That's correct.
You	Thank you very much.
Both	Goodbye.

Check your answers

London King's Cross d	08:24	08:45	**09:00**	**09:24**	**09:54**	10:00	10:25
Cambridge a	09:28	09:42	**10:12**	**10:16**	**10:46**	11:09	11:16

→ Verb *get*

In the exercise above *get* means **a** take **b** arrive

Check your answer

b

→ Answer these questions about meaning and form of the **verbs** in **bold** (* to *) in the text of Recording 9 on page 245.

Meaning

In the exercise above the journey to Cambridge is **a** in the past

                                                        b in the present

                                                        c in the future.

Form

The tense of the verbs is **a** Present Simple

                                b Present Progressive

                                c Future Simple

☑ **Check your answers**

Meaning c. Form a

Q *Tomorrow is in the future? Why are these verbs in the present simple?*

A Because we are talking about a **timetable**.

★   When we talk about organized future activities and they are part of a timetable or like a timetable, we use the **present simple**.

→ Let's look at another example.

Situation Monica is going on a business trip to Scotland next week. Her secretary, Angie, is telling her the itinerary.

Angie   **You leave** on the 10:30 flight on Monday and **you arrive** in Edinburgh at 11:10. **You have** a lunch meeting with Mr. Jones at 12:30 and then at 3:30 **you take** the train to Glasgow.

All these verbs are in the **present simple** because they are Monica's itinerary or schedule.

→ Now look at the next part of the conversation.

Monica Where **am I staying** in Glasgow?
Angie   I've got you a room at the King's Hotel. **You're staying** there for two nights.

Why are these verbs in the present progressive?

These are personal future arrangements (see Topic 5).

Summary
To talk about fixed future events we use: **a** Present progressive if it's a personal arrangement.   **b** Present simple if it's a timetable or like a timetable.

★ Sometimes both the present simple and present progressive are correct. The focus is a little different.

For example: '**I go** home next week' – more factual, more focus on the itinerary.
'**I'm going** next week' – more personal.

In this situation, can I also say, for example, 'I will go home next week'? (future simple)

No, not in this situation. ☹

★ 'I will go home' is grammatically correct.
★ It has a different meaning.

→ Answer these questions about 'I'm going home next week' and 'I go home next week.'

1 In both sentences, the decision is   **a** in the past?
                                              b in the present?
                                              c in the future ?

2 Actions to organise the trip home are   **a** in the past?
                                              b in the present?
                                              c in the future?

Check your answers

1 a in the past. **2 a** in the past. For example, you've got your ticket.

'I'll go home next week' is only correct at the moment of making the decision. For example,

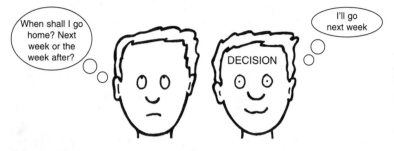

Itineraries – present simple

Situation   Fred is at a travel agent's, picking up his tickets for a short trip to Italy. The assistant talks about his itinerary.

→ Write the verbs in the correct tense.

Travel agent   Here are the tickets for your trip to Italy. You (fly)_____(1) to Naples with Alitalia on the 12th of next month. The flight (leave) _____ (2) Heathrow at l0:15. When you get to Naples a coach (pick you up) _____(3) from the airport and they (drive)_____ (4) you direct to your hotel. The next morning the coach (take)_____(5) you on an excursion to the ruins of Pompeii. In the afternoon you (get) _____ (6) the Eurostar train to Rome.

Fred   What (happen) _____ (7) when we arrive in Rome? How (get) _____(8) to the hotel?

Travel agent   A bilingual guide (meet) _____ (9) the train and (take) _____(10) you on a city tour. They (show)_____(11) you all the important sights such as the Coliseum and the Vatican and then the coach (leave)_____(12) you at your hotel. On the Sunday you (be)_____(13) free in Rome and you (come) _____(14) back to London on the evening flight.

Fred   What time (get)_____ (15) back?

Travel Agent   I think it's twenty-past nine. Just let me check – yes, nine twenty-five.

Fred   That all sounds wonderful. I'm looking forward to it.

Check your answers

1 fly **2** leaves **3** picks you up **4** drive **5** takes **6** get **7** happens **8** do we get?
9 meets **10** takes **11** show **12** leaves **13** are **14** come **15** do we get?

All these verbs are in the present simple because it is an itinerary.

In the mini-dialogue below, are the verbs in 'B' in the present simple?

A Can you tell me how I get to Waterloo, please?
B <u>Go</u> to Oxford Street and <u>take</u> the Bakerloo Line.

No. These verbs are in the **imperative** (verb without *to*).

★ People who work in transport often use the imperative to give instructions.
★ Here the imperative is impersonal and short.
(For more information and practice on the imperative, see Topic 9.)

Summary of travel questions

There are a lot of different questions in this topic. How many can you use now?

→ Read the questions below.
→ Write the correct questions for the answers on page 250.

Example: You *How can I get to Windsor?* (j)
'Take the train at Platform 5 and change at Egham.'

a Could you tell me how to get to London from here, please?
b How often do the trains run to Waterloo?
c When's the next coach to Glasgow, please?
d How long does it take to get to Cambridge from London?
e Is this the right train for Birmingham?
f Which platform is it for Brighton, please?
g I want to go to Cardiff. Where do I change?
h Do you know if this train stops in Reading?
i How much is a single* to Hull, please?
j How can I get to Windsor?

*single = one-way ticket

1 **You** *Excuse me, how can I get to Windsor?*
   Take the train at Platform 5 and change at Egham.
2 **You** _____?
   No, this is a non-stop to Paddington.
3 **You** _____?
   Number 7, sir.
4 **You** _____?
   £22.
5 **You** _____?
   Every half an hour – at ten to and twenty past the hour.
6 **You** _____?
   No, this is the Liverpool train.
7 **You** _____?
   It's not necessary, this bus goes all the way there.
8 **You** _____?
   In ten minutes at half past.
9 **You** _____?
   Yes, take the next train from Platform 10.
10 **You** _____?
   On a fast train? – just under an hour.

☑ **Check your answers**

1 j 2 h 3 f 4 i 5 b 6 e 7 g 8 c 9 a 10 d

Asking for information – transport

→ Listen to Recording 10 and ask the questions from the exercise above in the spaces.

🎧 *Recording 10*

1	**You**	Excuse me, how can I get to Windsor?
		Take the train at Platform 5 and change at Egham.
2	**You**	Do you know if this train stops at Reading?
		No, this is a non-stop to Paddington.
3	**You**	Which platform is it for Brighton, please?
		Number 7, sir.

4 **You** How much is a one-way ticket to Hull, please?
        £22.

5 **You** How often do the trains run to Waterloo?
        Every half an hour – at ten to and twenty past the hour.

6 **You** Is this the right train for Birmingham?
        No, this is the Liverpool train.

7 **You** I want to go to Cardiff. Where do I change?
        It's not necessary, this bus goes all the way there.

8 **You** When's the next coach to Glasgow, please?
        In ten minutes, at half past.

9 **You** Could you tell me how to get to London from here, please?
        Yes, take the next train from Platform 10.

10 **You** How long does it take to get to Cambridge from London?
        On a fast train? – just under an hour.

About your country: public transportation

→ Write answers to these questions or prepare to tell a friend.

1 How do you go to work and/or the shops?

_____

2 How do people travel long distances without a car?

_____

3 What are the names of the big train and bus companies in your country?

_____

4 Is public transportation cheap or expensive?

_____

5 Is there a subway in your town or capital?

_____

6 On the buses does the fare depend on distance?

_____

7 **a** When do you pay if you want to travel by bus?
      b Can you buy a round-trip ticket?
      c If you need to take two buses, can you use one ticket?

_____

_____

What would you say?

1 You are a tourist in London. You are at a station. Someone asks you, 'Excuse me can you tell me how to get to Wimbledon, please?'

_____

2 It's late at night. You want to get a train ticket from the machine – the ticket office is closed. You've only got a £20 bill. The machine takes only coins and £5 and £10 bills.

_____

Possible answers

1 I'm sorry but I'm not from here. **2** Excuse me, have got change for a £20 bill, please? I need to buy a ticket from the machine.

Review

How do you say it in your language?

→ Here are some examples of the important points in this topic.
→ Translate the sentences below into your language in the spaces.
→ Remember – translate the idea, not the words.

1 a Excuse me, can you tell me how to get to the center of town, please?

_____

   b Yes, you can go by bus, by train or by taxi.

_____

2   Which part of the town are you going to?

_____

3 a Where do I pay? **b** Over there, please, at the cash desk.

_____

4   Where do I go to get a ticket?

_____

5   Who are you talking to?

_____

6   Which excursions would you like to go on?

_____

7   You get a ticket before you get on the bus.

_____

8 **a** Excuse me, have you got the time, please?

_____

   b Yes, it's just after ten.

_____

9 **a** How often do the buses go to the station?

_____

10 How long does it take to get downtown?

_____

11 Take the train on track 6 and change at the next stop.

_____

Join the conversation

→ Look at Recording 1 (page 213) again.
→ Listen to Recording 11.
→ Read **Oliver's** words in the spaces.

TEST 8

Which one is right?

→ Choose **a** or **b**.

1 I go to work   **a** with   **car**.
                     b by

2 The bus   **a** leaves   every hour.
            b is leaving

3 **a** Do you know what is the time?
   b Do you know what the time is?

4 **a** How long does it take to get to the park?
   b How long takes it for go to the park?

5 **A** **a** How often go the trains to London?
      b How often do the trains go to London?
   B **a** Three times in an hour.
      b Three times an hour.

6 **a** How much is it for go and come back?
   b How much is a return ticket?

7 **a** What do I do now?
  b What I do now?

8 **a** Take that train and change at Broad Street.
  b You will take that train and then you are changing at Broad Street.

9 **a** West Road, 24.
  b 24, West Road.

10 My friend has a new baby.
   a What am I writing in this card?
   b What do I write in this card?

Write a dialogue

Situation   You are at the ticket office at Waterloo Station.
You want two tickets to Hampton Court, a famous palace near London.

1 **Travel clerk**

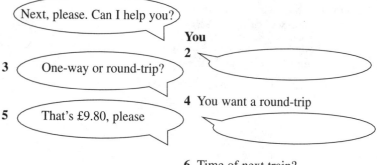

Next, please. Can I help you?

You

2

3 One-way or round-trip?

4 You want a round-trip

5 That's £9.80, please

6 Time of next train?

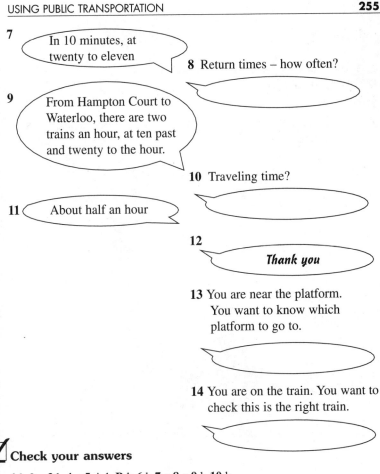

7 In 10 minutes, at twenty to eleven

8 Return times – how often?

9 From Hampton Court to Waterloo, there are two trains an hour, at ten past and twenty to the hour.

10 Traveling time?

11 About half an hour

12 *Thank you*

13 You are near the platform. You want to know which platform to go to.

14 You are on the train. You want to check this is the right train.

Check your answers

1 b 2 a 3 b 4 a 5 A b B b 6 b 7 a 8 a 9 b 10 b

Dialogue: model answers

2	**You**	Two tickets to Hampton Court, please.
3	**Clerk**	One-way or round-trip?
4	**You**	Round-trip, please.
5	**Clerk**	That's nine pounds eighty please.
6	**You**	When's the next train? OR
		At what time does the next train leave?
7	**Clerk**	In 10 minutes, at twenty to eleven.
8	**You**	And to come back, how often do the trains run?

9   **Clerk** There are two trains an hour, at ten past and twenty to the hour.
10 **You**   How long does the trip take?
11 **Clerk** About half an hour.
12 **You**   Thank you.

13 **You**   Excuse me. Which platform is it for Hampton Court, please?
14 **You**   Excuse me. Is this the right train for Hampton Court, please?
OR
            Excuse me. Does this train go to Hampton Court, please?

9 | **MEETING FRIENDS**

Grammar and communication	**Vocabulary**
◆ Impersonal *it*	◆ Public signs
◆ Asking for opinions – *how was?*	◆ Large numbers
◆ Adjectives + *-ed* or *-ing*	**Pronunciation**
◆ Saying *thank you*	◆ Intonation
◆ Obligation and necessity – *have to*	– expressing strong
◆ The imperative	feelings
◆ Offering, rejecting, insisting, accepting	
◆ Introducing something negative politely	

Tasha leaves customs. Who's there to meet her?
What happens next?

FLIGHT AA427 FROM MONTEVIDEO
VIA BUENOS AIRES, LANDED 7:15

Understanding the important information

→ Cover the text of Recording 1, *The Story*.
→ Read the sentences below. Only one is correct.
→ Listen to the recording and choose the correct answer.

a Tasha gets the bus with Oliver.
b Tasha's friend, Helen, is at the airport to meet her.
c Helen is at the airport with her husband and children.
d Tasha goes to Helen's house by taxi.

🎧 *Recording 1 – The Story*

Helen	Tasha, Hi, how are you? It's lovely to see you again!
Tasha	Hello, Helen! It's great to see you too. How are things?
Helen	I'm fine. We're all fine. How was your flight?
Tasha	It was all right – 13 hours is a bit long and tiring, but I'm here now. Thanks for picking me up, by the way.
Helen	That's O.K. We're glad you could come. The car's in the parking lot, this way. David and the children are at home, waiting for you.

✔️ Now check your answer

b

Understanding more

→ Cover the text of Recording 1 again.
→ Read the sentences below.
→ Listen and answer *True/False/We don't know*.

1 Tasha's flight was terrible.	True/False/We don't know
2 David is at home with the children.	True/False/We don't know
3 Tasha knows David and the children.	True/False/We don't know
4 Helen meets Oliver.	True/False/We don't know
5 Tasha tells Helen about Oliver.	True/False/We don't know
6 Helen can't drive.	True/False/We don't know

Check your answers

1 False **2** True **3** We don't know **4** False **5** False **6** False

What do they say?

→ Cover the text of Recording 1 again.
→ Read the sentences below.
→ Listen and try to complete the words.
→ Then read the text of the recording if necessary.

1 Helen says, 'Hello' but Tasha says 'H _ !'

2 a Helen is happy to see Tasha.
  She says, ' I _ ' _ / l _ _ _ _ y / t _ / s _ _ you again.'

  b Tasha is happy to see Helen.
  She says, ' _ t' s / g _ _ _ t / _ _ / _ _ _ / you / t _ _.'

3 Helen asks, 'How are you?' but Tasha asks 'H _ _ / a _ _ / t _ _ _ _ s?'

4 a Helen asks Tasha about her journey.
  She says, 'H _ _ / w _ _ / y _ _ r / flight?'
  b Tasha responds, ' I _ / w _ _ / a _ _ / _ _ _ _ _ .'
  c Tasha talks about the flight.
  She says ' 13 hours is a b_ _ / l _ _ _ / and /t_ _ _ _ _ but I'm here now.'

5 a Tasha is happy Helen is at the airport to meet her. During the conversation Tasha decides to thank her friend.
  She says: 'Thanks / f _ _ / p _ _ _ _ _ g / m _ / u _ , b_ / t _ _ / w _ _.'
  b When Tasha says, 'Thanks', Helen responds,
  ' T _ _ _ '_ O.K. W_'_ _ / g _ _ _ / you / c _ _ _ d / c _ _ e.'

Check your answers

1 Hi. (informal) **2 a** It's lovely to see you again. **b** It's great to see you too. **3** How are things ('things' is informal) **4 a** How was your flight? **b** It was all right. **c** 13 hours is a bit long and tiring but I'm here now. **5 a** Thanks for picking me up **b** That's O.K. We're glad you could come.

! Common mistake – impersonal *it*

Example from *The Story*:
Helen is happy to see Tasha again.
She says, '**It's** lovely to see you again.'
Tasha says, '**It's** great to see you too.'

(Not: ~~Is lovely~~ to see you again.
OR ~~Is great~~ to see you too.)

Q *Why do we say 'it' here?*

A All verbs need a subject in English (except imperatives).

'*It*' is the impersonal subject.

Q *What's the negative? Can I say, 'It's nice <u>to not work</u> on the weekend?'* ☹

A No – *not* is before *to*. '*It's nice **not to** work on the weekend.*'

Grammar summary – impersonal *it*			
Impersonal subject	**Verb *be***	**Adjective**	**Verb + *to/not to***
It	is	lovely	to see you again
	's	frustrating	not to understand

→ Complete the sentences on page 261 with
   – one adjective from **Box 1** and
   – one verb from **Box 2**.
→ Use your dictionary if necessary.

Box 1

difficult   wonderful
expensive   frustrating
useful   hard   correct   ~~cheap~~
interesting   tiring   boring
kind   important

Box 2

go   know   say   work   eat
understand   arrive   ~~travel~~
get   invite   see   visit

Example:

It doesn't cost much – in fact it's quite ***cheap*** to ***travel*** by coach.

1   It's too_____ to _____ by plane. Let's go by train.

2 **A** Is it _____to _____ 'Where are you live?' or 'Where do you live?'

    B 'Where do you live.'

3   At first it's _____ to _____a foreign language because people speak fast.

4   For some people it's very _____ to _____ museums – they really enjoy it.
For others it's the opposite. They find it really _____

5   I've got an invitation to stay with my friend abroad. It's very _____ of him to _____ me.

6   When you travel abroad, it's always _____ to _____ a few words of the language.

7   It's _____not to _____ late for an exam.

8   It's _____ to _____ long hours.

9   It's _____ to see old friends after a long time.

10   Every time I try to telephone him there's no reply It's really _____ not to _____ an answer.

11   If you are on a diet, it's _____ not to _____sweet things!

Check your answers

1 expensive to go.   2 correct to ask.   3 difficult/hard to understand.
4 interesting to visit/boring. 5 kind of him to invite. 6 useful to know.
7 important not to arrive. 8 tiring to work. 9 wonderful to see. 10 frustrating not to get. 11 difficult/hard not to eat.

It's + adjective + verb with *to/not to*

→ Write these words in the correct order.

1 _____

to/again/nice/talk/it's/you/to

2 _____

better/not/it's/go/to

3 _____

with/contact/easy/to/it's/people/e-mail

4 _____

for/wait/it's/someone/time/for/long/boring/to/a

5 _____

country/to/exciting/it's/visit/a/foreign

6 _____

normal/language/understand/not/it's/in/foreign/to/everything/a

☑ **Check your answers**

1 It's nice to talk to you again. **2** It's better not to go. **3** It's easy to contact people with e-mail. **4** It's boring to wait for someone for a long time **5** It's exciting to visit a foreign country. **6** It's normal not to understand everything in a foreign language.

Grammar and communication 1

Asking for opinions – *how was...?*

Example from *The Story*:
Helen asks Tasha about her journey.
She says: '**How was** your flight?'
Tasha answers: 'It was all right'.

→ Answer these questions about *How was...?*

Meaning

1 Is the flight   **a** in the present?
                b in the future?
                c in the past?

2 In 'How was your flight?' Helen is asking,
   a for a long description of the flight or
   b if the flight was O.K. or not for Tasha.

Form

Was is the past of **a** verb *be*
      b verb *do*?

Check your answers

Meaning: 1 c 2 b
Form: a

Grammar summary – Past of *be*		
Affirmative		
I He/she/it } was	You We They } were	
Negative		
I He/she/it } wasn't	You We They } weren't	
Affirmative		

Was {   I
   he/she/it?
	Were { you?
	   we?
	   they	

→ Complete these mini-dialogues with *was* or *were* + *not* where necessary.

1 **A** How _____ your vacation?
 B The hotel _____ bad but the food _____ terrible.

2 **A** _____ your parents all right last night?
 B My mother _____ fine but my father _____ very well at all, actually.

3 A _____ that film boring!
  B Yes, it _____ very good at all, _____ it?

4 A [On Monday morning] How _____ your weekend?
  B Really relaxing and quiet thanks. And yours?
  A It _____ nice, very nice.

5 A Why _____ you at school yesterday, David?
  B I _____ ill, Ma'am.

6 A How many people _____ at the party?
  B About 20, I suppose.

7   Nobody _____ at home – the answering machine _____ on.

☑ **Check your answers**

1 A was B wasn't, was 2 A were B was, wasn't 3 A wasn't B wasn't, was it?
4 A was A was 5 A weren't B was 6 A were 7 was, was

How do you pronounce it?

Was

The vowel 'a' in *was* has two pronunciations.

– reduced / ə / when *was* is with an adjective or noun
– full /ʌ / when *was* is the important word.

For example: '*Was* your flight O.K.?' – reduced / ə /.
'Yes, it *was*, thanks.' – full / ʌ /.

The pronunciation of the 'a' in strong *was* / ʌ / and *wasn't* is the same.

→ Look at the text of Recording 2, with the stress.
→ What is the pronounciation of *was* in each one?
→ Choose 'full' or 'reduced'.

Recording 2

1	How was your **day**?	full/reduced
2	Your **party** – how **was** it?	full/reduced
3	It was fan**tas**tic, thanks.	full/reduced
4	Was your hotel **com**fortable?	full/reduced
5	Yes it **was**, thanks.	full/reduced

Check your answers

1 reduced 2 full 3 reduced 4 reduced 5 full

→ Now listen to Recording 2 and repeat the sentences.

Intonation – big falls to express strong feelings

In Topic 4 we practice intonation to sound positive. In this topic we practice intonation to express strong feelings.

Examples from *The Story*:
Helen is happy to see Tasha.
She says, 'It's lovely to see you again.'

Tasha responds, 'It's great to see you, too.'

Remember, with flat intonation you express that actually you are not very happy to see the person.

To express strong feelings, the voice moves a lot on the syllable with stress.

→ Read the sentences below.
→ On Recording 3 you will hear each sentence twice.
→ Which expresses stronger feelings, **a** or **b**?

Recording 3

1	It's **won**derful to see you again.	**a** or **b**
2	It's **great** to hear from you.	**a** or **b**
3	I think it's a good i**de**a.	**a** or **b**
4	It's so **kind** of you to invite me.	**a** or **b**
5	I don't know **what** to do.	**a** or **b**
6	But I **can't**!	**a** or **b**
7	I'm so **sorry**!	**a** or **b**
8	Happy **Birth**day!	**a** or **b**

✓ **Check your answers**

1 a 2 a 3 b 4 a 5 b 6 b 7 a 8 b

→ Listen to Recording 3 again and repeat the sentences. Pay special attention to the big falls in the sentences with strong feelings.

Grammar and communication 2

Feelings – adjectives + -ed or -ing

Example from *The Story*:

Tasha talks about the flight. She says, 'It was a bit long and **tiring**...'

In other words, Tasha is **tired** because the flight was **tiring**.

! **Common mistake**

Tasha: 'The flight was a bit long and tiring....'

NOT: ~~'The flight was a bit long and tired'~~.....

BUT: 'Tasha was tired after her flight' is correct

Meanings and forms – adjectives + -ed and -ing

How is Tasha? She feels **tired**.

Why does Tasha feel tired?
What's the source of her tiredness?

The flight. The flight was **tiring**.

Summary		
Adjectives with -ed/-ing		
The feeling	Tasha is tired	adjective + -*ed*
Reason or source of the feeling	The flight was tiring	adjective + -*ing*

Here's another example:

INTERESTING

INTERESTED

| How does John feel? | Interested | Internal Feeling + *-ed* |
| Why? | His book is interesting | Source of feeling + *-ing* |

→ Complete the dialogue below.
→ Choose the correct form of the adjective in the brackets ( ).
→ Use your dictionary if necessary.

A I feel a bit _____1 (tired/tiring) actually – it was a very long journey. And the plane was completely full!

B Oh! That's _____2 (surprised/surprising) at this time of year. When I travel, I go to sleep if I'm _____3 (bored/boring) on a plane. But sometimes it's _____4 (interested/interesting) to talk to the person next to you.

A Oh, the man next to me on this flight was really _____5 (bored/boring). The conversation was all about his business trips – I wasn't very _____6 (interested/interesting) at all, really.

A Yes, but it is _____7 (fascinating/fascinated) to travel and visit different countries, isn't it?

B Absolutely! I just find it _____8 (frustrated/frustrating) if I can't speak the language at all.

A Yes, I was a bit _____9 (disappointed/disappointing) with our last vacation because of that.

Check your answers

1 tired **2** surprising **3** bored **4** interesting **5** boring **6** interested **7** fascinating **8** frustrating **9** disappointed

→ Correct the *-ed/-ing* adjectives in these sentences, if necessary.

1 The journey was very tired.
2 I'm very exciting about my trip.
3 I was really surprising about the new job.
4 The film was bored.
5 It's a fascinating story.

✓ **Check your answers**

1 tiring – source 2 excited – feeling 3 surprised – feeling 4 boring – source
5 *Correct*

Grammar and communication 3

Saying *Thank you*

Example from *The Story*:

Tasha is happy that Helen is at the airport to meet her.
She says, 'Thanks **for** pick**ing** me up.'

Summary – saying *Thank you*		
	Preposition '*for*'	**Verb + *-ing* – gerund**
Neutral Thank you Thank you very much **Formal** Thank you very much indeed **Informal** Thanks Many thanks	for	picking me up

Can I also say

a *'Thank you to meet me?'* ✗

b *'Thank you for meet me?'* ✗ OR

c *'Thank you for to meet me?'* ✗

No, 'Thank you for meeting me' } is the only correct expression.
Thank you + for + verb -ing.

→ Complete these sentences.

1 Thanks _____/_____ (help) me.
2 Thanks ____/_____(come) to pick us up.
3 Thank you very much _____/_____ (wait) for me.
4 Thank you _____/_____ (meet) us.
5 Thanks _____/_____ (calling). (on the telephone)

Check your answers

1 Thanks for helping me. 2 Thanks for coming to pick us up. 3 Thank you very much for waiting for me. 4 Thank you for meeting us. 5 Thanks for calling.

Saying *Thank you*

→ Use the verbs in the box to say *thank you* in the situations below.

| let me know   go   tell   come   help   call   invite   wait   ask |

Example:

A friend tells you something very important.
You *Thank you for telling me.*

1 A friend in another country invites you for a holiday.
   You _____

2 You arrange to meet a friend at 2 o'clock. You arrive at 2:20.
   You _____

3 Your colleague shows you how to use the new computer in the office.
   You _____

4 You've got an appointment for tomorrow – but something happens and you can't go. You telephone and tell them. The other person says,

_____

5 Your colleague's friend was ill yesterday. Today you ask about her. Your friend says, 'She's much better today.' _____

6 Your friend goes to the doctor's. You go with her. Later, at home she says,

_____

7 You call a business friend. At the end of the conversation he/she says,

_____

8 You invite some friends to your house. When they leave you can say,

_____

☑ **Check your answers**

1 Thanks for inviting me. **2** Thanks for waiting for me. **3** Thank you for helping me. **4** Thanks for letting me know. **5** Thank you for asking. **6** Thanks for going with me. **7** Thanks for calling. **8** Thanks for coming.

Responding to *Thank you*

→Read the formal, neutral and informal expressions in the box.
→Choose an appropriate expression for the situations **1–6** below.

Formal – *You're welcome*	OR	*Not at all*
Neutral – *That's O.K.*	OR	*That's all right*
Informal – *No problem*	OR	*Any time*

1 Your friend says, 'Thank you for helping me with my English.'
You respond, _____

2 On the bus, you give your seat to an old lady.
She says 'Thank you so much. You're very kind!'
You respond, _____

3 A young person talks to you in the street. She says 'Excuse me, where's the station, please?' You say, 'Just there.' She says, 'Thank you.'
You respond, _____

4 The bus is at the bus stop. A woman is getting on the bus with three young children. You help her. She says, 'Thank you ever so much.'
You respond, _____

5 In a class you lend your dictionary to a friend. He says, 'Thanks.'
You respond, _____

6 You're in a shopping center. You open the door for someone. The person says, 'Thank you.'
You respond, _____

Check your answers

1 Informal: Either *No problem* or *Any time* **2** Formal: Either, *You're welcome* or *Not at all* **3** Neutral: *That's O.K.* or *That's all right* **4** Neutral: *That's O.K.* or *That's all right* **5** Informal: *No problem* or *Any time* **6** Formal: *You're welcome* or *Not at all*

$\boxed{i}$ **Culture – meeting people at the end of a journey**

- **Clothes**
  In your country, do you wear formal clothes to meet a friend or family member at the end of a journey? In the U.S., it is usual to wear everyday clothes.

- **Saying *Hello***
  When we meet a family member or friend, it is common to **kiss them on the cheek (1)** and sometimes **hug them (2)**.
  Men often **shake hands (3)** or just say *Hello*. Good friends or family members sometimes shake hands and **hold the other person's arm (4)**, or **pat each other on the back (5)**. When we meet a business friend, it is common to shake hands.

Adults often hug and/or kiss children.
- In the U.S., some friends and families touch each other. Others don't. Touching isn't always the norm.

About your country: meeting people you know

→Read the questions below.
→Either write your answers or prepare to tell a friend.

What do you do when you meet someone after a journey?

a a family member? _____
b a friend? _____
c business friend? _____
d child? _____

What's the right word?

Saying large numbers – *and*

i	**Culture – Airports**

- The U.S. is a very big country, and some of the world's largest airports serve major U.S. cities. Chicago's O'Hare International Airport serves 180,000 passengers per day. It has 162 gates in four terminals. In 1997, 70,000,000 passengers used this airport.

→ How do we say the numbers below? Choose the correct expression from the box.

10   100   1,000   10,000
100,000   1,000,000   1,000,000,000

> a million   a hundred   ten thousand   ten   a billion
> a hundred thousand   a thousand

Check your answers

10 – ten
100 – a hundred
1,000 – a thousand
10,000 – ten thousand
100,000 – a hundred thousand
1,000,000 – a million
1,000,000,000 – a billion

→ Now look at these numbers – where's the **and**?

120
A hundred
and twenty

1,358
One thousand
three hundred
and fifty-eight

10,579
Ten thousand
five hundred
and seventy-nine

150,550
One hundred
and fifty thousand,
five hundred
and fifty

1,350,425
One million, three
hundred
and fifty thousand,
four hundred
and twenty-five

→ Read the sentence about *and* and choose True or False.

With big numbers we say *and* before the 'tens'.
('Tens' are twenty, thirty, forty, etc.) True/False

Check your answer

True

Saying large numbers

→ Write these numbers in words – don't forget the *and*.

1 594,000 _____

2 611,420 _____

3 4,601 _____

4 827 _____

5 32,158 _____

6 24, 250,000 _____

7 6,368 _____

8 923,750 _____

 Check your answers

1 Five hundred **and** ninety-four thousand. **2** Six hundred **and** eleven thousand, four hundred **and** twenty. **3** Four thousand, six hundred **and** one. **4** Eight hundred **and** twenty-seven. **5** Thirty-two thousand, one hundred **and** fifty-eight. **6** Twenty-four million, two hundred **and** fifty thousand. **7** Six thousand, three hundred **and** sixty-eight. **8** Nine hundred **and** twenty-three thousand, seven hundred **and** fifty.

→ Read aloud the numbers in the text about O'Hare Airport on page 272.

Check your answers

one hundred and eighty thousand passengers, one hundred and sixty-two gates, seventy million

About your country: large numbers

→ Read the questions below.

→ Either write your answers or prepare to tell a friend.

1 What is the population of your country/the capital/your town/village, etc.?

_____

2 If you work, how much do you earn a year?

_____

3 How much does a room/apartment/house cost in your area? – to rent a month/to buy?

_____

4 How much does a new car cost in your country?

_____

Our story continues ... Helen and Tasha go to the airport parking lot to get Helen's car

Understanding the important information

→ Read the sentences below.

→ Listen to the Recording 4, *The Story* and choose *True/False/ We don't know*.

1 Tasha pays for the parking lot.　　　　　　True/False/We don't know
2 They can't find the car.　　　　　　　　　True/False/We don't know
3 They ask a man for help with the suitcase.　True/False/We don't know

🎧 *Recording 4 – The Story*

Helen	The car's on level 2. We can take the luggage cart with us in the elevator. We have to pay on the way out, so I had better get the ticket and my money ready. Here's the ticket in my pocket. One hour, $8.50. Let me see if I've got the correct change.
Tasha	I'm afraid I haven't got any change. I've only got bills.
Helen	No, don't worry. I'll pay for this. I'm sure the attendant can make change. So, let's find the car. …There it is … it's the green Ford. Now let's get your luggage in the trunk. Can I help you with your suitcase?
Tasha	No, really. It's all right thanks. I can manage. Could you just hold this bag for a minute while I get the suitcase in? Then we can put the bag on top.
Helen	Come on! Let me help. Don't lift that suitcase on your own.
Tasha	O.K. – Thanks – it is quite heavy… Ready? One, two, three…
Helen	We can put our coats in the back seat.
Tasha	I think I'll keep mine on. I'm really cold.
Helen	I expect that's because you're tired after your long flight. Let's get home and you can have a rest. •

☑ Check your answers

a False **b** False **c** False

Understanding more

→ Cover the text of Recording 4.
→ Read the sentences on page 277. Some are True , some are False.
→ Listen and put a check mark ✓ by the True sentences.

1   The car is on level 4.
2   First they pay, then they get the car.
3   Parking costs $3.60.
4   They take the elevator.
5   They leave the luggage cart on the ground floor.
6   Helen's got a red Honda.
7   Tasha's suitcase is heavy.
8   They put the luggage on the back seat.
9   Helen helps Tasha with her luggage.
10 They put their coats in the trunk.
11 They're going straight to Helen's house.

trunk

front seats

back seats

Check your answers

1 False **2** False **3** False **4** True **5** False **6** False **7** True **8** False **9** True **10** False **11** True

→ Now listen again and correct the wrong information in **1, 3, 5, 6, 8, 10**.

Check your answers

1 The car is on level 2. **3** The car park costs $8.50. **5** They take the luggage cart in the elevator. **6** Helen's got a green Ford. **8** They put the suitcase in the trunk. **10** Helen puts her coat in the back but Tasha keeps her coat on.

What do they say?

→ Read the sentences below
→ Listen to Recording 4 again and try to complete the words.
→ Then read the text of the recording to help you if necessary.

1   Parking isn't free. Helen says,
    'I / h _ _ / b _ _ _ _ _ / g _ _ / the ticket and my money ready.'

2   Helen needs time to see if she's got $8.50 in change. She says,
    'L _ _ / m _ / s _ _ / i _ / I've got the / c _ _ _ _ _ _ / c _ _ _ _ _ .'

3 a Tasha is sorry she hasn't got change. She says,
'I' _ / a _ _ _ _ _ / I haven't got any change.'
b Helen tells her it isn't a problem.
She says, 'D _ _ ' t / w _ _ _ _ .'

4 Helen tells Tasha she's paying. She says,
'I' _ _ / p _ _ / f _ _ / t _ _ _.'

5 a Helen offers to help with Tasha's suitcase twice. The first time, she says,
'C _ _ / I / h _ _ _ / y _ _ with your suitcase?'
b Tasha says no. She says,
'No, / r _ _ _ _ _ , / it's / a _ _ / r _ _ _ _ / thanks./ I / c _ _ / m _ _ _ _ e .'
c Helen insists. She offers Tasha help again. She says,
'C _ _ _ / _ n! / L _ _ / m _ / help. D _ _ ' _ / l _ _ t / that suitcase...'
d Tasha accepts. She says,
'O. _. / T _ _ _ _ _ /. It / _ _ / q _ _ _ _ / h _ _ _ y.'

☑ **Check your answers**

1 I had better get the ticket and my money ready. **2** Let me see if I've got the correct change. **3 a** I'm afraid I haven't got any change. **b** Don't worry. **4** I'll pay for this. **5 a** Can I help you with your suitcase? **b** No, really, it's all right, thanks. I can manage. **c** Come on! Let me help. Don't lift that suitcase... **d** O.K. Thanks. It <u>is</u> quite heavy.

Find the words and phrases

→Read the sentences below.
→Read the text of Recording 4 and complete the words and phrases.

1 Helen finds the parking ticket.
She says, 'H _ _ _'s / t _ _ / t _ _ _ _ _ / i _/, in my p _ _ _ _ _.'

2 It's not necessary to pay the exact change because the attendant gives / c _ _ _ _ _ /. You can pay with /b _ _ _ _ .

3 Tasha needs help with the bag. She says,
'C _ _ _ _ / you / j _ _ _/ h _ _ _ / this bag for a minute?'

4 Helen holds the bag /w _ _ _ _ / Tasha puts the suitcase in.

5 They put the suitcase in the trunk first.
Then they put the bag / o _ / t _ _ / t _ _ .

6 Helen wants to help Tasha with the suitcase. She says,
'Don't lift it / o _ / y _ _ _ / o _ _ .'

7 Is the suitcase very heavy? No, but it's q _ _ _ _ heavy.

8 Tasha decides not to take her coat off. She's cold.
She says, 'I / think / I ' _ _ / k _ _ _ / m _ _ _ / o _ .'

9 Tasha's tired. When they get to the house she can go to her room and
relax – she can h _ _ _ / a / r _ _ t.

10 Verb *get*. In the sentences below *get* means **a** go/arrive
                                                      b put – with difficulty

i Let's **get** your luggage in the car.
ii Let's **get** home.

Check your answers

1 Here's the ticket, *in* my pocket. (preposition!) 2 change/bills 3 Could you just
hold this bag for a minute? 4 while. 5 *on* the top (preposition!). 6 on your own.
7 quite. 8 I think I'll keep mine *on*. (preposition!) 9 have a rest. 10 Get **i b ii a.**

Using these words and phrases

→ Match the following **1–10** with **a–j**.

1 Why don't you take your jacket off?	**a**	Yes, it's quite interesting, actually.
2 Where's John?	**b**	I can give you two ten dollar bills
3 Don't go on your own.	**c**	with chocolate sauce on the top.
4 The trunk is full.	**d**	Oliver is going downtown by bus.
5 I'll pay for the drinks.	**e**	I'll go with you.
6 I love vanilla ice cream.	**f**	I'll put the bag on the back seat then.
7 Have you got change for $20?	**g**	No, thanks, it's all right. I can manage.
8 Is that a good T.V. program?	**h**	He's upstairs, having a rest.
9 While Tasha is going to Helen's,	**i**	I prefer to keep it on, thanks. I'm a bit cold.
10 Do you need help with that?	**j**	No, it's my turn. I'll get them.

☑ **Check your answers**

1 i **2** h **3** e **4** f **5** j **6** c **7** b **8** a **9** d **10** g

Q What's the difference between 'parking lot' and 'parking'?

A Parking lot is a noun. It's a public place to leave a car.

For example: 'When I go to the airport, I leave the car in the parking lot at the airport.'

Not: '~~I leave the car in the parking~~'.

Park is a verb, for example, 'You can't park here'.

The phrase *No parking* means 'You can't park here'. This is a **verbal noun** (a verb used as a noun).

Grammar and communication 4

Obligation and necessity – *Have to*

Example from *The Story*:

The parking lot isn't free. Helen says,
'We **have to** pay on the way out …'

Meaning

Is it necessary to pay?   Yes, it is a regulation of the parking lot.
And if Helen doesn't pay? She'll have a problem – she is obliged to pay.

Grammar Summary – *have to* – obligation and necessity					
Affirmative			**Negative**		**Questions**
I	have	to + verb	I don't	have to + verb	Do I
S/he	has		S/he doesn't		Does s/he

(last two columns) Do I / Does s/he : have to + verb

Look at these examples:
1 **I don't have to** go now. I can stay until 1:00.
    Meaning It's not necessary for me to go now.

2 Do I have to enroll before the next course or can I just come on the first day?

Meaning Is it an obligation to enroll before the next course or is it possible to just go to the class on the first day?

Tip: Learners of English often say, *Is it necessary for me to...?* ☹
  ★ This isn't wrong but *Do I have to....?* is more common.

What's the difference between 'Where <u>do I have to go</u> now?' and 'Where <u>do I go</u> now?'? (Topic 8)

The difference is small:

a asks more about obligation – rules and regulations
b asks more about systems – what is the custom/norm?

★ In some situations both are appropriate.

  Examples:

  1 You are filling in a form:
    'Where do I sign?' and
    'Where do I have to sign?' are both correct and appropriate.

  2 You are using a new photocopier:
    'Which way do I put the paper?' and
    'Which way do I have to put the paper?' are both correct and appropriate.

Obligation and necessity – *have to*

→ Complete these sentences with the correct form of *have to*.

1 My husband _____ travel a lot for his job. He's always away.

2 How many times a day _____ take this medicine, doctor?

3 We _____ go if you don't want to. I really don't mind.

4 **Mother** Come on Tommy – it's time for bed.
  Tommy Oh, Mom _____? I'm not tired.

5 You _____ say 'yes' or 'no' now. You can tell me later.

6 I _____ come back again tomorrow, do I? Can't we finish all the work today?

7   A What time _____ be at the airport for your flight?
      B Half past ten.

8 I'm sorry but I really _____ go now, or I'll miss my train.

9   A Could you please tell me why I _____ fill this form in?
      B I'm sorry, sir. It's a company regulation.

10 Which number _____ phone to confirm my return flight?

✓ **Check your answers**

1 has to. **2** do I have to. **3** We don't have to. **4** Do I have to? **5** you don't have to. **6** I don't have to. **7** do you have to. **8** have to. **9** have to. **10** do I have to.

Grammar and communication 5

The imperative

Examples from *The Story*:

1 Helen needs time to find the parking ticket.
   She could say, '**Wait** a minute.'

2 Tasha wants to help with the money. Helen says it isn't a problem.
   She says, '**Don't worry**.'

Meanings

1 '*Wait*.'   Helen is telling Tasha to do something.

2 '*Don't worry*.' Helen is telling Tasha not to do something.

'*Wait*' is the imperative. '*Don't worry*' is the negative imperative.

Grammar Summary – the imperative		
		Examples
Positive imperative	Verb without *to*	Stop!
Negative imperative	*Don't* + verb without *to*	Don't forget!

The negative imperative – Prohibition – *don't*

→ Use the correct form of the verbs in the box below to complete the sentences.

write	wait	forget	worry

1 _____ for me. I'll be home late tonight.
2 _____ it's Mom's birthday tomorrow.
3 _____! Everything will be all right.
4 _____ to me. It takes too long. Can't you e-mail me instead?

Check your answers

1 Don't wait. **2** Don't forget. **3** Don't worry! **4** Don't write.

The positive imperative

★ Be careful! The imperative is a **danger zone** for communication in English. In many languages it is very common to use the imperative in many situations.

★ In English we use the imperative in some situations. In other situations it is impolite.

When do we use the positive imperative?

→ Look at the examples **1–6** below and match with **a–f** from the box on page 284.
→ Use your dictionary if necessary.

1 A doctor 'Stay in bed for two days.' _____
2 'Come in!' _____
3 'Have a good weekend!' _____
4 'Be careful!' _____
5 'Stay in touch.' _____
6 'Go to the end of the road and turn right.'

a invitations and offers
b instructions – telling someone to do something
c giving street directions
d asking for contact
e hopes and wishes
f warnings

☑ Check your answers

1 b 2 a 3 e 4 f 5 d 6 c

What are they saying? What are they communicating?

→ Match the situations (**A–E**) on page 285 with the correct imperative phrase from **Box 1** and the correct communication from **Box 2** on page 286.

Example: 'Have a good holiday'
            Hopes and wishes

Situation A

Situation B

Situation C

Situation D

Situation E

Situation F

Box 1

1 'Take the second on the left'
2 'Go ahead. Help yourself!'
3 'Put the cup here and press that button'
4 'Write to me'
5 'Enjoy yourselves!'
6 'Look out!'

Box 2

a Instructions
c Street directions
c Offers and invitations
d Hopes and wishes
e Warnings
f Asking for contact

✓ Check your answers

Situation A	2 'Go ahead. Help yourself!	c Offers and invitations
Situation B	6 'Look out!'	e Warning
Situation C	4 'Please write to me'	f Asking for contact
Situation D	5 'Enjoy yourselves!'	d Hopes and wishes
Situation E	3 'Put the cup here and press that button.'	a Instructions
Situation F	1 'Take the second on the left'	b Street directions

★ For instructions and street directions, you can also use *you* + verb (the present simple, Topic 8).
This form is also very common.

Examples:

A Instructions

1 You put your cup here then you press that button.
2 First you fill this form in, then you pay over there.

B Street Directions:

1 You take the second on the left.
2 You go as far as the station and then you turn right.

Be careful with the positive imperative

Q When is the positive imperative impolite?

A When we ask people to do things.

→ Look at these examples.

Situation   You are eating with friends or colleagues. A person at the table says,

a 'Give me some bread.'   ☹
   'Can you give me some bread, please?'   ☺
b 'Put this on the table.'   ☹
   'Could you put this on the table, please?'   ☺

(See Topic 7 for more practice with *Can you...?*, *Could you...?* for asking people to do things.)

Telling people to do things – The imperative

★   The positive imperative is appropriate in some situations.

→ Match sentences (**1–4**) below with situations **a–d**.

1 Do your homework first.	**a** with a close friend
2 Empty your pockets onto the table.	**b** an adult to a child
3 Sit, Jack, sit.	**c** a policeman
4 Don't go home yet! Stay a bit longer.	**d** to an animal

Check your answers

1 b 2 c 3 d 4 a

★   To make an imperative more polite, add *please*.
   For example, 'Please tell me' or 'Tell me please'.

Summary – The use of the imperative – spoken English

→ Read these sentences about the use of the imperative.
→ Choose true or false.

1 The negative imperative is appropriate in many situations, e.g. 'Don't say that!' True/False
2 The positive imperative can be impolite, e.g. 'Sit here.' True/False
3 We use the positive imperative for wishes, e.g. 'Have a good journey!' True/False

4 We use the positive imperative for invitations and offers, e.g. 'Come and join us.' True/False

5 We use the imperative with good friends and children. True/False

 Check your answers

1 – 5 are all True.

What's the right word?

Public signs – the imperative

The positive imperative

★ The positive imperative is common in written instructions and warnings.

→ Look at the pictures below and the imperative phrases in the box on page 289.

→ Write the correct imperative phrase for each picture.

→ Use your dictionary if necessary.

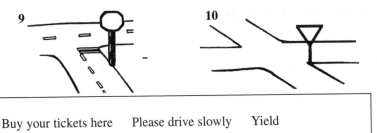

Buy your tickets here	Please drive slowly	Yield
Watch your head Stop	Look both ways	Beware of the dog
Cut along the dotted line	Insert your card here	Line up here

✓ Check your answers

1 Watch your head **2** Insert your card here **3** Line up here **4** Look both ways **5** Please drive slowly **6** Cut along the dotted line **7** Beware of the dog **8** Buy your tickets here **9** Stop **10** Yield

Verb *mind*

★ In the exercise above, *watch* means 'be careful of…' This verb is common for warning people.

You can use the verb 'watch' with both

a the person or thing in danger:
For example, 'Watch your head'.

b the dangerous thing:
For example, 'Watch the door'.

→ Write an expression with the verb *watch* for the following situations.

1 You are crossing the road. A bus is coming. Warn your friend.

2 There's a step. Warn your friend.

3 A child is sitting in a car, his legs outside the car. You want to shut the car door.

4 Your friend is in the car with the door open. Another car is coming.

✓ Check your answers

1 Watch the bus! **2** Watch the step! **3** Watch your legs! **4** Watch your door! OR Watch the car!

Find the right word

Public signs – Negative imperative

★ The negative imperative is not common in signs.

★ 'No + verb + ing' or 'No + noun' is more common.

→ Label the signs below with the correct expression from the box.

→ Use your dictionary if necessary.

No entry   No photography   No left turn

No swimming   No smoking

1

2

3

4

5

☑ **Check your answers**

1 No smoking **2** No swimming **3** No entry **4** No left turn **5** No photography

Grammar and communication 6

Offering, rejecting, insisting, accepting

Examples from *The Story*:

a Helen offers to help Tasha with her suitcase.
  She says, 'Can I help you with your suitcase?'
b Tasha says no.
  She says, 'No, really, it's all right thanks. I can manage.'
c Helen insists. She offers Tasha help again.
  She says, 'Come on! Let me help.'
d Tasha accepts.
  She says, 'O.K. Thanks. It is quite heavy.'

Rejecting an offer

Example from *The Story*: 'No really, it's all right. I can manage.'

★ We use *manage* when the action is difficult but possible.
  Manage is about effort and success.

In the sentence above, 'manage' means 'It's difficult to lift the suitcase because it's heavy, but I can lift it with effort.'

→ Listen to these mini-dialogues on Recording 5.
→ Repeat B's responses in the spaces.

Recording 5

1	**A**	Can I help you with that?
	B	Thanks very much, but I think I can manage it on my own.
2	**A**	Let me do that.
	B	No, honestly, I can manage thanks.
3	**A**	I'll take that if you like.
	B	No, really, I'm fine thanks. I can manage.
4	**A**	Shall I do that?
	B	It's O.K. I can manage, thanks.
5	**A**	Would you like me to carry that for you?
	B	Thanks for the offer, but I think I can manage it.

Verb *manage*

→ Complete the mini-dialogues below with the correct sentence from the box.

Example: How often do you go home to see your parents?
   B *I usually manage to go about once a month.*

1 A The meeting is now at three o'clock and not four. Can you manage to get here one hour earlier?
   B _____

2 A That's a big box! Be careful of your back!
   B _____

3 A I'm sorry I can't help.
   B _____

4 A I've got no idea how to do this.
   B _____

5 A Tom worries so much about exams.
   B _____

6 A How much do you understand when you watch a film in English now?
   B _____

7 A Do you play a sport?
   B _____

8 A Do you see your children in the evenings?
   B _____

---

a I try to get to the gym twice a week but I don't always manage it.
b Don't worry! I'll manage on my own.
c It's alright. I think I can manage it. Where shall I put it?
d If we work together, we'll manage something.
e Yes, I usually manage to spend an hour or so with them before they go to bed
f ~~I usually manage to go about once a month~~.
g I can try.
h Yes, but he always manages to get good marks.
i I manage to understand quite a lot, actually.

Check your answers

1 g 2 c 3 b 4 d 5 h 6 i 7 a 8 e

c Offering again – insisting

Example from *The Story*:

Helen insists. She offers Tasha help again.
She says, 'Come on! Let me help.'

Verb *let*

Form: | Verb *let*, imperative form | person | verb.

★ The expressions 'Come on!' and 'Go on!' make the phrase stronger.

→ Look at the situations 1–7 below. You are the person
→ Complete the dialogues with sentences from the box.

Let me call an ambulance.

No, it's heavy. Let me take it!

Wait a second. Let me open the door for you.

Come on! It's my turn. Let me pay this time.

Come on! Let me have a look at it.

No, really. Let me do something to help.

Come on, its late! Let me take you.

---

1 A Can I carry that for you?
  B I'm all right thanks.
  A _____
  B Thank you. It is very heavy, actually.

2 A I'll get this.
  B _____
  A O.K. Thanks.

3 **A** Can I take some of those
for you?

  B No, it's all right. I can manage.

  A _____

  B Thanks.

5 **A** Do you know where the
nearest bus stop is?

  B It's O.K. I've got the car. I
can drive you home.

  A No, I can get the bus. It's no
problem.

  B _____

  A Thanks. It's really nice of you
to offer but I can get the bus.

4 **A** Can I just sit down for a
minute?

  B Of course. Would you like
me to get you anything?

  A No, I'm… oh, the baby…

  B _____

6 **A** Can I do anything?

  B No, you go and sit down.

  A _____

  B Thanks, could you peel the
vegetables?

7 **A** Oh! My eye!

  B What's the matter?

  A I think I've got something
in it.

  B _____

Check your answers

1 No, it's heavy. Let me take it! **2** Come on! It's my turn. Let me pay this time.
3 Wait a second. Let me open the door for you. **4** Let me call an ambulance.
5 Come on, it's late! Let me take you. **6** No really. Let me do something to
help. **7** Come on! Let me have a look at it.

Grammar and communication 7

Introducing something negative in a polite way – *I'm afraid*

Example from *The Story*:
Tasha is sorry she hasn't got any change. She says,
'**I'm afraid** I haven't got any change.'

★   Use *I'm afraid* to introduce something negative in a polite way.

→ Match **1–8** below with the correct response **a–h**.

1 Excuse me, are you the manager?	**a** I'm afraid I can't. I'm driving.
2 Could you tell me the time please?	**b** I'm afraid I don't know. I'm not from here.
3 Excuse me, where I can get a taxi?	**c** I'm afraid I've got some bad news.
4 Could I borrow your dictionary?	**d** I'm afraid we can't. We're going to my mother's.
5 Come on! Have another glass of wine.	**e** No, actually I'm not. I'm afraid he's not here at the moment.
6 Would you like to come to dinner on Saturday?	**f** I'm afraid I can't eat another thing!
7 Do have some more cake	**g** I'm afraid I haven't got a watch.
8 What's the matter?	**h** I'm afraid I haven't got one.

Check your answers

1 e 2 g 3 b 4 h 5 a 6 d 7 f 8 c

Short answers – *I'm afraid so, I'm afraid not*

★   To respond to questions with *Yes* or *No* alone can sound rude.
★   To express that you are sorry about a situation, use *I'm afraid so* and
I'm afraid not.

I'm afraid so

Meaning
I'm sorry but yes.

Examples:

He's drunk, isn't he?
He isn't ill, is he?
It's a big problem, isn't it?
It's too expensive, isn't it?

Response: I'm afraid so.

I'm afraid not

Meaning
I'm sorry but no.

Examples:

Is he here?
You haven't got a car, have you?
Have you got any change?
Can you help me?

Response: I'm afraid not.

→ Respond with *I'm afraid so* or *I'm afraid not*.

1	**A**	It's a bad accident, isn't it?	**B**	_____
2	**A**	This isn't right, is it?	**B**	_____
3	**A**	Do you know where he lives?	**B**	_____
4	**A**	You don't like this, do you?	**B**	_____
5	**A**	You can't swim, can you?	**B**	_____
6	**A**	Do we have to pay?	**B**	_____

✓ **Check your answers**

1 I'm afraid so. **2** I'm afraid not. **3** I'm afraid not. **4** I'm afraid not. **5** I'm afraid not. **6** I'm afraid so.

Using these words and phrases

Get for buy

Example:

John tells Bill he's buying a new car. He says,
'I'm **getting** a new car.'

★ *Get* is an indirect verb for *buy*.
→ Put the words in the right order to make sentences.

1 **A** You need a new computer.
   B _____
   next week/one/getting/I'm

2 Ice cream sounds good._____
   I/some/us/shall/get?

3 _____ It was your turn last week.
   me/ice cream/the/get/today/let

4 _____
   card/get/I'll/on/credit/it/my

✓ Check your answers

1 I'm getting one next week. **2** Shall I get us some? **3** Let me get the ice cream
today. **4** I'll get it on my credit card.

Q *What's the difference between 'I'll get this' and 'I'm getting this'?*

A *I'll get this* is an offer.
I'm getting this insists more.

What would you say?

1 You come to the U.S. to stay with an American family. You don't know
   whether to use their first names or their surnames. You ask.

   _____

2 Your friend hasn't got any change for parking. You have.

   _____

Possible answers

1 What shall I call you? Advanced alternative: What would you like me to call
you? **2** I've got some change. Here you are.

Review

How do you say it in your language?

Here are some examples of the important points in this topic.

→ Translate the sentences below into your language in the spaces.
→ Remember – translate the idea, not the words.

1 It's lovely to see you again.

_____

2 How was your journey?

_____

3 I'm tired! My job is very tiring!

_____

4 Thank you for inviting me.

_____

5 Don't wait for me. I have to finish this.

_____

6 A Shall I do that?
  B Thanks but I think I can manage.

_____

  C Come on! Let me help you.

_____

7 I'm afraid the manager's not here.

_____

8 Have a good weekend!

_____

Join the conversation

→ Look at Recording 1 (page 258) again.
→ Listen to Recording 6.
→ Read **Tasha's** words in the spaces.

TEST 9

Which one is right?

→ Choose **a** or **b**.

1 a It's nice to have a vacation.
  b Is nice to have a vacation.

2 **a** How was your day?
   b How were your day?

3 **a** I'm very interesting in football.
   b I'm very interested in football.

4 **a** Thank you for to ask me to go with you.
   b Thank you for asking me to go with you.

5 **a** I'm have to leave now.
   b I have to leave now.

6 **a** Can I get this on my credit card?
   b Can I get on my credit card this?

7 **a** Please come with us today.
   b Please to come with us today.

8 **a** Let me to do that.
   b Let me do that.

9 Can you come with us?
   a I afraid no.
   b I'm afraid not.

10 Can I help with that?
   a Thanks but I can manage.
   b Thanks but I manage.

Write a dialogue

Meeting someone after a journey

Situation   You travel to visit a friend. Your friend is at the station to meet you.

1 **Your friend**
    greets you. She is happy
    to see you.

You
greet your friend. You are happy
to see her.

3   Your friend asks about your journey

4   Say something positive.
You ask about her life in
general

5   Your friend replies and shows
you the way to the taxis

6   You thank your friend for meeting
you

7   Your friend responds and then says

___ Look, here's a taxi.
Go on! You get in first.

8   You arrive. Your friend asks the
driver how much it is.

9   You decide to pay

10 Your friend says <u>she's</u> paying

☑ **Check your answers**

1 a 2 a 3 b 4 b 5 b 6 a 7 a 8 b 9 b 10 a

Dialogue: model answers

1	**Your friend**	Hello, X. It's great to see you again.
2	**You**	Hi, X. It's lovely to see you too.
3	**Your friend**	How was your journey?
4	**You**	It was good thanks. How are things with you?
5	**Your friend**	I'm fine. The taxis are this way.
6	**You**	Thank you for picking me up, by the way.
7	**Your friend**	That's O.K. Look, here's a taxi. Go on! You get in first.
8	**Your friend**	How much is it, please?
9	**You**	Let me pay.
10	**Your friend**	No, <u>I'm</u> getting this.

10 | FINDING ACCOMMODATIONS

Grammar and communication	Vocabulary
◆ Asking *Who?* + short answers	◆ Hotel language
◆ Talking about the number of people	◆ Ordinal numbers
◆ Talking about the same thing – *one, ones*	**Pronunciation**
◆ Asking for an alternative	◆ *Schwa / ə /*
◆ Negative comparisons	
◆ Decisions – buying things	
◆ Verb *hope*	
◆ Talking about the past – past simple	
◆ Past experience – present perfect	

Oliver is at the hotel reservations desk in the tourist information center in the Denver airport.
He needs a room.

Understanding the important information

→ Read the sentences on page 302.
→ Listen to Recording 1 *The Story* and answer *Yes* or *No* to the sentences.

1 Oliver reserves a hotel room.	Yes/No
2 They talk about	
– type of room	Yes/No
– hotel facilities	Yes/No
– prices	Yes/No
– one particular hotel	Yes/No

🎧 Recording 1 (and 8) – The Story

Assistant	Who's next, please?
Oliver	I think I am. I'd like to reserve a room, please.
Assistant	Yes, how many of you are there?
Oliver	It's just for me.
Assistant	And how long is it for?
Oliver	I need a room from tonight until the end of next week.
Assistant	O.K. So that's a single room for 14 nights altogether.
Oliver	Yes, that's right.
Assistant	In any specific area?
Oliver	I don't mind, as long as it's near the Tech Center.
Assistant	What sort of price are you looking to pay?
Oliver	Between $90.00 and $125.00 a night.
Assistant	There's the Courtyard, Denver Tech Center.
Oliver	How much is that one?
Assistant	$100.00 a night.
Oliver	That would be fine.
Assistant	I'll just see if they have any vacancies. Would you like to take a seat for a moment?
Oliver	Thanks.

☑ Check your answers

1 No 2 a Type of room	Yes
b Hotel facilities	No
c Prices	Yes
d One particular hotel	Yes

Understanding more

Finding a room

→ Cover the text of Recording 1.
→ Read the table below.
→ Listen to the recording and complete the table.

Number of nights	Oliver's price range	Location (where?)	Name of hotel	Price
	$..... – $.....			

Check your answers

Number of nights: 14; Price range: $90.00–$125.00 a night; Location: near the Tech Center; Name of hotel: Courtyard; Price: $100.00

What do they say?

→ Read the sentences below.
→ Listen to Recording 1 again and try to complete the words.
→ Then read the text to help you if necessary.

1 A   The assistant starts the conversation.
      She asks, 'W _ _ 's / n _ _ _?'
   B   Oliver responds, 'I think _ / _ m.'
2 A   The assistant asks about the number of people.
      She says, 'H_ _ / m _ _ y / o _ / y _ _ / a _ e / t _ _ r _?'
   B   Oliver responds, 'It's / j _ _ _ / f _ _ / m _.'
3 A   The assistant suggests a Courtyard and Oliver asks the price.
      He says, 'How much is /t _ _ _ / o _ _?'
   B   The assistant responds, '$100 / _ / n _ _ _ t.'

Check your answers

1 a Who's next?   **b** I think I am.
2 a How many of you are there?   **b** It's just for me.
3 a How much is that one?   **b** $100 a night.

Find the words and phrases

→ Read the sentences below.
→ Read the text of Recording 1 and complete the words and phrases.

1 Oliver is looking for a room.
He says, 'I'd like to / r _ _ _ _ _ _ / a room, please.'

2 **a** The assistant asks about the number of nights.
She says, 'H _ _ / l _ _ g / _ s / i _ / f _ r?'
b Oliver responds, 'F _ _ _ / tonight / u _ _ _ _ / the end of the week.'

3 Oliver needs a room for one person. He needs a /s _ _ _ _ _ / room.

4 The location of the hotel isn't very important to Oliver, but he wants to be near the Tech Center. He says, 'I don't mind, / a _ / l _ _ _ / a _ / it's near the Tech Center.'

5 **a** The assistant asks how much Oliver wants to pay.
She says, 'W _ _ _ / s _ _ _ / o _ / price / are / you / l _ _ _ _ _ g / t _ / p _ _ ?'
b Oliver's minimum is $90 and his maximum $125.
He says, 'B _ _ _ _ _ n / $90 and $125 / _ / n _ _ _ t.'

6 When you need a room, you can say,
'Have you got any rooms free?' or
'Have you got any v _ _ _ _ _ _ _ _?'

7 The assistant asks Oliver to sit down.
☑   She says, 'Would you like to t _ _ _ / a / s _ _ _ / for a moment?'

Check your answers

1 I'd like to reserve a room, please. **2 a** How long is it for? **b** From tonight until the end of next week. **3** He needs a single room. **4** I don't mind, as long as it's near the Tech Center. **5 a** What sort of price are you looking to pay? **b** Between $90 and $125 a night. **6** Have you got any vacancies? **7** Would you like to take a seat for a moment?

Using these words and phrases

1 Questions with *for* at the end

Example from *The Story*:
The assistant asks about the number of nights.
She says, '**How long** is it **for**?'

How long asks about the number of days.
It refers to 'the room'.

She can also say, *How long for?* but this is more direct. It can sound abrupt.

Summary – Questions with *for* at the end			
How many	is	it/this/that	
How long	are	they/these/those	for?
When			
Who			

→ Complete these dialogues. Make questions from the words in the table above.

1 **A** Good evening, sir.

   _____?

  B There are four of us.

  A If you would like to follow me, I'll show you to your table.

2 **A** Here are our tickets to New York.

  B _____?

  A Next Wednesday.

3 **A** Here's the bill.

  B Let's pay half each.

   _____?

  A $20.50.

4 **A** They're beautiful.

   _____?

  B Oh, that's my little secret.

5 A   If you want to go out on
            the lake you can rent a
            boat. It costs $10.
B   _____?

A   One hour.

☑ Check your answers

1 How many is it for? (it' refers to 'table') **2** When are they for? **3** How much
is it for? **4** Who are they for? **5** How long is that for?

2 As long as

The location of the hotel isn't very important to Oliver, but he wants to be
near the Tech Center.

The assistant asks, 'In any specific area?'
Oliver says, 'I don't mind, as long as it's near the Tech Center.'

As long as talks about condition. It means 'if' but we use *as long as* when
the condition is important to us.

→ Complete the mini-dialogues on page 307.
→ Use *as long as* + the correct phrase from the box.
→ Change the verb if necessary.

as long as …	be in a non-smoking area get there by twenty past be back before 11 o'clock go to Aspen find me a room rain take me home afterwards ~~be careful~~

Example:
A   Dad, can I borrow the car?
B   Yes, *as long as you're careful.*

1 A Can we go on a trip to England?
  B Why not, _____we_____

2 A Could you baby-sit for us on Saturday evening?
  B Of course,_____ you _____

3 A We're going to the open-air theater this evening.
  B That can be really good, _____it_____

4 A The train leaves at 3:30.
  B So, _____we_____ we'll be O.K.

5 A Would you like a table by the window, sir?
  B I don't mind, _____it_____

6 A Mom, can I go out?
  B Yes , _____you_____

7 A I'm sorry sir, but the hotel is full. I understand you've got a reservation but...
  B I don't mind how long I have to wait, _____you
_____

Check your answers

1		we go to Aspen.
2		you take me home afterwards.
3		it doesn't rain.
4	as long as	we get there by twenty past.
5		it is in a non-smoking area.
6		you are back by 11 o'clock.
7		you find me a room.

3 Talking about how much you want to spend

Example from *The Story:*
The assistant asks Oliver how much he wants to pay.
She says, 'What sort of price are you looking to pay?'

What's the difference between
a *'How much do you want to pay?'*
  and
b *'What sort of price are you looking to pay?'*

The grammar is correct in both questions. The meaning is the same.

a 'How much do you want to pay?' is more direct.
b 'What sort of price are you looking to pay?' is indirect.

Question **b** is common in shops and when you are buying a service.

Q *Can I say, 'What kind of price...?' instead of 'sort'.*

A Yes, *What kind of ...?* and *What sort of ...?* are the same.

Responses – The price

Oliver's minimum is $90.00 and his maximum is $125.00.
He says, 'Between $90.00 and $125.00.'

Other possible responses:

Anything up to $90 is all right Anything under $90 is O.K. As long as it's less than $90 $\Big\}$	These expressions mean $90 is your maximum
About $90 Around $90 $\Big\}$	It can be a little more or a little less than $90.00

Prices, quantities and time

How much is a room at the Courtyard? '$90.00 **a** night.'

★ We use *a/an* for measurements of time, units of quantity etc.
For example, 50 cents **a** pack.

→ Complete the mini-dialogues below. Use one picture from the top of
page 309 and one word from the box under the pictures.
→ Use your dictionary if necessary.

Example: A He's very good at his job. How much does he charge?
      B *$25 an hour*

1   **A**   How much does it cost to have a car?
      B   About_____.
         Expensive, isn't it?
2   **A**   Can you tell me how much those flowers cost, please?
      B   Yes,_____
3   **A**   How much are these bananas, please?
      B   Yes,_____

> 1 hour
>
> **$25**

| month | kilo | bunch | packet | bottle | box | ~~hour~~ |

4 A Those strawberries look nice. How much are they, please?

B _____

5 A Can you tell me the price of these cookies, please?

B _____

6 A Let's get some more of that wine, shall we? How much is it?

B _____

Check your answers

1 $90 a month. **2** $3 a bunch. **3** 90 cents a pound. **4** $1.49 a box. **5** 65 cents a pack. **6** $3.99 a bottle.

Can I also say 'per', for example, '$20 per hour'?

A/an is normal in spoken English.

Per is formal. It is more common in written English.

How do you pronounce it?

Schwa / ə /

★ This is the most common sound in English.

★ Why? The vowel in unstressed syllables is often pronounced *schwa*.

★ In the words and phrases on the next page, all the letters with the *schwa* symbol / ə / on the top have the same sound *schwa*.

→ Listen to Recording 2 and repeat the words and phrases.
The stress is underlined in each phrase.

→ Pay special attention to the pronunciation of the *schwa* / ə /.

🎧 *Recording 2*

1 to, to <u>reserve</u>, a, a <u>room</u>, to <u>reserve</u> a <u>room</u>,

   I'd <u>like</u> to <u>reserve</u> a <u>room</u>

2 to<u>night</u>, from, from to<u>night</u>

3 of, the <u>end</u> of, the <u>end</u> of next <u>week</u>

4 as, as <u>long</u> as, as <u>long</u> as it's <u>central</u>

5 <u>sort</u> of, sort of <u>price</u>, what sort of <u>price</u> are you, to <u>pay</u>,

   What sort of <u>price</u> are you <u>looking</u> to <u>pay</u>?

6 a <u>night</u>, $55 a <u>night</u>

7 <u>vacancies</u>

8 to <u>take</u>, to take a <u>seat</u>, for a <u>moment</u>,

   Would you like to take a <u>seat</u> for a <u>moment</u>?

What's the right word?

In a hotel

→ Complete these mini-dialogues with the correct response from the box on page 311.

→ Use your dictionary if necessary.

1 **A** There are two of us.

   B _____

2 A Does the room have a private bathroom?
  B _____

3 A Is dinner included?
  B _____

4 A Are all meals included?
  B _____

5 A I see B & B signs everywhere. What does B & B mean?
  B _____

6 A What does 'No vacancies' mean?
  B _____

7 A I'm very sorry but the elevator isn't working.
  B _____

8 A Don't I need a key to open the door of my room?
  B _____

9 A Where could I have a business meeting, please?
  B _____

10 A We're really thirsty and I'd like something to eat, too.
  B _____

---

a No, sir. Just put this card in the slot on the door.
b Yes, the price includes dinner.
c Do you prefer a double or twin room?
d Yes, all our rooms have private facilities, madam.
e It means there are no rooms free. The hotel is full.
f The conference room is always open to visitors, madam.
g Yes, that price includes a light lunch and a 3-course dinner.
h It stands for 'bed and breakfast'. It's very common in Britain.
i The bar is open all day for refreshments, sir.
j Oh, dear ! We'll have to go up the stairs.

Check your answers

1 c **2** d **3** b **4** g **5** h **6** e **7** j **8** a **9** f **10** i

Grammar and communication 1

Asking *Who?* + short answers

Example from *The Story*:

The assistant asks, 'Who's next?' Oliver responds, 'I think I am.'

★ Short answers are very common in English.

Who works in this office?	→	I do
Who likes coffee?	→	Peter does
Who can drive?	→	David and Sally can
Who hasn't got a sister?	→	Tom hasn't
Who's hungry?	→	We are
Who's going to Italy?	→	I am

Look at the examples below.

→ Complete the short answers in these mini-dialogues.

→ Choose from

am/am not	*is/isn't*	*are/aren't*
do/don't	*does/doesn't*	
have/haven't	*has/hasn't*	
can/can't	*could/couldn't*	

1 **A** Who lives at No. 12?
    B John and Sheila _____. You don't remember them, do you?

2 **A** Who's coming to the movies with us tonight?
    B I _____. Have you got my ticket?

3 **A** Who's not here yet?
    B Sue _____ – she's always late.

4 **A** Who's got a watch?
    B I _____. It's six o'clock.

5 **A** Who can cook tonight?
    B We _____, if you like.

6 **A** Do you all like pizza?
    I'm afraid Mike _____. He can't eat cheese.

7 A Who has to go to work tomorrow?
  B I _____ but my friend _____
  Isn't she lucky?

8 A Who's using the computer?
  B Robert _____, as usual.

9 A Who thinks it's a good idea?
  B I _____ – I think it's great!

10 A Who understands her?
  B No-one _____ . She talks so fast.

11 A Who's got a car?
  B Kate _____
  A Good! Perhaps she can take us there.

12 A Who watches T.V. in your house?
  B We all _____

Check your answers

1 John and Sheila do. **2** I am. **3** Sue isn't. **4** I have. **5** We can. **6** I'm afraid
Mike doesn't. **7** I do but my friend doesn't. **8** Robert is. **9** I do. **10** No-one
does. **11** Kate has. **12** We all do.

Grammar and communication 2

Talking about the number of people – *How many?*

Example from *The Story*:
The assistant asks about the number of people.
She says, '**How many of you are there?**'
Oliver responds 'It's just for me.'

How many of you are there?

→ Answer the following questions about you.

1 How many of you are there in your family?
  There are _____ ***of us.***

2 How many of you are there in the room at this moment?
  T _____/ are / _____/ o _/ u _
  OR
  J_____/ m_____

3 If you are a student – how many of you are there in your class?

_____

4 If you work – how many of you are there in the company?

_____

☑ **Check your answers**

All answers: 'There are XXX of us.' If you're alone, the answer to question **2** is: 'Just me.'

Grammar and communication 3

Talking about the same thing – *one/ones*

Example from *The Story*:

The assistant suggests a Courtyard Hotel and Oliver asks the price.

He says 'How much is that one?'

★ Don't repeat the noun. Use 'one' or 'ones' instead.

→ Complete the speech balloons.
→ Choose from the sentences in the box on page 315.

5

---

a I think I'll take this one.   **b** Have you got any smaller ones?
c I prefer the white one.   **d** A large one, please.
e Excuse me, can you tell me how much the small one is, please?

Check your answers

1 e 2 d 3 c 4 a 5 b

Common mistake – *One/Ones*

Example from the exercise above:

'A small or a large Coke?'

Answer: 'A large, please.' ✗
       'A large one, please.' ✓

→ Look at these examples.

1 A Would you like a large Coke? **B** No, can I have a small one?

2 I like the green car but I prefer the white one.

3 This bag is too big. Can I see that one, please?

4 A Peter's out on his new bike. **B** A new bike? Who's got his old one?

5 A I like green apples. **B** Do you? I prefer red ones.

Example sentence	Grammar Summary – *One/Ones*		
1	*a*	adjective	*one*
2 4	*the* *my* etc. }	adjective	*one* or *ones*
3	*this/that*	(adjective)	*one*
5	*these/those* no article }	adjective	*ones*

Let's look at sentence **4** on page 315, about the bike.

Q *Can't I say, 'The old is in the garage?'* **✗**

A No, with *the* + adjective, say *one* or *ones*.
'**The old one** is in the garage'

→ Complete the mini-dialogues below. Use *a*, *the*, *my* etc. + *one*, *ones*.

1 A Would you like a hot or a cold drink?
  B Could I have /_____/ cold_____, please?
2 A Which umbrella is yours?
  B _____black_____
3 A Do you like your new computer?
  B Not really, I prefer _____/ old /_____
4 A Do you like that blue hat?
  B It's too expensive. How about _____ red _____?
5 A Are you going on a long trip?
  B No, it's just _____ short _____ this time.
6 A Which shoes shall I wear?
  B Why don't you wear _____new _____?
7 A Can I borrow a pen?
  B I've only got _____ red _____
8 A Where do I put the clean plates?
  B Here.
  A And _____ dirty _____?
  B They go over there.
9 A How many children have you got?
  B Two. They're both girls. The oldest one's called Marie and _____ other _____'s name's Danielle.

☑ Check your answers

1 a cold one. **2** the black one. **3** the/my old one. **4** the/this/that red one. **5** a short one. **6** the/your new ones. **7** a red one. **8** the dirty ones. **9** the/my other one's.

Q *Where's the stress in the sentences above?*

A Stress is always on the important or new information.

So, in these sentences, the stress is on the adjectives, for example, *cold*, *black*, *old*, etc. A *cold* one, the *black* one, my *old* one etc.

*Our story continues... the assistant telephones the Courtyard,
Denver Tech Center and talks to Oliver again*

Understanding the important information

→ Cover the text of Recording 3.
→ Read the sentences below.
→ Listen to the recording and answer the questions.

1 Oliver books a room at a Courtyard Hotel? Yes/No.
2 They talk about two, three, four or five hotels?

Recording 3 – The Story

Assistant	Sorry to keep you waiting sir. I'm afraid the Courtyard has no vacancies.
Oliver	Have you got anything else?
Assistant	How about these two? Summerfield Suites or TownePlace Suites. Both are in the Denver Tech Center.
Oliver	Are they about the same price?
Assistant	Let me see. Summerfield Suites is $95.00 a night and TownePlace Suites is a bit cheaper, $85.00. They both have the same facilities. Breakfast is included, of course, and both have private bathrooms, television, direct-dial telephones and a mini-bar in the room.
Oliver	Which one is closer to the Denver Tech Center?
Assistant	They are about the same, but you may need a rental car.
Oliver	I think I'll take a room at Summerfield. It costs more and it might be a little more comfortable.

Check your answers

1 No   2 three

Understanding more

→ Cover the text of Recording 3 again.
→ Read the grid below.
→ Listen to Recording 3 again and complete the grid.

Name of Hotel	Summerfield Suites	TownePlace Suites
Price per night	$	$
Private bathrooms		
Direct-dial telephones		
Mini-bar		
Breakfast included	Yes/No	Yes/No
Oliver chooses		

 Check your answers

Name of Hotel	Summerfield Suites	TownePlace Suites
Price per night	$95.00	$85.00
Private bathrooms	✓	✓
Direct-dial telephones	✓	✓
Mini-bar	✓	✓
Breakfast included	Yes	Yes
Oliver chooses	✓	

What's the right word?

Other hotels

→ Choose words from the box below to complete the sentences below.
→ Use your dictionary if necessary.

1 My hotel is very _____ because it's ___ a park. There's not much traffic.

2 **A** How much is that hotel?
B I don't know but it's in the center of town. That means it's

_____

A I prefer to pay a bit more and be _____ so I can walk to the museums, shops and all the other places I want to visit. I also need a hotel that is _____ – being a tourist is tiring.

3 I really like my hotel. Everything looks so _____ and the staff is very _____ – they always talk to me.

---

small	modern	traditional	big	comfortable	friendly
clean	central	expensive	quiet	near	

Check your answers

1 quiet… near **2** expensive…central…comfortable **3** clean...friendly

What do they say?

→ Read the sentences below.
→ Listen to Recording 3 again and try to complete the words.
→ Then read the text of the recording to help you if necessary.

1 Oliver waits and the assistant comes back. She starts the conversation. She says, 'S _ _ _ y / t _ / k _ _ p / y _ _ / w _ _ _ _ _ g.'

2 When she says the Courtyard is full Oliver asks about other possibilities. He says, 'H _ _ _/ y _ _ / g _ t / a _ _ t h _ _ g / e _ s _?'

3 The assistant compares the hotels. What does she say about them? She says, 'They are a _ _ _ t / t _ _ / s _ _ _ but you may n _ _ _ / a / r _ _ _ _ l / c _ _.'

4 Oliver decides on the Summerfield Suites He says ' I t _ _ _ k / I'll /
t _ _ _ / a / r _ _ _ / at / S _ _ _ _ _ _ _ _ _.'

How do they pronounce it?

Schwa (Part 2)

→ Listen to Recording 4 and repeat these words and phrases from the conversation above.

→ Pay special attention to the letters with the *schwa* symbol / ə / on the top. Two of the vowels with / ə / are not *schwa* on the recording.

→ Can you find the two vowels that are not *schwa*?

→ Stressed syllables are <u>underlined</u>.

🎧 *Recording 4*

1 <u>Roy</u>ạl	7 conti<u>nen</u>tạl
2 <u>Holl</u>ạnd <u>Park</u>	8 <u>nec</u>ẹssary
3 <u>Ox</u>fọrd Street	9 ạ<u>bout</u>
4 fạ<u>cil</u>ities	10 <u>tel</u>evisiọn
5 trạ<u>di</u>tiọnạl	11 in<u>clud</u>ẹd
6 <u>break</u>fạst	12 <u>Ol</u>ivẹr

✓ Check your answers

3 Oxford Street 11 included

Grammar and communication 4

Asking for an alternative

1 A general alternative

Example from *The Story*:
The Courtyard Hotel is full. Oliver asks about other possibilities.
He says, 'Have you got **anything else**?'

★ This question is very general.
★ You can use it to ask about everything.

2 A more specific alternative

→ Look at this example. Fred is going to London on business.

Receptionist: I've got one room at £100 a night.
Fred: Have you got **anything cheaper?**

★ We can use the **comparative** with this question.

→ Ask questions in these situations. Use the comparative.

1 In a store
   You _____?

2 In a store
   You _____?

3 Your travel agent suggests a flight at 10:00 p.m. It's too late.
   You _____?

4 You book a hotel room in London. Your friend tells you it's far from the center of the city. You phone your travel agent.
   You _____?

Check your answers

1 Have you got anything smaller? **2** Have you got anything longer? **3** Have you got anything earlier? **4** Have you got anything /nearer the center? / more central?

Grammar and communication 5

Negative comparisons

Fred chooses The Park Hotel because it's **smaller**, **quieter**, **more comfortable**, it is **more traditional** and it's **nearer** the office than the Royal Hotel.

Why doesn't Fred choose the Royal?

The Royal's **not as quiet** (as The Park) OR
The Royal **isn't as quiet** (as The Park).
The pronunciation of 'as' is also with *schwa* / ə /.

→ Complete the sentences below. Use adjectives from the box.

quiet	comfortable	big	traditional	good	near	expensive

1 The Royal's not___/_____. It's in a really busy street.
2 The Royal's _____as_____/___ the Park. The beds are hard.
3 The Royal's _____/____ traditional. The style is more modern.
4 The Royal's ___/___ good ____ the Park for Fred because it isn't
   /____/n_____his office.

☑ Check your answers

1 not as quiet. 2 not as comfortable as. 3 not as traditional. 4 not as good as,
as near.

ⓘ Culture – lodging for visitors in the U.S.

Where to stay

■ **Hotels**   Traditional hotels are usually in a city or town.
They normally have one or more restaurants, some parking
(for a fee) and a swimming pool. They are in good
locations for tourists and business people. In general,
breakfast is not included in the price. They usually have
private bathrooms.

■ **Motels**   Traditional motels are near a highway. They
usually have lots of free parking and a swimming pool.
They often have a restaurant or café. Rooms always have a
private bathroom. Highway travelers often use motels.

- **All-suite Hotels** All-suite hotels are usually in the suburbs, often near newer businesses and office buildings. They usually have lots of free parking, a swimming pool, an exercise room, voice mail and data connections in each room, and a full kitchen. They always have private bathrooms, one for each bedroom in the suite. A complete buffet breakfast is usually included. All-suite hotels don't always have a restaurant. This is because all the suites have a kitchen.

- **Bed and Breakfast (B. & B.)** Typical B. & B.s are usually in a city or town. They are usually rooms in private homes. It is common to share the bathroom. B. & B.s always offer a light breakfast.

Fred Wilson needs a place to stay in London.

→ Now read about this London hotel.

The Royal Scot Hotel, London

→ Look at the map below. Where is the Royal Scot Hotel?

→ Read the text from a London Tourist brochure and choose **A, B, C, D,** or **E.**

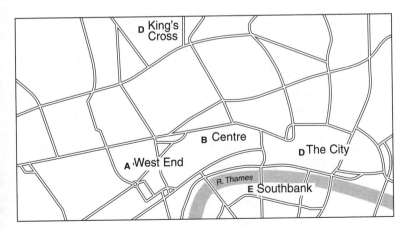

KINGS CROSS

ROYAL SCOT
★ ★ ★
A THISTLE ASSOCIATE HOTEL

142

Situated between the West End and the City of London, close to Kings Cross station, this modern hotel with 87 refurbished deluxe rooms, provides the ideal base for a shopping and sightseeing visit to the capital. London Zoo and Madame Tussaud's famous waxworks are within easy reach and local attractions include the British Museum and Sadler's Wells.

Check your answer

C – Close to (near) King's Cross Station.

→ Read the questions below.
→ Read the text again and put a check mark ✓ by each right answer.

The Royal Scot is:
- ☐ small
- ☐ large
- ☐ traditional
- ☐ modern
- ☐ good for visiting London's shops
- ☐ good for tourists
- ☐ good for sports enthusiasts
- ☐ hot in the summer
- ☐ air-conditioned

It has:
- ☐ a swimming pool
- ☐ a big parking lot
- ☐ limited car parking
- ☐ three restaurants
- ☐ views of the park
- ☐ more than 80 rooms

Check your answers

The Royal Scot is:
large
modern
good for visiting London's shops
good for tourists (sightseeing)
air-conditioned

It has:
limited parking
more than 80 rooms

Grammar and communication 6

Decisions – buying things

Example from *The Story*: Oliver decides on Summerfield Suites.
He says, '**I'll take** a room at Summerfield.'

★ Say *I'll take* when you decide to buy.

Situation   You are in a store and you decide to buy.

1 You look at two boxes of chocolates, a big one and a small one.
You decide to buy the small one.
You _____

2 You look at two pictures – one in black and white, one in color.
You decide to buy the one in black and white.
You _____

3 You look at two watches – a more expensive one and a cheaper one.
You decide to buy the more expensive one.
You _____

☑ **Check your answers**

1 I'll take the small one, please. **2** I'll take the black and white one please.
3 I'll take the more expensive one, please.

*Our story continues. Oliver arrives at Summerfield Suites.
He checks in*

Understanding the important information

→ Cover the text of Recording 5.
→ Read the sentences below.
→ Listen to the recording and choose *Yes* or *No*.

They talk about

    a Oliver's passport   Yes/No
    b his room number   Yes/No
    c the restaurant   Yes/No
    d the breakfast room   Yes/No
    e the cost of the room   Yes/No
    f Oliver's luggage?   Yes/No

Recording 5 – The Story

Room clerk	Good afternoon. Can I help you?
Oliver	Yes, I've got a room reserved.
Room clerk	In what name, sir?
Oliver	Rees, R – double E – S, Oliver.
Room clerk	Yes, here it is, a single room for 14 nights.
Oliver	That's right.
Room clerk	Could you sign this registration card, please?
[Oliver signs]	
Oliver	There you are.
Room clerk	Thank you. Here's your key. Room 508's on the fifth floor. Breakfast is served in the breakfast room downstairs from 7 to 10 o'clock and the elevator is around the corner to your right. Do you need help with your luggage?
Oliver	No thanks, I'm fine.
Room clerk	I hope you enjoy your stay with us, Mr Rees.
Oliver	Thank you.

Check your answers

a passport – no **b** room number – yes **c** restaurant – no **d** breakfast room – yes
e cost – no **f** luggage – yes

Understanding more

→ Cover the text of Recording 5 again.
→ Read the questions below.
→ Listen to the recording and write short answers.

1 What does Oliver sign? _____
2 What's his room number? _____
3 Where's the breakfast room? _____
4 What time's breakfast? _____
5 How much luggage does Oliver have?_____

☑️ **Check your answers**

1 the registration card. **2** 508. **3** downstairs. **4** 7:00 – 10:00. **5** Not much.

What do they say?

→ Read the sentences below.
→ Listen to Recording 5 again and try to complete the words.
→ Then read the text of the recording to help you if necessary

1 Oliver says he has a reservation.
He says: 'I've / g _ _ / a / _ _ _ _ / r _ _ _ _ _ _ d.'

2 The room clerk asks his name.
She says, 'I _ / w _ _ _ / n _ _ e / sir?'

3 Where is room 508?
'Room 508's / _ n / the / f _ _ t _ / floor.'

4 Where can Oliver have breakfast?
She says, 'Breakfast / i _ / s _ _ _ _ d /
in the breakfast room.'

5 Where's the breakfast room?
'D _ _ _ _ _ _ _ s.'

6 Where's the elevator?
'A _ _ _ _ _ / the / c _ _ _ _ _ / t _/
y _ _ _ / r _ _ _ t.'

7 The room clerk wants Oliver to enjoy his stay.
She says: 'I / h _ _ _ / you enjoy your stay with us, Mr Rees.'

☑️ **Check your answers**

1 I've got a room reserved. **2** In what name? **3** … on the fifth floor. **4** Breakfast is served in the breakfast room. **5** Downstairs. **6** Around the corner to your right. **7** I hope you enjoy your stay.

Common mistake

'**On** the first floor'

Not: ~~In the first floor~~
or ~~At the first floor?~~

To say 'where', *on* is the only correct preposition with *floor*.

What's the right word?

Ordinal numbers

Example from *The Story*:
'Room 508 is on the **fifth** floor.'

→ Look at this elevator sign and complete the words on the right.

■	12th	◄————	twelfth
■	11th		eleventh
■	10th		_ _ _ th
■	9th		_ _ _ _ h
■	8th		e _ g _ _ _
■	7th		_ _ _ _ _ _ _
■	6th		_ _ _ t _
■	5th		_ _ f _ _
■	4th		_ o _ _ _ h
■	3rd		third
■	2nd – Restaurant/Bar		second
■	1st – Lobby		first
■	B – Breakfast room		basement

Check your answers
10th – tenth; 9th – ninth; 8th – eighth; 7th – seventh; 6th – sixth; 5th – fifth;
4th – fourth

→ Look at the lift notice above and complete these mini-dialogues.

Example: [617] Where's your room? *I'm on the sixth floor.*

1 **A** Excuse me, where's the reception desk?
   B It's / _ _ / t _ _/ g _ _ _ _ _ / f _ _ _ _ .

2 A Can you tell me where the restaurant is, please?
  B Yes, / i _ ' _ / o_ / t _ _ / s _ _ _ _ _ / floor.

3 A Where do we go for breakfast?
  B Downstairs. The breakfast room's /_ n / t _ _ / b _ _ _ _ _ _ _ .'

4 A Excuse me, where can I get a drink?
  B The bar's / on / t _ _ / s _ _ _ _ _ / f _ _ _ _ .

☑️ **Check your answers**

1 It's on the first floor. **2** Yes, it's on the second floor. **3** Downstairs, the breakfast room's in the basement. **4** The bar's on the second floor.

→ Complete the rule below.

For ordinal numbers in English, add the letters _ _ to the number.

The ordinals f _ _ _ _, s _ _ _ _ _ and _ _ _ _ d are irregular.

☑️ **Check your answer**

For ordinal numbers, add the letter 'th' to the number.
The ordinals *first*, *second*, and *third* are irregular.

On which floor?

→ Answer these questions.

1 If you live an apartment– where is your apartment? On which floor?
  You _____

2 If you live in a house – where is your bedroom? On which floor?
  You _____

3 Where do you work or study – on which floor?
  You _____

4 Where are you now?
  You _____

Grammar and communication 7

Verb *Hope*

Example from *The Story*:

The room clerk wants Oliver to enjoy his stay.
She says, 'I **hope** you enjoy your stay.'

→ Write sentences for these situations. Use the verb *hope*...

1 It's the end of the week.
What do you say to your colleagues when you leave work?
I hope _____

2 Your friend is going out for the evening.
You _____

3 Your friend is going on vacation.
You _____

4 Your friend is going on a journey.
You _____

5 Your friend is taking an exam/having a baby/taking a driving test etc.
You _____

Check your answers

1 I hope you have a good weekend. **2** I hope you have a nice evening. **3** I hope you enjoy your vacation. **4** I hope you have a good journey. **5** I hope everything goes well.

What's the difference between 'I hope you have a good weekend' and 'Have a good weekend'? (Topic 9)

They are very similar. Both are appropriate in most situations. *I hope* can be more formal.

Our story continues ... Oliver is in his hotel room in Denver. He phones his mother.

Understanding the important information

→ Cover the text of Recording 7.

→ Read the sentences below.

→ Listen to the recording and choose *Yes* or *No*.

Oliver and his mother talk about

a	the weather	Yes/No
b	Oliver's hotel	Yes/No
c	his trip	Yes/No
d	his work in Denver	Yes/No
e	Tasha	Yes/No
f	Oliver's father	Yes/No
g	a message	Yes/No

Recording 6 – The Story

Oliver	Hi Mom! It's Oliver. How are you?
Mother	Hello, dear. Where are you?
Oliver	I'm in a hotel in Denver, the Summerfield Suites. I haven't stayed here before. It's quite nice – comfortable and quiet. I've just got here from the airport.
Mother	How was your trip?
Oliver	It went quite well, actually. First, I visited our new representative in Chile, and then on Tuesday, Wednesday and Thursday I went to the Computer Fair in Buenos Aires. I talked to a lot of people there and had lots of meetings. And then on the flight on the way back I met a very interesting girl.
Mother	Oh, did you?
Oliver	Yes, she's an English teacher in South America. She's on vacation here, staying with friends, just outside Denver. I've got her number there so I can contact her again. I'm going to call her one day next week. We might have dinner together, or something. Anyway, how are you?

Mother	Did you get my message?
Oliver	What message?
Mother	I left a message at your hotel in Argentina two days ago.
Oliver	What was it about, Mom? Come on! What's happened?

Check your answers

a No b Yes c Yes d No e Yes f No g No

Understanding more

→ Cover the text of Recording 7 again.
→ Read the sentences below.
→ Listen to the recording and choose the correct answer.

1 The name of Oliver's hotel is a the Centerfield Suites
                                                 b the Summerfield Suites
                                                 c the Seinhartfelt Suites
                                                 d the Simmerland Suites.

2 a This is Oliver's first visit to this hotel.
    b This isn't Oliver's first visit to this hotel.
    c Oliver always stays at this hotel.

3 Oliver thinks the hotel is
    a excellent
    b good
    c poor.

4 Oliver's business trip was
    d good
    e not very good
    f terrible.

5 Oliver is thinking about inviting Tasha
    a for lunch
    b for a drink
    c for dinner
    d to the movies.

6 Oliver doesn't know about …
  a a letter
  b a problem
  c a ticket
  d an invitation.

☑ **Check your answers**

1 b **2** b **3** b **4** d **5** c **6** b

What do they say?

→ Read the sentences below.
→ Listen to Recording 7 again and try to complete the words.
→ Read the text to help you, if necessary.

1 This is Oliver's first visit to the Summerfield Suites.
    He says, '/ I / h _ _ _ n ' _ / s _ _ _ _ d / here before.'

2 Oliver talks about this trip.
    a He says, 'First / I / v _ _ _ _ _ d / our new representative…'
    b … then on Tuesday, Wednesday and Thursday I / w _ _ _ / to the Computer Fair…'
    c He talks about his activities there.
    He says, 'I / t _ _ _ _ d / t _ / a / l _ _ / o _ people there and h _ _ / l _ _ _ / o _ / meetings.'

3 a Oliver tells his mother about Tasha.
    He says, 'On the flight on the way back / I / m _ _ / a very interesting girl.'
    b His mother is interested. She says, 'Oh, d _ _ / y _ _?'

4 Oliver plans to phone Tasha next week.
    He says, 'I ' _ / g _ _ _ _ / t _ / call her one day next week.'

5 Oliver talks about the possibility of dinner with Tasha.
    He says, 'We / m _ _ _ _ / h _ _ _ / dinner together.'

6 a Verb *get*: Oliver's mother asks him about her message.
    She says, 'Did you get my message?
    Here, 'get' means *find, buy, receive*?

b Oliver says no. His mother gives more information about the message. She says, 'I / l _ _ _ / a message at your hotel two days / a _ _ /.
c Oliver asks about the message.
He says, 'W _ _ _ / w _ _ / _ _ / a _ _ _ _ ?'

7 He wants to know what the situation is.
He says, 'W _ _ _ ' _ / h _ _ p _ _ e _ ?'

Check your answers

1 I haven't stayed here before. **2 a** First I visited our new representative…
b then on Tuesday, Wednesday and Thursday I went to the Computer Fair.
c I talked to a lot of people there and had lots of meetings **3 a** On the flight on the way back I met a very interesting girl. **b** Oh, did you? **4** I'm going to call her one day next week. **5** We might have dinner together. **6 a** Here, *get* means *receive* **b** I left a message at your hotel two days ago. **c** What was it about? (preposition!) **7** What's happened?

Find the words and phrases

→ Read the sentences below.
→ Read the text of Recording 7 again and complete the words and phrases.

1 When Oliver's mother starts the conversation, she says, ' Hello, / d _ _ _ /' to her son.

2 a What's the hotel like? It's q _ _ _ _ / n _ _ _ .
b Is there a lot of traffic noise? No it's a /q _ _ _ _ / hotel.

Check your answers

1 Hello dear.
(Older people often say *dear* to be friendly.)
2 a quite nice **b** No, it's a quiet hotel.

What's the difference in pronunciation between 'quite' and 'quiet'?

Quite has one syllable / kwaɪt /.
Quiet has two. (qui-et) / kwaɪət /

Grammar and communication 8

Talking about the past – Past simple

Example from *The Story*:

Oliver talks about his trip.
He says, 'First I **visited** our new representative.
Then on Tuesday, Wednesday and Thursday I **went** to the Computer Fair.
I talked to a lot of people there and I **had** a lot of meetings
On the flight on the way back, I **met** a very interesting girl.'

All the verbs in **bold** are in the **past simple tense**.

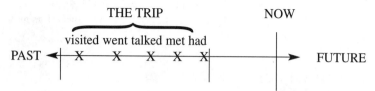

→ Read these questions and answers about the past simple.

Meaning:

Q Is the trip **a** in the past?
           b in the present?
           c in the future?

A In the past.

Q Oliver **visited** the new representative. Do we know when?
A Yes, during his trip. His trip is in the past.

Q Oliver **went** to the Computer Fair. Do we know when?
A Yes, on Tuesday, Wednesday and Thursday.

Q Oliver **talked** to lots of people and **had** lots of meetings. When?
A During the Computer Fair. The Computer Fair is in the past.

Q Oliver **met** Tasha. When?

A On the way to the U.S.

All these activities were during his trip. His trip is in the past.

Is there a connection with the present? No. The trip is finished.

Form – past simple

Regular verbs – verb + *-ed*	Irregular verbs
visit – **visited** talk – **talked**	go – **went** have – **had** meet – **met**

Note: The verbs in **bold** are the past simple.

Summary – Past Simple		
Affirmative I, you, he, she, it we, they	talked (verb + -ed or irregular verb)	
Negative I, you, he, she, it we, they	didn't	talk (verb)
Questions Did	I, you, he, she, it we, they	talk? (verb)
Tag questions, echo questions and short answers I talked, didn't I? Yes, I did, etc.		

Past simple

→ Complete the dialogue below.

Situation It's Monday morning. Two colleagues, Natalie and Dan are talking about the weekend.

Is the weekend in the past? Yes
Is it finished? Yes
So, the verbs are in the past simple.

Natalie   Hi, Dan, _____ you _____(have/had) a good weekend?

Dan   Yes, I _____ thanks. It _____ (be/was) really nice, actually. On Saturday, I _____ (wash) the car. Then in the afternoon I ____(take/took) the children to the park. Yesterday I ____ (play) tennis in the morning and for lunch we ____ (have/had) a barbecue in the back yard.

Natalie   Great!

Dan   How about you? What _____ you _____ ?(do/did)

Natalie   I _____ (be/was) so tired after last week. I really ____ / ____ (do/did) much at all. I ____ (see/saw) a good film on the T.V. on Saturday night and yesterday I just _____ (relax) at home. My husband's sister ____ (come/came) to see us. We ____/ ___ (want) to cook so we ____ (get/got/got) some Chinese food. Later, in the evening we ____ (go/went) out for a drink and then we _____ (drive/drove) her home.

✔ Check your answers

Natalie   Hi, Dan, **did you have** a good weekend?
Dan   Yes, I did thanks. It **was** really nice, actually. On Saturday, I **washed** the car. Then in the afternoon I **took** the children to the park. Yesterday I **played** tennis in the morning and for lunch we **had** a barbecue in the garden.
Natalie   Great!

Dan   How about you? What **did** you **do**?

Natalie **I was** so tired after last week. I really **didn't do** much at all. I **saw** a good film on the T.V. on Saturday night and yesterday I just **relaxed** at home. My husband's sister **came** to see us. We **didn't want** to cook so we got some Chinese food. Later, in the evening we **went** out for a drink and then we **drove** her home.

Grammar and communication 9

Experience up to now – present perfect

Examples from *The Story*:

1 This is Oliver's first visit to the Summerfield Suites
He says, 'I **haven't stayed** here before.'

2 Oliver asks what was in the message.
He says, 'What**'s happened**?'
                        has

Now look at this example:

'I've **stayed** in this hotel three times.'

Meaning

→ Read these questions and answers about '*I have stayed*.'

1 Is the action in the past? Yes.

2 Do we know when? No. When is not the focus.
We use the present perfect to connect past actions with the present.

3 Is there a connection between staying in the hotel and now? Yes.
I know the hotel now because of my three visits in the past.

Form

The name of this tense is **present perfect**.

Q *Why is it called the present perfect?*

A Let's look at another example.

I	**have**	**lived**	**in France**
subject	*have* in present	past participle	

Half the verb is present (*have*) and half is the past participle (*lived*).
This tense connects the past and the present.
My time in France is in the past, but the experience is with me today.

Grammar Summary – Present Perfect		
I/you/we/they	+ have ('ve)	+ past participle
He/she/it	has ('s)	(regular verb + 'ed') or irregular
Negative		
I/you/we/they	haven't	+ past participle
He/she/it	hasn't	
Question		
Have	I/you/we/they	+ past participle
Has	he/she/it	
Tag questions, echo questions and short answers		
Have(n't)	I/you/we/they?	
Has(n't)	He/she/it?	

The past and the present are connected = present perfect.

★ Asking questions with the **present perfect**:
The **present perfect** is the same as all other two-word verbs in
English. To make questions you change the word order.

For example: (1) *He* → (2) *has* → (3) *visited*
For questions, say (2) *Has* → (1) *he* → (3) *visited*?

> (2) auxiliary, *Has* (1) the subject, *he* (3) the past
> participle, *visited*.

★ The past participle is the third in a list of irregular verbs.
  For example: see – saw – **seen**
    write – wrote – **written**

'I have **seen** this film before.'
'She has **written** three books.'

→ Put the words in the right order to make sentences about Oliver.

1 _____ at his hotel.
arrived/Oliver/has/

2 _____ to his mother.
spoken/has/he

3 _____ Tasha? No, not yet. He's going to call her next week.
called/he/has

4 _____ the office. He's going there later.
contacted/hasn't/he

5 How many times _____ to South America? About six times.
he/been/has

Check your answers

1 Oliver has arrived. **2** He has spoken. **3** Has he called. **4** He hasn't contacted.
5 has he been.

→ Use the verbs in brackets in the present perfect to complete these
  mini-dialogues.

1 **A** ____ you _____(see/saw/seen) the film 'Titanic'?
    B Yes I ___.

2 **A** How many times ____ you _____ (go/went/been) to France?
    B I '___ / ___ lots of times.

3 **A** How many countries ____ you _____ (visit)?
    B Me? I' ___/_____ to the U.S. but I _____/_____ anywhere else.

4 A   How many jobs ____ your brother ____(have/had/had)?
   B   He _____n't / ____ many, actually.

5 A   How many English books ___ you _____ (read/read/read)?
   B   I' ___ / _____ hundreds!

6 A   ____ they _____ (finish)?
   B   No, not yet.

7 A   You ____ _____ (forget/forgot/forgotten), have you?
   B   No, of course not.

8 A   My sister '__ / _____ (buy/bought/bought) a new house.
   B   Oh! _____ she? Whereabouts?

✓ Check your answers

1 A Have you seen the film 'Titanic'?
  B Yes, I have.

2 A How many times have you been to France?
  B I've been lots of times.

3 A How many countries have you visited?
  B Me? I've been to the U.S. but I haven't been anywhere else.

4 A How many jobs has your brother had?
  B He hasn't had many actually.

5 A How many English books have you read?
  B I've read hundreds.

6 A Have you finished?
  B No, not yet.

7 A You haven't forgotten, have you?
  B No, of course not.

8 A My sister's (has) bought a new house.
  B Oh! Has she? Whereabouts?

Tip: If you can't answer the question *when* about the past, use the present perfect.

Goodbye!

Leaving the hotel

→ Put this conversation in the right order. Use the letters.

_____	**A**	Certainly. What room number is it, please?
_____	**B**	Good morning. Can I help you?
_____	**C**	Room 201.
_____	**D**	Of course. If you wait at the front door, one will be here in a few moments. Goodbye. I hope you have a good flight.
_____	**E**	Let me see... Here's your bill. How would you like to pay?
_____	**F**	Thanks. Goodbye.
_____	**G**	Morning. Yes, I'd like to check out, please.
_____	**H**	There you are. Could you possibly call me a taxi to go to the airport?
_____	**I**	If I could ask you to just sign here, please.
_____	**J**	By credit card, if that's O.K.

→ Listen to Recording 8 and check your answers.

Check your answers (Recording 7)

Receptionist	**B**	Good morning. Can I help you?
Guest	**G**	Morning. Yes, I'd like to check out, please.
Receptionist	**A**	Certainly. What room number is it, please?
Guest	**C**	Room 201.
Receptionist	**E**	Let me see... Here's your bill. How would you like to pay?
Guest	**J**	By credit card, if that's O.K.
Receptionist	**I**	If I could ask you to just sign here, please.
Guest	**H**	There you are. Could you possibly call me a taxi to go to the airport?
Receptionist	**D**	Of course. If you wait at the front door, one will be here in a few moments. Goodbye. I hope you have a good flight.
Guest	**F**	Thanks. Goodbye.

About your country: hotels

→ Write answers to these questions or prepare to tell a friend.

1 When was the last time you stayed in a hotel?

_____

2 Talk or write about   **a** the place
                               b how long you stayed
                               c who you went with
                               d why you went there.

_____

_____

_____

3 What was the hotel like? Describe it and talk or write about the facilities.

_____

_____

4 How much did you enjoy your stay there?

_____

What would you say?

1 You are in a hotel. You would like to watch T.V. You turn the T.V. on and nothing happens. You call the front desk.

_____

2 You can't find your hotel key. You look everywhere but you can't find it. You're at the front desk.

_____

Possible answers
1 The television in my room doesn't work. **2** I'm very sorry but I can't find my key. Advanced alternative: I'm terribly sorry but I think I've lost my key.

Review

How do you say it in your language?

Here are some examples of the important points in this topic.

→ Translate the sentences below into your language.
→ Remember – translate the idea, not the words.

1 A Who's next? **B** I think I am.

_____

2 A How many of you are there? **B** There are four of us.

_____

3 A How much is this one?

_____

4 $3 a pack.

_____

5 I don't mind where we go as long as you come too.

_____

6 Have you got anything cheaper?

_____

7 On the 6th floor.

_____

8 I haven't been to Singapore.

_____

9 He telephoned last week.

_____

10 I got the letter yesterday.

_____

Join the conversation

→ Look at the text of Recording 1 (page 302) again.
→ Listen to Recording 8 and say **Oliver's** words in the spaces.

TEST 10

Which one is right?

→ Choose **a** or **b**.

1 I've seen that film on video.
   a Did you? What's it like?
   b Have you? What's it like?

2 **a** My room is in the 1st floor.
   b My room is on the 1st floor.

3   **a** This ice cream costs $2 a container.
    b This ice cream costs $2 the container.

4   **a** Could I see the red one, please?
    b Could I see the red, please?

5   **a** I hope you to enjoy your trip.
    b I hope you enjoy your trip.

6   **a** Yesterday I went to the movies.
    b Yesterday I was to the movies.

7   **a** Where you met my brother?
    b Where did you meet my brother?

8   **a** How would you like to pay?
    b How would you like to paying?

9   **a** With credit card, please.
    b By credit card, please.

10 **a** The bar is in the upstairs.
    b The bar is upstairs.

11 **a** What did you at the weekend?
    b What did you do at the weekend?

12 **a** When have you arrived?
    b When did you arrive?

13 **a** I'll take this one, please.
    b I buy this one, please.

14 **a** In which floor is the restaurant, please?
    b What floor is the restaurant on, please?

Write two dialogues

1   **A In the travel agency**
    The travel agent asks about the
    type of hotel you want.

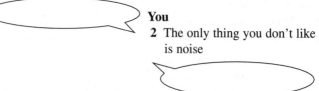

You
2 The only thing you don't like
  is noise

3 She asks about the number of people

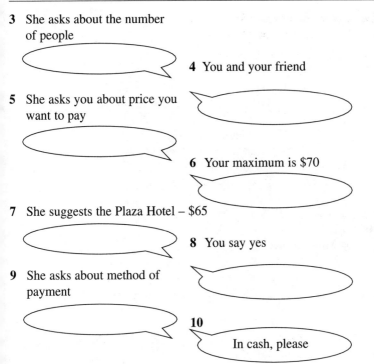

4 You and your friend

5 She asks you about price you want to pay

6 Your maximum is $70

7 She suggests the Plaza Hotel – $65

8 You say yes

9 She asks about method of payment

10 In cash, please

B You pay and then you go to the shop next door to buy a suitcase. You are looking at a small suitcase

1 Sales clerk

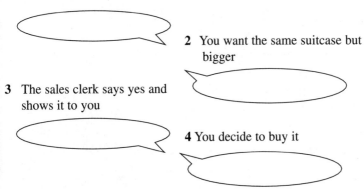

2 You want the same suitcase but bigger

3 The sales clerk says yes and shows it to you

4 You decide to buy it

☑ **Check your answers**

1 b 2 b 3 a 4 a 5 b 6 a 7 b 8 a 9 b 10 b 11 b 12 b 13 a 14 b

Dialogues: model answers

A 1 **Travel agent** What sort of hotel are you looking for?
  2 **You** I don't mind, as long as it's quiet.
  3 **Travel agent** How many of you are there?
  4 **You** There are two of us.
  5 **Travel agent** What sort of price are you looking to pay?
  6 **You** Anything up to $70.
  7 **Travel agent** How about the Plaza Hotel? It's $65 a night.
  8 **You** O.K.
  9 **Travel agent** How would you like to pay?
 10 **You** In cash, please.

B 1 **Shop assistant** Can I help you?
  2 **You** Yes, have you got a bigger one like this?
  3 **Shop assistant** Yes, I have – this one.
  4 **You** I'll take that one, please.

To the learner

We hope you have enjoyed learning with *Teach Yourself English* and that you are happy with the progress you have made. We enjoyed finding a method to help you learn English in English, without a teacher, and writing this course for you.

We wonder what will happen to Oliver and Tasha
in the future?
Will Tasha enjoy her holiday?
Will Oliver and Tasha meet again?
What do you think?
We'll see!

With best wishes

Sandra Stevens

Sandra Stevens

GLOSSARY

Auxiliary (verb) A verb used with another verb. The auxiliary (verb) shows tense etc. For example:

*She **is** reading*	Present progressive
*He **can** drive*	Modal auxiliary/ability
*I **have** finished*	Present perfect

Reading, *drive* and *finished* are the main verbs – they give the meaning. ***Is**, **can't**, **have*** are the auxiliaries.

- The auxiliary for the present simple is ***do/does***
- The auxiliary for the past simple is ***did***
- Auxiliaries are always part of the verb in all other tenses

We use auxiliaries to make questions. We change the word order: the auxiliary goes *before* the person. For example:

*She **is** reading*
***Is** she reading?*
She likes Coke
***Does** she like Coke?*

To make the verb negative, we add '*n't*' (*not*) to the auxiliary. For example:

*He **can't** drive*
*She **doesn't** like Coke*

Some auxiliaries have a short form or contraction (see **Contraction**), for example *he's*, *they're*, *we've*. Contractions are common in spoken English and informal written English.

Auxiliaries are very important in English because we use them a lot to make conversation: **Question tags** and **short answers** both use **auxiliaries**.

Some examples of **auxiliaries** in **question tags** are:

> *He's working,* **isn't** *he?*
> *They're married,* **aren't** *they?*
> *She's got a cat,* **hasn't** *she?*

And here are some examples of **auxiliaries** in **short answers**:

A *He's here*	**B** *Oh, is he?*
A *They can't come*	**B** *Can't they? Why not?*
A *She's had the baby*	**B** *Has she? Is it a boy or a girl?*

Comparative Comparing two things. For example:

> *Peter is older than his brother.* Short adjective *old* + *er* (*than*)
> *A house is* **more** *expensive* **than** *an apartment.* Longer adjective, *more* + adjective (+ *than*)

Contraction A short form of verbs *be* and *have*, some auxiliary verbs and *us* in *let's*. We write an apostrophe (') in the place of the missing letters. For example:

> *I am =* **I'm**
> *It is* and *it has =* **it's**
> *He would not =* **He wouldn't**

Contractions are very common in spoken and informal written English.

Direct language Can be impolite in English. For example: *Give me a glass of water* is often impolite. It is more polite to use indirect language, for example, *Could you give me a glass of water, please?*

Echo questions Help conversation. They show you are interested and want to continue the conversation. Echo questions have two words: the auxiliary + subject. For example:

A *I live in Paris*	**B** *Do you?*
A *He hasn't got a car*	**B** *Hasn't he?*

Formal language Is appropriate with people you don't know, people in authority and official situations and documents. (see **Informal language** and **Neutral language**). For example: *Thanks* is informal language. *Thank you very much indeed* is formal.

Gerund The verb + *ing*, used like a noun. For example:

> *I enjoy* **traveling**.

Imperative The verb without *to*, for example, **Wait** *a minute*.

Remember the imperative is a danger zone for learners of English. We often use other forms of the verb to ask/tell someone to do something.

The imperative is common for:

Wishes:	**Have** *a nice day!*
Instructions:	**Take** *this train*
Directions:	**Turn** *left at the end of the road*
Warnings:	**Be** *careful!*

Informal language Appropriate with family, friends and children. For example, *Hi!* is informal, *Hello* is neutral/formal.

Intonation Is the pitch and movement in the pitch of the voice on the syllable with stress. English expresses different meanings through intonation. For example:

Yes ⟶

Flat intonation. The person isn't interested.

Yes ↘

A big movement in the pitch of the voice. The person is interested.

Less direct language – English uses indirect language a lot. It helps conversation and communication. Direct language with flat intonation can sound rude. For example:

Dialogue 1 – direct	**Dialogue 2 – less direct**
A *Where's John?*	**Do you know where John is?**
B *I've got no idea*	**I'm afraid I've got no idea**

The words in Dialogue 1, with flat intonation, can sound rude. The words in Dialogue 2 are less direct.

Neutral language Appropriate in most situations. For example, *Hello* is appropriate with people you know, people you don't know, people in authority and children (see **Formal language** and **Informal language**).

Past participle The verb + *ed*. The third part of an irregular verb, for example *see/saw/seen – seen*, is the past participle. We use the verb *have* + past participle to form the perfect tenses. For example, *I have eaten* – present perfect.

Plural More than one. For example, *sandwiches*, *grapes*.

Preposition Little words that connect nouns, etc., with other words. For example, *to the station* (direction), *at the restaurant* (place), *before two o'clock* (time).

The preposition is sometimes part of a phrase. For example, *interested in*, *I'm interested in sport* or *to be married to*, *She's married to a Frenchman*.

There are lots of prepositions in English. They are a problem zone for learners because it's often difficult to know which preposition to use. To help you:

- Try to learn the meanings of the prepositions (for example direction = *to*)
- When you learn a phrase with a preposition, remember to learn the preposition, too!

Question tag A short question form at the end of a sentence. This question form with falling intonation isn't really a question. It *is* a way of starting or making conversation. For example:

   A *Terrible weather, **isn't it?***   **B** *Yes. It's not very good, **is it?***

The speakers know that the weather is terrible. They are not really asking questions. They are using question tags to start/continue the conversation.

Reduced form In some short, common words (for example *but, for, from, to, was, does*), the vowel has two pronunciations: one full (when the word has stress), for example, *who is it for?*; and one reduced (when the word doesn't have stress), for example, *it's for you, but not now, from Tom, to Paris, Was it good? Does she know?* In all these words, the pronunciation of the vowel is *schwa* – it is very short and weak.

Schwa – The vowel sound / ə /, as in *a* book, *nut, just*.

Short answers *Yes* and *No* alone can often sound rude in English. Short answers are: *Yes/No* + person + auxiliary. For example:

   A *Is Sue here?*   **B** *Yes, she is.*
   A *Can you drive?*   **B** *No, I can't.*

Singular One only, for example, a *bus*, a *biscuit*.

Stress Emphasis or force on a syllable or word. In all words with two syllables or more in English, one syllable has stress. Example, _En_ - glish, fan – _tas_ – tic.

In sentences, the stress is on the important words, the words with a lot of meaning. For example, _I've bought some <u>bread</u>, some <u>cheese</u> and some <u>fruit</u>._

In English we also use stress to give a particular meaning or emphasis: _Could I have a <u>cold</u> drink?_ (meaning not a _hot_ one).

We also use it to correct people. For example, _The books <u>on</u> the desk, not <u>under</u> it._

Syllable Part of a word with a vowel sound. For example, the word _question_ has two syllables, **_ques – tion_**. And the word _popular_ has three, **_pop – u – lar_**.

Uncountable Nouns that you can't count – mass nouns. For example, _rice_ and _money_ are uncountable nouns. You can't say one, two, three + noun.

QUICK REFERENCE: COMMUNICATIVE FUNCTIONS

The figure in brackets ( ) is the topic number.

Ability (3)
Questions: *Can you + verb?*
Do you + verb?
Responses: *No, not at all*
Yes, but not very well
Yes, not too badly

Asking about the same topic (3)
And you?
How about you?

Asking for an alternative – general (10)
Have you got anything else?

Asking for an alternative - specific
Can I/ Could I have X instead, please? **(2)**
Have you got anything… (+ short adjective + *er*?)
Example: *Have you got anything cheaper?* **(10)**
(+ more + long adjective)
Example: *Have you got anything more suitable?*

Asking for help – Indirect questions (7)
Can you tell me where X is, please?
Do you know how much X costs, please?
Could you tell me if …

Asking for help, systems – Present simple (8)
What/Where/When/How do I … + verb?
Example: *Where do I sign?*

Asking for information (6)
Could you tell me …? I'd like (to know) … What's the …?

$$\left.\begin{array}{l}\textit{Could you tell me}\\ \textit{I'd like (to know)}\\ \textit{What's}\end{array}\right\}\ \textit{the time of the next train, please?}$$

Asking for opinions (9)
How is/was …?
Example: *How was your meal?*

Asking for things (2)
Could I have …?
Example: *Could I have a glass of water, please?*

Asking someone to do something
Can you …, Could you …, Would you mind + verb -ing **(7)**

$$\text{Examples: }\left.\begin{array}{l}\textit{Can you}\\ \textit{Could you}\end{array}\right\}\ \textit{wait a moment, please?}$$

Would you mind waiting a moment?

If you would like to … (very indirect) (7)
Example: *If you would like to call again tomorrow …*

Attracting attention (1)
Excuse me …
Example: *Excuse me, could I have the bill, please?*

Buying things, decisions (10)
I'll take …
Example: *I'll take this one*

Choosing – responding to offers (2)
X, please
X for me, please
I'd like X, please
Could I have X, please?
I'll have X, please

Decisions (2)
I'll …

Negative decisions – I don't think I will **(2)**

Decisions, buying (10)
I'll take …
Negative decision – *I think I'll leave it*

Insisting, offering help (9)

Come on! Let me ... + verb
Example: *Come on. Let me do that!*
Response: Yes: *Thank you/ Thanks*
          No: *No thank you/thanks. I can manage*

Invitations and offers

Question: *Would you like a ...?*   **(1)**
Example: *Would you like some ice cream?*
Responses: Yes: *Yes, please. That would be nice*
                  Yes, please. I'd love one/some
         No: *No, thank you*
               No, thanks. I'm fine
Question: *Would you like to...?*   **(7)**
Response: Yes: *Yes, that would be nice*
         No: *I'm sorry, I'm ... (reason)*
Question: *If you would like to ...* (a very indirect way of asking
       someone to do something)
Responses: Yes: *Thank you*
              Yes, of course
              Yes, that's fine
              Yes, I'll...
        No: *I'm sorry but I can't*

Likes and dislikes – *like, enjoy, mind, be keen on*   **(4)**

Question: *Do you like/enjoy X/verb + ing?*
         Do you like your job?
         Do you enjoy being a mother/father?
Responses: Very positive: *Yes, I really enjoy it*
         Yes: *Yes, I quite like it*
         Neutral: *I don't mind it*
         No: *I'm not very enthusiastic about it, actually*
         Very negative: *Actually, I don't like it at all*

Making conversation

actually   **(3)**
Actually, I + verb or *I + verb, actually*
Example: *I live in Miami, actually*
echo questions   **(3)**
auxiliary + person
Do you? / Have you? / Can she? / Aren't they? etc.

Number of people, talking about the   (10)

Question: *How many of you are there?*

Response: *There are X of us*

Offers (see **Invitations and offers**)

Offering help   (6)

Offers: *I can...*

　　　I could...

　　　I'll...

　　　Shall I...?

　　　Would you like me to...?

Example: *I can*

　　　　I could　} *do that for you,* (if you like)

　　　　I'll

Example: *Shall I*

　　　　Would you like me to } *do that for you?*

Responses: Yes: *Thanks*

　　　　　　Thank you

　　　　　　That's very kind of you

　　　　　　Can you? Could you? Would you?

　　　　　No: *Thanks for the offer but it's all right*

　　　　　　Thanks but I can manage

Offering more

(some) more, another (**1**)

Question: *Would you like some more coffee?*

　　　　　Would you like another sandwich?

Responses:(see **Invitations**)

Permission, asking for (**2**)

Questions: *Is it all right if I ,...?*

　　　　　Could I...?

　　　　　Can I...?

Example: *Is it all right if I*

　　　　Could I　} *use your phone?*

　　　　Can I

Responses: Yes: *Of course*

　　　　　　Go ahead

　　　　　No: *I'm sorry but...* + reason

Possibilities and suggestions (6)
  We could...
  Example: *We could go to the movies*
  You can...
  Example: *You can tell me tomorrow*

Possibilities, suggestions and offers (see **Offering help**)

Price, talking about the   (10)
  Question: *What sort of price are you looking to pay?*
  Response: Maximum: *Anything up to XXX*
                        Anything under XXX
                        As long as it's less than XXX
              Approximately: *About XXX*
                        Around XXX

Rejecting an offer of help   (9)
  No, really. It's all right thanks
  No, really. I can manage

Requests (see **Asking for things/Asking people to do things**)

Same, asking for the   (2)
  The same for me, please
  I'll have X, too, please

Starting a conversation – Question tags   (1)
  Adjective +, *isn't it?*
  Example: *Nice, isn't it?*
  Not very + adjective +, *is it?*
  Example: *Not very interesting, is it?*
  Sentence + question tag
  Example: *He isn't playing very well, is he?*
          It was a good film, wasn't it?

Suggesting doing something together   (7)
  Let's ... + verb
  Example: *Let's go to the movies*
  Responses: Yes: *OK*
                  All right
                  Yes, why not?
                  That's a good idea
                  Yes, why don't we?

No: *Do you really want to?*
I'm not too sure
Perhaps not
Actually, I don't think so

Negative suggestion: *Let's not ...*
Example: *Let's not go to the party. I'm too tired*

Suggestions, possibilities and offers (see **Offering help**)

Thanking (9)

Neutral:	*Thank you*	
Formal:	*Thank you very much*	*for* + verb *-ing*
Informal:	*Thanks*	e.g. *for inviting me*
	Many thanks	
	Thanks a lot	

Responses:

Neutral: *That's OK*
That's all right

Formal: *You're welcome*
Not at all

Informal: *No problem*
Any time

Why, saying (5)

Question: Why are you...?
Responses: *to... + verb*
because I want to...
because I need to...
because I like to...
so (that) (I can)
because...
because of... + noun

Example: **A** *Why are you going to Italy?*
B *To*
Because I want to
Because I need to } *visit my Italian friends*
Because I like to
So (that) (I can)

Because of my friends – they're Italian
Because I'm going to visit my Italian friends

INDEX

TEACH YOURSELF

ENGLISH GRAMMAR

John Shepheard

Teach Yourself English Grammar helps you to learn and understand English grammar without a teacher. It makes learning English grammar easy and enjoyable, because it:

- gives you tips on how to learn the rules
- presents the grammar in clear and interesting situations
- shows you the common mistakes students make
- gives you practice in choosing the correct forms and making sentences
- helps you to write about yourself and your own life
- has the answers to all the exercises at the back of the book.